Savoring
Spain & Portugal

WILLIAMS-SONOMA

Savoring Spain & Portugal

Recipes and Reflections on Iberian Cooking

Recipes and Text
JOYCE GOLDSTEIN

General Editor
CHUCK WILLIAMS

Recipe Photography
NOEL BARNHURST

Scenic Photography
STEVEN ROTHFELD

TIME
LIFE
BOOKS

CANARY ISLANDS

ALEGRANZA
LANZAROTE
LA PALMA
FUERTEVENTURA
TENERIFE
GOMERA
HIERRO
GRAND CANARY

28°
15°

ASTURIAS
CONSORCIO
BASQUE COUNTRY
PAMPLONA
NAVARRA

BURGOS
OLD CASTILE
SARAGOSSA
GALICIA

MINHO
TRÁS-OS-MONTES
SALAMANCA
SPAIN
ARAGON

PORTO
BEIRA ALTA
MADRID
CUENCA

BEIRA LITORAL
BEIRA BAIXA
NEW CASTILE

RIBATEJO
ESTREMADURA
EXTREMADURA

LISBON
ALENTEJO
CÓRDOBA
GRANADA

ANDALUSIA
SEVILLE
ALGARVE
JEREZ
GIBRALTAR

ATLANTIC
17°
33°
MADEIRA
OCEAN
MEDITERR
MOROCCO

9°
6°
3°
45°
42°
39°
36°

Contents

INTRODUCTION

The Iberian Table

Above top: Near Consuegra, on the golden plains of La Mancha, stand the now-rusting windmills immortalized by Cervantes in *Don Quixote*. **Above bottom:** Pear season fills outdoor markets with the aromatic fruits, many of which will be simmered together with poultry or meats in a *cazuela*. **Right:** In the lively Basque port of Fuenterrabía, a tuna fisherman unloads his morning catch.

HISTORY AND GEOGRAPHY have conspired to define the tables of Spain and Portugal. For centuries, the Iberian Peninsula, a patchwork of rugged mountains and dramatic seacoasts, green valleys and arid plains, saw waves of invaders—Phoenicians, Celts, Greeks, Romans, Visigoths, Moors—wash over its shores, each new arrival leaving its culinary footprint.

The Phoenicians planted the first vineyards. The Greeks established olives and olive oil, wheat, and honey. The Celts raised pigs, leading to a rich tradition of sausage and ham, and the Romans put in more vineyards, olive trees, and wheat. The Moors, who were Arabs and their Berber cohorts, grew rice in Valencia, sugarcane in Levante, and almonds, citrus, eggplants (aubergines), spinach, and artichokes in the Algarve and Andalusia. Indeed, the impact of the Moors, who arrived in the eighth century, cannot be underestimated. Their culinary influences are evident everywhere today, from the use of cumin, saffron, nutmeg, and black pepper to the bread-based soups, egg-based sweets, and nut-thickened sauces that are signature dishes in Portugal and Spain.

Slowly the Moors were expelled, however, and by 1252, the reconquest of Spain was nearly complete. Portugal became a separate nation, with its boundaries permanently established by the mid–thirteenth century. Granada fell to Spain's Catholic rulers,

Below top: In addition to the well-known Manchego, Spain produces a wealth of other delicious cheeses: hard, soft, mild, piquant, smoked, blue-veined, rubbed with paprika and oil. **Below bottom:** A patron of one of Seville's many cafés gets a shoeshine and conducts a little business while waiting for a *café solo*. **Right:** On a typical wrought-iron balcony, two suits of armor stand watch over a quiet Toledo street.

Ferdinand and Isabella, in 1492, a doubly triumphal moment because it also marked Columbus's discovery of the New World. Yet it was a tragic time as well, for that same year Jews who had been living in Spain and Portugal for centuries were expelled and the Inquisition began.

Although Columbus had discovered America under the Spanish flag, it was the Portuguese who spearheaded the Age of Discovery. They ventured into the Atlantic to Madeira, the Azores, and the Cape Verde Islands; visited the west coast of Africa; and continued around the tip of the continent to open a sea route to India, the Spice Islands, and the Far East. They sought to control the holy trinity of spices—cloves, nutmeg, and pepper—by wrestling away the spice trade from the Arabs, and for a time they succeeded.

Yet even more important than the opening of the spice route was the impact New World foods had on the way Europeans cooked then and now. Spanish and Portuguese explorers brought on a culinary revolution with their introduction to Europe of peppers (capsicums) and chiles, corn, green beans and kidney beans, tomatoes, avocados, summer and winter squashes, pumpkins, regular and sweet potatoes, pineapples, vanilla, chocolate, cashews, Brazil nuts, peanuts, and even turkeys. While not all of the foods were adopted with equal passion, their gradual assimilation into the Iberian pantries dramatically changed the dinner table.

These new foodstuffs joined with geography to define the development of regional cuisines. Portugal is a narrow swatch, with mountains isolating it on one side and the Atlantic on the other. Spain, in contrast, is mountainous in the northern regions, but a great central plain dominates the center. The cold Atlantic laps Spain's northern border, while the milder Mediterranean lines its southern and eastern flanks. Early on, regional cooking took hold because people could prepare only what was produced locally. Today, these rustic dishes persist because of a profound respect for tradition.

A closer look at the countries' regional divisions illustrates the role of geography at the table. Minho, in Portugal's far north, is an area

of small family farms and vineyards, pine forests, groves of chestnuts and oaks, and delightful country fairs and festivals. *Caldo verde* ("green" soup) is the region's best-known dish, and *couve,* a leafy green that goes into the soup, is cultivated on every spare patch of earth. Also common to the Minho table are *vinhos verdes,* young white table wines. Douro, directly south of Minho and with a similar cuisine, harbors Oporto, the center of port production. Forty percent of the grapes grown in the demarcated wine region are used for port, with the remainder going into table wines, including the excellent Barca Velha reds.

To the east of Minho lies Trás-os-Montes, a sparsely populated province of high plateaus, deep valleys, and remote villages. Fruit trees thrive in a handful of valleys and some good red table wines are produced, but the best-known specialties of the area are the sausages and the *presunto* (air-cured ham).

The three Beiras—Alta, Baixa, and Litoral —are mountainous central regions. Beira Alta is home to the old Roman town of Viseu, which stands at the heart of the Dão wine region and is a treasure trove of egg-rich

confections. Castelo Branco, the principal town of Beira Baixa, is a center for the production of honey, cheese, and olive oil, while Beira Litoral, with its picturesque university town of Coimbra, is known for *leitão assado,* roast suckling pig cooked in a brick oven.

Lisbon lies near the center of Estremadura, a coastal region that also boasts the lovely medieval hill town of Obidos, the Roman village of Colares with its camellia-dressed terraces and precipitous streets, and the large port of Setúbal. Not surprisingly, fish and shellfish abound here. To the south lies Alentejo, Portugal's largest province, its land

richly planted with olive and almond groves, cork trees, and wheat fields.

Stretched along Portugal's southern coast is the Algarve, where idyllic villages share the landscape with busy beach resorts at Lagos, Faro, and Albufeira, and the local table is laden with seafood and delectable sweets such as marzipan and *bolos de figo* (fig-and-almond candy). Far off the southern coast lies the volcanic island of Madeira, the source of some of Portugal's most esteemed wines.

To the east of the Algarve is the Spanish region of Andalusia, home of flamenco and bullfighting, sherry and olive oil, the intricate

Left top: *Pastelerías* all over Spain feature cakes, cookies, and pastries that are usually enjoyed in the afternoons with coffee or tea, while a fruit, a custard, or an ice cream usually caps off dinner. **Right top:** The owner of one of the many popular bars in Barcelona's La Boquería market greets shoppers with a big smile.

Moorish architecture of the Alhambra and the simple whitewashed villages of a stark countryside. From the city of Cádiz, North Africa is visible, and, not surprisingly, most Andalusian cuisine shows a strong Moorish imprint.

Northwest of Andalusia, sparsely populated Extremadura supports wheat fields, herds of sheep, and chestnut, oak, and beech forests. Its pantries are filled with locally produced *jamón serrano* and chorizos, and clay deposits in the south are used for making the earthenware *cazuelas* sold countrywide. To the east, Levante, on the Mediterranean coast, has long, hot summers and mild temperatures year-round, ideal conditions for growing the rice, sugarcane, citrus fruits, peaches, figs, apricots, and grapes that flourish there.

The two Castiles, Old and New, stretch over Spain's broad central plateau. Old Castile, with its bitter cold winters and furnace-hot summers, is the "zone of roasts"—suckling pig, kid, lamb—and of *cocidos* (stews) and is where much of the best Spanish wine is made. New Castile, also known as La Mancha, is Don Quixote country. The country's most famous cheese, Manchego, originates here, and the vast plains are populated with flocks of sheep and cultivated with chickpeas (garbanzos) and lentils. As in Old Castile, *cocidos* are everyday fare.

Catalonia, wedged between the sea, France, and the rest of Spain, has its own language and boasts scores of classic dishes with many regional variations. The Balearic Islands, an overnight ferry ride away, share many Catalan culinary customs.

Aragon and Navarre, adjacent to the French border, are ribboned with vineyards and wheat fields, orchards and vegetable patches. Zaragoza, Aragon's capital, is home to some good restaurants for sampling the local dishes, such as roast kid or lamb and grilled rabbit. The capital of Navarre is medieval Pamplona, made famous by Ernest Hemingway for its annual running of the bulls. The mountainous north produces lamb of exceptional quality, while the town of Tudela, in Navarre's south, is famous for its asparagus.

Next door lies Basque country, a prosperous area of excellent dairy products, fine produce, a bounty of fish from the Bay of Biscay, and one of the most well-regarded and diverse cuisines in all of Spain. So passionate are the Basques for their local dishes that a network of gastronomic societies flourishes in the region. In neighboring Asturias and Galicia, which anchor Spain's northwest corner, strong Celtic influences persist in local pantries. Verdant Asturias, replendent with apple orchards, is the home of fine hard cider, as are Brittany and Normandy, its Celtic counterparts in France. Fish and shellfish are popular and are often paired with cider at the stove. Beyond the Cantabrian Mountains lies Galicia, a land of first-rate vegetables, meats, cheeses, and fish and shellfish. Indeed, shellfish is where Galicia shines, providing everything from lobsters and scallops to barnacles and cockles to restaurants all over the country.

The Portuguese in adjacent Minho and Trás-os-Montes find much on the Galician table that is familiar, such as the *caldo gallego,* a cousin of *caldo verde,* and young white wines. One can cite many more similarities between the two national cuisines, of course: the appreciation of seafood, cured hams and sausages, hearty stews, and rich egg sweets and the everyday use of olive oil, garlic, and wine. Still, an unwavering pride in the strong regional kitchen makes the differences as striking as the similarities.

Left top: The frescoes of Madrid's famed seventeenth-century Plaza Mayor frame a handsome equestrian statue of King Philip III of Spain. **Left middle:** Brilliant yellow sunflower fields blanket stretches of Catalonia and Old Castile. **Left bottom:** Many sweet shops in Segovia proudly display *florones,* delicate, flaky cookies native to the city. **Above:** At his family-owned bodega in Pedrosa del Duero, wine maker José Manuel Pérez tastes the fruits of his labor—a rich, aromatic Ribera del Duero wine.

APPETIZERS

The Spanish cook has elevated the making of tapas to an art form.

A COOK'S GREATEST CREATIVITY is often most evident in the small dishes that begin a meal, and the cooks of Spain and Portugal are no exception. In Portugal these opening plates are called *acepipes,* while in Spain, where they have been elevated to an art form, they are known as tapas.

The word *tapa* comes from *tapar,* to cover, and it originated with a barkeep's habit of placing a little plate or slice of bread on top of a glass of wine to keep out flies. Soon a tidbit of food was set on the plate—a slice of ham, a piece of cheese—and thus an enduring tradition was born. Today, *el tapeo,* the custom of traveling from bar to bar and sampling just a dish or two—the bar's specialties—at each one, is a popular ritual, especially in picturesque Andalusia, the home of the tapa. In Seville, the acknowledged capital of these small plates, wise visitors thread their way through the narrow, untouristed streets of La Macarena, pausing to admire a fifteenth-century palace that once housed the Dukes of Alba, stopping to buy marmalade from nuns at the Convento de Santa Paula, and then perhaps beginning their *tapeo* at the tile-faced El Rinconcillo, the oldest bar in the city.

This elaborate "course" grew out of the dining habits of Spaniards—habits that differ from those of the neighboring Portuguese. In Portugal, for example, breakfast is at about eight o'clock, followed by lunch, or *almoço,* which begins around twelve-thirty, and finally dinner at eight or so. The Spanish routine is more complicated. Breakfast is taken twice, with *café con leche* and a roll consumed quite early and the heartier *almuerzo,* perhaps a *bocadillo* (small sandwich), eaten around eleven. Lunch, or the *comida,* begins at two, followed by a siesta, and then at about six o'clock a snack, the *merienda,* which is usually a pastry or sandwich and coffee or tea. Between seven or eight and ten o'clock in Seville, Madrid, Barcelona, and elsewhere, the tapas bars are filled. Then it is time for dinner, *la cena,* at ten or even later.

Tapas fall into three major categories: *cosas de picar, pinchos,* and *cazuelas. Cosas de picar,* the biggest group, are essentially finger foods— a bowl of marinated olives or fried almonds,

Preceding spread: This cathedral ceiling in Avila soars to the heavens in an otherworldly display of Gothic craftsmanship. **Left:** From early morning until late into the night, the outdoor cafés on Barcelona's elegant Passeig de Gràcia are filled with city dwellers enjoying everything from a *café con leche* and a sweet roll to a selection of tapas. **Above top:** Here, labels depicting a *corrida de toros* grace a collection of wine bottles. **Above bottom:** Residents of the Portuguese city of Evora live among a profusion of tiled patios, Moorish arches, and balconies such as this one.

a wedge of cheese, slices of sausage. *Montaditos,* spreads on bread; *empanadillas,* foods encased in a crust; *tartaletas,* tiny filled pastry shells; *bocadillos;* slices of *tortilla;* and deviled eggs all fall under this banner, as do *fritos* (fried foods) and *buñuelitos* (small fritters), both of which are usually served with *alioli.*

Pinchos, including *banderillas* (named for the dart thrust into the bull at a bullfight) and *palillos,* are skewered foods, whether on tooth-picks or larger rods. *Cazuelas* or *cazuelitas,* dishes cooked in earthenware pots of the same names, require utensils for eating. All three types are usually accompanied with sherry or another wine, or with cider in Asturias.

Acepipes have never achieved the culinary extravagance or the social importance that tapas enjoy in Spain. The Portuguese custom-arily consume their small plates in a local bar, which, even in Lisbon or Oporto, is often no more than a small room with a wooden counter and barrels from which rough red wine is released into narrow tumblers. Small dishes holding olives, almonds, *bolinhos de bacalhau,* or perhaps slices of ham or cheese, may be lined up on the bar top.

In Spain and Portugal, hams and cheeses are important players at the start of the meal, and

Left: Merseguera and Moscatel white wine grapes are harvested in Valencia, where hot, dry summers and cool winters prevail. **Above top:** The ruins of the Scala Dei in the Priorat region of Spain. **Above bottom:** Extremadura's prized cork oak woods yield one of the region's most important exports, a high-quality bark valued for its excellent density and fine pores.

exquisite products are made in both countries. *Jamón serrano* (mountain ham) is the general term for a cured Spanish ham similar to Italy's prosciutto, although perhaps a bit deeper and gamier in flavor. The hams are cured with salt for as long as two weeks and then hung to mature, sometimes for up to two years. The best of these is *jamón ibérico,* made from a native black pig raised in forests in Extremadura, western Andalusia, and western New Castile, where it dines on grasses, acorns, and olives. Around the whitewashed Extremaduran village of Jerez de los Caballeros, rich in belfries and history—two great explorers, Balboa and de Soto, were born here—hams hang in drying

halls and cellars, filling the mountain air with a rich, nutty fragrance. So highly regarded are the nation's cured hams that the Spanish Ministry of Agriculture grants *denominaciones de origen* to the best of them, such as those from Teruel in Aragon, Guijuelo in Salamanca, and Jabugo in Andalusia.

Portuguese *presunto* is treated to a more elaborate curing ritual. After an initial salting, it is rubbed with a mixture of salt, paprika, garlic, and wine and then placed in a smoking chamber called a *fumeiro,* literally "chimney," where it takes on a dark brown color and smoky flavor. The best *presunto* comes from the Trás-os-Montes towns of Chaves, known

for its striking black pottery, and Valpaços, home to full-bodied red wines that complement the local ham. Another excellent *presunto*—sweeter than the others—is made in the town of Monchique, in the Algarve.

Cheeses are sometimes served as a dessert course in Spain and Portugal, but they are more commonly bar offerings—presented in cubes or wedges. Many different types are produced throughout both countries. A discussion of only a handful of them illustrates the considerable variety.

Manchego is the best known of the Spanish cheeses. Made from the milk of sheep that graze on the vast plains of La Mancha and

Left: Lisbon's Antiga Confeitaria de Belém, renowned for its flaky custard-filled pastry cup called *pastéis de Belém,* is a regular stop for dessert lovers of all ages. **Above top:** Bushels of sun-ripened tomatoes remain in the fields near Santiago do Cacém, in Alentejo, waiting for transport to local markets. **Above bottom:** Basque Idiazábal cheese, produced from sheep's milk, attains its intriguing flavor from an age-old smoking process.

Below top: Spaniards add just a squeeze of lemon juice to silvery sardines preserved in oil, or coat the fresh fish with fruity olive oil, chopped herbs, and garlic and then grill them quickly over a hot fire. **Below bottom:** No true Spaniard can pass a day without stopping in at his or her favorite tapas bar for a morsel or two accompanied with a glass of sherry or cider, wine or beer. **Right:** Evidence of Spain's Catholic heritage is visible in its simple sidewalk shrines, tranquil cloisters, and richly ornamented altars.

produced in large rounds, it has a rich, complex flavor and ivory to golden color. Zamorano, another Castilian sheep's milk cheese, is slightly salty and has a pleasing grainy texture, while Idiazábal, a Basque sheep's milk cheese, is smoky and sharp. Blue-veined Cabrales, made from three different milks, is matured in limestone caves in Asturias, where steady winds blowing off the surrounding mountains cool the rounds. Mahón, a full-flavored butterfat-rich cow's milk cheese, is a specialty of the Balearic Islands.

Although the most popular Spanish cheeses are exported, few Portuguese cheeses cross the border. They are primarily the products of sheep's milk, sometimes with the addition of goat's milk. Castelo Branco, from Beira Baixa, is a white sheep's milk cheese eaten fresh or aged. Cabreiro, a soft goat cheese, or sometimes a mixture of goat's and sheep's milk, is from the same area. Serra, the most celebrated of the Portuguese cheeses, is buttery and is as runny as Brie when ripe. Alentejo produces three highly regarded sheep's milk cheeses: Evora, a smallish cheese eaten both young and aged; Beja, also enjoyed both young and aged; and Serpa, a semihard cheese with a peppery flavor. In the Azores, cow's milk is used for making cheeses, with São Jorge, a cheddarlike cheese from the island of the same name, one of the best examples.

While cheese and ham invariably turn up on the tapas or *acepipe* menu, salads are not as common, with the exception of such favorites as *ensaladilla rusa* (Russian salad) and *cogollos* (lettuce hearts) with vinaigrette. In Iberian homes, however, salads regularly open the meal. The Romans introduced salad to the peninsula, but it was the Arabs who created the tradition of serving it at the beginning of the repast. While you will find simple green salads, more often they are embellished with sliced oranges, cooked eggs, asparagus, strips of ham, canned tuna, olives, or pimientos. In most cases, they are served on big platters placed at the center of the table and eaten communally. And, in their own way, these colorful starters showcase the creativity of the Iberian cook just as the better-known tapa and *acepipe* do.

Catalonia

Tortilla de Espárragos

asparagus omelet

I ate this wonderful omelet at Casa Leopoldo in Barcelona early one spring, when the season's first asparagus and green garlic appeared at La Boquería market. If you cannot find green garlic (ajos tiernos in Spanish), a combination of garlic chives and garlic cloves will capture a similar aroma.

½ lb (250 g) pencil-thin asparagus, tough ends removed

6 tablespoons (3 fl oz/90 ml) olive oil

8 green (spring) onions, including tender green tops, finely chopped

½ cup (1½ oz/45 g) coarsely chopped green garlic shoots, or 2 or 3 cloves garlic, minced

12 garlic chives, if using garlic cloves

7 large eggs

salt and freshly ground pepper to taste

❧ Bring a saucepan three-fourths full of water to a boil. Add the asparagus, boil for 3–4 minutes, and drain. Place under cold running water to halt the cooking. Drain again and cut into 1-inch (2.5-cm) lengths. Set aside.

❧ In a frying pan over low heat, warm 3 tablespoons of the olive oil. Add the green onions and the green or regular garlic and sauté until tender, about 8 minutes. Add the chives, if using, and the asparagus and sauté to warm through, about 2 minutes. Remove from the heat. In a bowl, lightly beat the eggs until blended. Add the asparagus mixture. Season with salt and pepper.

❧ In an omelet pan or a frying pan over high heat, warm the remaining 3 tablespoons oil until very hot. Pour in the egg mixture and reduce the heat to medium. Cook until the underside is golden, about 6 minutes. Run a spatula around the edges of the pan a few times during cooking to loosen the eggs. Invert a large plate on top of the pan, invert the pan and plate together, and lift off the pan. Slide the omelet back into the pan and return it to low heat. Cook until pale gold and just set, 2–3 minutes longer.

❧ Slide the omelet onto a serving plate, let cool slightly, and then cut into wedges to serve.

serves 6

Basque Country

Champiñones al Ajillo

garlicky fried mushrooms

Mushrooms grow wild in the abundant forests of the Basque country and Catalonia, and the people of both regions are crazy for setas (wild mushrooms). Boletus edulis (porcini or cepes), girolles (chanterelles), and rabassoles (morels) are among the most prized. While this dish is served all over Spain, in these regions it reaches its apex of flavor and appreciation.

Al ajillo is used to indicate a style of cooking in which foods are fried in oil with garlic and maybe a bit of chile. Shrimp (prawns), squid, chicken, and mushrooms are often served this way. These garlicky mushrooms are wonderful eaten just as they are, with bread for sopping up the juices, or spooned over grilled bread. Chanterelles, portobellos, and cremini combined with the more common white cultivated mushrooms will result in a flavorful dish.

5 tablespoons (2½ fl oz/75 ml) olive oil

2 tablespoons minced garlic

¼ cup (1½ oz/45 g) diced bacon or ham (optional)

1 lb (500 g) assorted fresh mushrooms (see note), brushed clean and halved if small or sliced ¼ inch (6 mm) thick

¼ cup (2 fl oz/60 ml) dry white wine or dry sherry, if needed

¼ cup (⅓ oz/10 g) chopped fresh flat-leaf (Italian) parsley

salt and freshly ground pepper to taste

❧ In a large frying pan over medium heat, warm the oil. Add the garlic and the bacon or ham, if using, and sauté until warmed through, about 2 minutes.

❧ Raise the heat to high, add the mushrooms, and sauté briefly, stirring occasionally, until tender, 4–6 minutes, depending upon the type of mushrooms and the thickness of the slices. If the mushrooms haven't given off much juice, add the wine or sherry and continue to cook until the liquid is absorbed. Add the parsley and stir well.

❧ Sprinkle with salt and pepper, transfer to a serving dish, and serve at once.

serves 4–6

Tortilla

Some French food historians insist that the omelet was the creation of a Gallic monk at work in the kitchen of a Carthusian monastery. But a number of Spanish scholars dismiss the claim, countering with a story set in the court of Louis XIV, where the queen's Spanish cook served what he called *tortilla a la Cartujana*—Carthusian omelet—to a chorus of royal raves. Whatever the omelet's true origin (nearly everyone else agrees that it dates back to ancient Rome), Spain's *tortilla española,* a large, thick cake of eggs, potatoes, and sometimes onion, is one of the simplest yet best representatives of the omelet world.

This classic *tortilla* is served many ways. Office workers might eat a wedge in the late morning to bridge the wait for lunch. Shepherds and schoolchildren like to slip a square between two slices of crusty bread for a hearty midday meal. In the evening, staffs at tapas bars such as Madrid's old, lively Taberna de Antonio Sánchez know that everyone who walks in the door expects to find a good supply of *tortillas* on the bar top. The ubiquitous *tortilla* even turns up on the dinner table, simply set out with bread and salad and usually washed down with a chilled local white wine.

New Castile

Tortilla Española

potato omelet

Unlike most omelets, a tortilla española is served at room temperature. It is the classic tapa, prepared all over Spain, but reputed to be best in La Mancha, a forbidding land of parched earth and aging windmills.

½ cup (4 fl oz/125 ml) plus 2–3 tablespoons olive oil

2 lb (1 kg) baking potatoes, peeled and sliced ¼ inch (6 mm) thick

salt and freshly ground pepper to taste

2 yellow onions, thinly sliced

6 eggs, lightly beaten

2–4 oz (60–125 g) serrano ham, diced (optional)

1 large red bell pepper (capsicum), roasted, peeled, seeded, and cut into strips (optional)

chopped fresh flat-leaf (Italian) parsley

In a large frying pan over low heat, warm the ½ cup (4 fl oz/125 ml) oil. Add half of the potato slices and fry, turning occasionally, until tender but not browned, 15–20 minutes. Transfer to a plate and season with salt and pepper. Repeat with the remaining potato slices. Leave the oil in the pan.

In another frying pan over medium heat, warm the 2–3 tablespoons oil. Add the onions and fry until soft and golden, about 15 minutes. Remove from the heat and let cool a bit.

In a large bowl, whisk the eggs until blended. Mix in the onions and the ham and roasted pepper, if using. Season with salt and pepper. Fold in the cooked potatoes.

Heat the oil remaining in the large pan over low heat and pour in the egg mixture. Cook until the bottom is set and golden, 8–10 minutes. Invert a plate on top of the pan, invert the pan and plate together, and lift off the pan. Slide the omelet back into the pan and return to low heat. Cook until the second side is set, about 4 minutes. Slide onto a plate, garnish with parsley, and cut into wedges.

serves 6–8

Catalonia

Boquerones

marinated anchovies

Most of the anchovies caught in the Atlantic off Spain's Cantabrian coast are packed for export, but the Costa Brava's Mediterranean waters yield excellent anchovies as well, many of which are reserved for domestic consumption. Local fleets set out from the small settlements of Palamós, Sant Feliu de Guíxols, and L'Escala, the last an important anchovy center for centuries because of the plankton-rich waters just beyond its port. Boquerones appear in nearly every tapas assortment in Catalonia and Andalusia. The small fresh fish are sometimes dipped in seasoned flour and deep-fried, or they are left uncooked to marinate in a tart vinaigrette such as this one.

1 lb (500 g) fresh anchovies (about 16)

kosher salt and freshly ground pepper to taste

⅔ cup (5 fl oz / 160 ml) extra-virgin olive oil

⅓ cup (3 fl oz / 80 ml) red wine vinegar

2 cloves garlic, finely minced

1 red (Spanish) onion, sliced paper-thin

3 tablespoons chopped fresh flat-leaf (Italian) parsley

❀ Lay the anchovies on a plate, sprinkle with kosher salt, cover, and refrigerate overnight. The next day, using a small, sharp knife, slit each fish along its belly and remove the entrails. Cut off the head in back of the gills and discard. Slip the knife under the backbone near the neck and slide it to the tail, separating the bone from the bottom fillet. Repeat with the top fillet. Discard the bone. Rinse the anchovies.

❀ In a bowl, whisk together the olive oil, vinegar, and garlic to make a simple vinaigrette. Pour just enough of it over the anchovies to cover them. Let stand for 35–45 minutes at room temperature. Place the onions in a shallow bowl and spoon the remaining vinaigrette over them. Let stand for 15 minutes.

❀ Divide the onion slices among individual plates, then lay the anchovies on top. Sprinkle with the parsley and pepper and serve.

serves 4

Levante

Ensalada de Arroz

rice salad with shrimp

In Spain, especially in the cities of Murcia and Valencia, rice salads appear on menus as a tapa or an appetizer. They are usually embellished with cooked shellfish or canned tuna. In Spain and Portugal, mayonnaise is the most popular dressing for rice salad, but vinaigrette is a close rival. Use long-grain rice, as it firms up and holds for a longer time than short-grain varieties. For maximum flavor, make sure the rice is still warm when it is tossed with the olive oil and lemon juice.

1 cup (7 oz/220 g) long-grain white rice

1½ cups (12 fl oz/375 ml) water

1 teaspoon salt, plus salt to taste

1¼ cups (10 fl oz/310 ml) olive oil, plus extra for tossing with the shrimp (optional)

about ⅓ cup (3 fl oz/80 ml) fresh lemon juice

½ lb (250 g) shrimp (prawns), peeled and deveined

2 egg yolks

1 teaspoon Dijon mustard

½ cup (2½ oz/75 g) finely minced red (Spanish) onion

¼ cup (1½ oz/45 g) diced jarred pimiento or roasted red pepper (capsicum)

¼ cup (⅓ oz/10 g) chopped fresh flat-leaf (Italian) parsley

2 teaspoons finely minced garlic

1 teaspoon chopped fresh tarragon

freshly ground pepper to taste

3 hard-boiled eggs, peeled and quartered lengthwise (optional)

½ cup (2½ oz/75 g) small black olives (optional)

❀ In a saucepan, combine the rice, water, and the 1 teaspoon salt and bring to a boil over high heat. Reduce the heat to low, cover, and cook until the rice absorbs the water and is tender, about 15 minutes. Transfer to a bowl. While the rice is still warm, add ¼ cup (2 fl oz/60 ml) of the olive oil and a few tablespoons of the lemon juice, toss gently to distribute evenly, and let cool completely.

❀ Meanwhile, bring a saucepan three-fourths full of salted water to a boil. Add the shrimp and boil until they begin to curl and are opaque throughout, 3–4 minutes. Drain and rinse under cold running water until cool. Set aside.

❀ To make the mayonnaise, in a food processor or blender, combine the egg yolks, mustard, and 2 tablespoons of the lemon juice. Process briefly to mix. With the motor running, very slowly add the remaining 1 cup (8 fl oz/250 ml) olive oil, first drop by drop until an emulsion forms. Then you can add the oil in a thin, slow, steady stream until the mixture is thickened to a mayonnaise consistency. Season with salt and more lemon juice to taste.

❀ When the rice is cool, fold in the red onion, pimiento or roasted pepper, parsley, garlic, and tarragon and mix well. Season with salt and pepper. Fold in the mayonnaise, reserving about ¼ cup (2 fl oz/60 ml) if desired, for mixing with the shrimp.

❀ Arrange the rice on a serving platter. In a bowl, toss the shrimp with the reserved mayonnaise or with a little olive oil, as desired. Arrange the shrimp on top of the rice. If using, garnish with the hard-boiled eggs and olives, then serve.

serves 4–6

Catalonia

Escalivada

eggplant salad with onions and peppers

Although escalivar *means "to grill," many restaurant cooks in Spain roast their vegetables, as it is easier and requires less maintenance. I have joined them.*

2 yellow or red (Spanish) onions, unpeeled

olive oil for rubbing on onions, plus 1 cup
(8 fl oz/250 ml)

3 eggplants (aubergines)

3 tomatoes

2 red bell peppers (capsicums)

½ cup (4 fl oz/125 ml) fresh lemon juice

3 cloves garlic, minced

salt and freshly ground pepper to taste

chopped fresh flat-leaf (Italian) parsley

☙ Preheat an oven to 400°F (200°C). Put the onions in a small baking pan and rub with olive oil. Roast until tender when pierced, at least 1 hour. Let stand until cool enough to handle, then peel and slice ½ inch (12 mm) thick.

☙ At the same time, prick the eggplants in several places with a fork and place them in a separate baking pan. Add the tomatoes to the pan and place in the oven along with the onions. Roast the tomatoes until the skins blacken, about 15 minutes, let stand until cool enough to handle, then peel and cut into cubes. Continue to roast the eggplants until soft but not mushy, about 45 minutes. Let cool, then peel and tear into large strips. Place in a colander to drain.

☙ Turn the oven to broil (grill). Cut the bell peppers in half lengthwise and remove the stems, seeds, and ribs. Place, cut sides down, on a baking sheet. Broil (grill) until the skins blacken and blister. Remove from the broiler (griller), drape the peppers with aluminum foil, let cool for 10 minutes, and then peel away the skins. Cut into long, narrow strips.

☙ Combine the onions, eggplants, tomatoes, and peppers in a large bowl. In a small bowl, whisk together the 1 cup (8 fl oz/250 ml) oil, the lemon juice, and the garlic. Season with salt and pepper. Pour over the eggplant mixture and toss to coat well. Taste and adjust the seasoning. Sprinkle the salad with parsley and serve.

serves 6–8

Andalusia

Croquetas de Pollo y Jamón

chicken and ham croquettes

Spaniards are fond of these bite-sized morsels with a crunchy, golden crust enclosing a creamy filling.

¼ cup (2 fl oz/60 ml) olive oil, plus extra for deep-frying

2 boneless, skinless chicken breast halves, about ¾ lb (375 g) total weight

1 small yellow onion, minced

⅓ cup (2 oz/60 g) all-purpose (plain) flour

2½ cups (20 fl oz/625 ml) milk

¼ lb (125 g) serrano ham, chopped

salt and freshly ground pepper to taste

pinch of ground cinnamon

1 egg, separated

fine dried bread crumbs

☙ In a frying pan over medium-low heat, warm the ¼ cup (2 fl oz/60 ml) olive oil. Add the chicken, cover, and cook, turning once, until opaque throughout, about 10 minutes total. Transfer to a cutting board, let cool, and then chop finely.

☙ Add the onion to the oil remaining in the pan and sauté over medium heat until golden, 12–15 minutes. Add the flour and stir until the mixture thickens, 3–4 minutes. Slowly pour in the milk, stirring constantly, then cook, stirring, until thick and creamy, about 5 minutes. Add the ham and chicken and season with salt, pepper, and cinnamon. Remove from the heat and let cool slightly. Lightly beat the egg yolk, then stir well into the mixture. Let cool.

☙ In a shallow bowl, beat the egg white until frothy. Place the crumbs in another shallow bowl. Using 1 or 2 spoons, scoop up an egg-shaped ball of the chicken mixture. Dip it into the egg white and then into the crumbs, coating evenly each time. Place on a rack or on a baking sheet lined with parchment (baking) paper. Repeat until all the mixture is used.

☙ In a deep frying pan, pour in oil to a depth of 3 inches (7.5 cm) and heat to 375°F (190°C). Working in batches, fry the croquettes until golden, about 4 minutes. Transfer to paper towels to drain; keep warm. Arrange on a platter and serve hot.

serves 4–6

Amêijoas à Bulhão Pato

clams in white wine

This Portuguese dish is named after the nineteenth-century Lisbon poet Bulhão Pato, a well-known gourmand, and today it is a popular first course in the capital's many tascas and restaurantes típicos. The Spanish, of course, make a similar dish, which they call almejas a la marinera, or clams "fisherman's style." It might mean spicy clams cooked with tomato and onion in Galicia; the addition of red bell pepper (capsicum) or even carrots in Bilbao; or white wine and garlic, with a few bread crumbs for thickening the pan juices, in Andalusia.

If you have sandy clams, place them in a large basin of salted water to cover and leave for about 2 hours, stirring around occasionally, so they will expel their sand. Drain and discard any open or broken clams before cooking. Serve with warm crusty bread to soak up the delicious juices.

⅓ cup (3 fl oz / 90 ml) olive oil

5 cloves garlic, finely minced

pinch of red pepper flakes (optional)

1 tablespoon fine dried bread crumbs, toasted

3 lb (1.5 kg) small clams, preferably Manila, well scrubbed

½ cup (4 fl oz / 125 ml) dry white wine

1 cup (8 fl oz / 250 ml) water

¼ cup (⅓ oz / 10 g) chopped fresh flat-leaf (Italian) parsley

¼ cup (⅓ oz / 10 g) chopped fresh cilantro (fresh coriander)

⚜ In a large sauté pan over medium heat, warm the olive oil. Add the garlic, the red pepper flakes, if using, and the bread crumbs and sauté until softened and pale gold, about 5 minutes. Add the clams, wine, and water, cover, and cook until the clams open, 5–8 minutes, depending upon the size of the clams. Discard any clams that failed to open.

⚜ Transfer the clams and pan juices to warmed soup bowls, dividing evenly. Sprinkle with the parsley and cilantro and serve at once.

serves 4–6

New Castile

Patatas Bravas

"fierce" potatoes

No one can resist these spicy potatoes. Found all over Spain, they are especially popular in the lively tapas bars of Madrid. Some versions of the recipe omit the stock, cooking the potatoes in a tomato mixture spiked with chiles, while others add alioli *(page 194) to the sauce for a smoother, richer consistency. Pour glasses of ice-cold beer to temper the heat of the peppers.*

olive oil for frying

2 lb (1 kg) new potatoes, cut into 2-inch (5-cm) chunks

2 tablespoons all-purpose (plain) flour

1 teaspoon sweet paprika

1 cup (8 fl oz/250 ml) beef stock

2 tablespoons red wine vinegar

½–1 teaspoon red pepper flakes

¼ cup (2 fl oz/60 ml) tomato sauce

salt to taste

❦ In a large frying pan over medium heat, pour in olive oil to a depth of 1½ inches (4 cm). When the oil is hot, add the potatoes and more oil if necessary to cover, reduce the heat to low, and cook until the potatoes are tender, 20–30 minutes. Raise the heat to high and allow them to brown. Using a slotted spoon, transfer the potatoes to a *cazuela* or baking dish and keep warm in a low oven.

❦ Drain off all but 1 tablespoon of the oil from the pan. Add the flour and paprika and stir over low heat for a few minutes. Slowly add the stock, stirring constantly. Then add the vinegar and red pepper flakes and simmer, uncovered, over low heat for about 10 minutes. Stir in the tomato sauce and salt. Taste and adjust the seasoning.

❦ Pour the sauce over the potatoes, toss to coat, and serve warm.

serves 8

Tapas Bars

The tapas bar is Spain's most enduring gastronomic icon. The bar itself can go under various names—*tasca*, *taberna*, *mesón*, *bodega*—and its character can vary as well, from Madrid's elegant José Luis, where caviar is on the menu, to Seville's rustic El Rinconcillo, where small plates have been served in an unchanging décor for over three hundred years. Some bars are attached to restaurants, some stand alone. Some have only a handful of choices, others produce scores of different dishes. Some are frequented by bullfight fans, others are the haunts of the intelligentsia. Some display all their culinary wares on a long bar, others have patrons order from a chalkboard list. Tapas bars are found in big cities and in the smallest villages, and a *tapeo*, visiting a number of spots in a single evening before heading off to dinner, is the best way to explore them.

Many Spaniards stop for a quick drink and tapa or two before the midday meal or in the afternoon, but the evening hours, between seven and ten, are when tapas bars are at their busiest and most convivial. Most customers stand at the bar, which is usually topped with wood, tile, or marble, and often has sawdust strewn below it.

A tapa is traditionally just a single bite. But if you favor a particular dish, you can order a *ración*, a larger portion. Some people skip dinner altogether, filling up on tapas and *raciones* and then wending their way home.

What you drink depends on where you are. In Andalusia, reputedly the birthplace of the tapa, the region's celebrated sherry is drunk. But in Madrid, table wines or beer are more common, and in Asturias, serious cider drinkers don't forsake their local beverage.

Catalonia

Xató

tuna and curly endive salad with romesco vinaigrette

Curly endive, with its pale green and white leaves and pleasantly bitter taste, is the basis for this wonderful winter salad of Barcelona. Here, the endive is topped with tuna and then dressed with a piquant vinaigrette adapted from the region's classic almond-based romesco sauce. The salad is also sometimes made with salt cod or a mixture of tuna and salt cod.

DRESSING

1 cup (5½ oz/170 g) almonds, toasted

1 tablespoon chopped garlic

2 teaspoons red pepper flakes or ½ teaspoon cayenne pepper, or to taste

1 large red bell pepper (capsicum), roasted, peeled, seeded, and chopped

½ cup (4 fl oz/125 ml) red wine vinegar

1 cup (8 fl oz/250 ml) olive oil

salt and freshly ground black pepper to taste

3 small heads curly endive (chicory), leaves separated and torn into pieces

2 cans (6 oz/180 g each) tuna in olive oil, drained

2 hard-boiled eggs, peeled and quartered lengthwise

½ cup (2½ oz/75 g) oil-cured black olives

❦ To make the dressing, in a food processor, combine the almonds, garlic, and red pepper flakes or cayenne pepper. Pulse until the mixture is the consistency of fine crumbs. Add the roasted pepper and pulse to combine. Pour in the vinegar and process until puréed. Gradually add the olive oil in a slow, steady stream, processing until the oil is emulsified and the dressing is the consistency of thick cream. If it is too thick, thin with a little water. Season with salt and black pepper.

❦ Distribute the endive leaves evenly among individual plates. Break up the tuna into bite-sized pieces and arrange it on top of the endive. Drizzle the dressing over the top and garnish with the hard-boiled eggs and olives. Serve at once.

serves 6

Catalonia

Pa amb Tomàquet

grilled bread with tomato

This classic Catalan tapa is the soulmate of the better-known Italian bruschetta. *It is nothing more than good rustic bread that is grilled, rubbed with garlic, then rubbed with a ripe tomato half and drizzled with a fruity olive oil. The tomatoes can also be very, very finely chopped, almost to a purée, and rubbed into the bread. If you wish to add a small embellishment, top with a chopped anchovy or a paper-thin slice of serrano* ham.

6 slices coarse country bread, each about ⅓ inch (9 mm) thick

extra-virgin olive oil, preferably Spanish

2 cloves garlic

2 very ripe tomatoes, halved

salt and freshly ground pepper to taste

❦ Preheat a broiler (griller), or prepare a fire in a charcoal or gas grill.

❦ Brush both sides of the bread lightly with oil. Place on a baking sheet and slip under the broiler, or place on the grill rack. Broil or grill, turning once, until golden brown on both sides, 4–6 minutes total.

❦ Transfer the bread to a platter. Rub the hot bread on one side with the garlic cloves, and then squeeze the tomato halves as you rub them across the surface. Drizzle with oil and season with salt and pepper. Serve immediately.

serves 6

Catalan vendors traditionally separate their tomatoes into two piles; one suitable for salads and the other for making pa amb tomàquet.

Basque Country

Pimientos Rellenos de Bacalao

peppers stuffed with salt cod

Many different kinds of sweet peppers are grown in Spain, but the piquillo is the most highly regarded. It is small and triangular, narrowing to a point at the bottom, and sweet with just a hint of heat. It is sold fresh and is also roasted and peeled and packed in cans and jars. In California and elsewhere, one can find a similar pepper called the gypsy pepper, but its season is quite brief. Don't hestiate to use the jarred or canned Spanish imports for this dish. Large fresh pimientos are also a good choice. If you must use fresh red bell peppers, select the smallest ones possible and cut away the thick inner ribs.

In this Basque version of salt cod–stuffed peppers, the peppers are bathed in a mild tomato sauce. Poached fresh cod can be used in place of the salt cod.

1½ lb (750 g) boneless salt cod, soaked (see glossary, page 249)

6 tablespoons extra-virgin olive oil

2 large yellow onions, finely chopped

¼ cup (2 fl oz/60 ml) tomato sauce

1 tablespoon sweet paprika

4 tablespoons (⅓ oz/10 g) chopped fresh flat-leaf (Italian) parsley

2 tablespoons all-purpose (plain) flour, plus extra for dusting

½ cup (4 fl oz/125 ml) dry white wine

½ cup (4 fl oz/125 ml) fish or vegetable stock

3 cloves garlic, minced

1 cup (2 oz/60 g) fresh bread crumbs, soaked in milk to cover and squeezed dry

salt and freshly ground pepper to taste

2 egg yolks, lightly beaten, plus 1 whole egg

8 canned or jarred roasted whole piquillo *peppers* or 8 large fresh pimiento peppers (capsicums), roasted and peeled

olive oil for deep-frying

☙ Drain the cod and place in a saucepan with water to cover. Bring to a simmer very slowly over low heat. When it comes to a boil, remove from the heat and let cool completely in the water. Drain well and break up the cod into small pieces with your fingers, removing any bits of skin and any small bones. Set the cod aside.

☙ In a sauté pan over medium heat, warm 3 table-spoons of the olive oil. Add half of the chopped onions and sauté until soft and pale gold, 10–12 minutes. Add the tomato sauce, paprika, 2 tablespoons of the parsley, and the 2 tablespoons flour. Stir well and pour in the white wine and stock. Bring to a boil, reduce the heat to low, and simmer until thickened, 5–8 minutes. Remove from the heat and set aside.

☙ In another sauté pan over medium heat, warm the remaining 3 tablespoons oil. Add the remaining onion and the garlic and sauté until translucent, about 8 minutes. Add the cod and the bread crumbs, season with salt and pepper, and cook gently, stirring from time to time, until well mixed and softened, 8–10 minutes. Add the egg yolks and the remaining 2 tablespoons parsley and remove from the heat. Let cool completely.

☙ Cut a slit down one side of each pepper and care-fully remove the seeds. Stuff the peppers with the cooled cod mixture. If you like, secure the stuffing with toothpicks.

☙ In a deep-frying pan, pour in olive oil to a depth of 1½ inches (4 cm) and heat to 375°F (190°C) on a deep-frying thermometer. Meanwhile, in a shallow bowl, beat the whole egg until blended. Put some flour for dusting in a separate bowl.

☙ When the oil is ready, dip the peppers, one at a time, into the beaten egg and then coat with the flour. Slip the peppers into the oil in small batches and fry, turning as necessary, until golden, 4–5 minutes. Using a slotted spoon, transfer the peppers to paper towels to drain.

☙ When all the peppers are fried, transfer the tomato sauce mixture to a large frying pan and place over low heat. Add the stuffed peppers and simmer, uncovered, for 10 minutes to blend the flavors.

☙ Transfer to a serving dish and serve hot or at room temperature.

serves 8

Galicia

Empanada Gallega

pork-and-pepper pie

*There are countless variations on what gets stuffed
into this famous double-crusted tart, the origins of
which lie with the early Celtic invaders.*

double recipe pastry dough (see page 54)

1 egg, beaten

FILLING

½ cup (4 fl oz/125 ml) olive oil or lard

2 yellow onions, chopped

*1 each red and green bell pepper (capsicum),
seeded and chopped*

½ lb (250 g) chorizo, diced

½ lb (250 g) boneless pork or veal, diced

¼ lb (125 g) serrano ham, diced

3 hard-boiled eggs, peeled and sliced

1 large tomato, thinly sliced

❧ Prepare the dough and let it rest as directed.
Preheat an oven to 400°F (200°C). Oil a 12-by-7½-
by-2-inch (30-by-19-by-5-cm) baking pan.

❧ To make the filling, in a frying pan over medium
heat, warm the olive oil or lard. Add the onions and
peppers and sauté until softened, about 10 minutes.
Remove from the heat. Ready the remaining filling
ingredients.

❧ Divide the dough into 2 pieces, one slightly larger
than the other. On a floured work surface, roll out
the larger piece into a rectangle just larger than the
baking pan and about ½ inch (12 mm) thick. Transfer
to the pan. Top the crust evenly with the chorizo, the
pork or veal, and the ham. Spread the onion mixture
over the meats and then top with the egg and tomato
slices. Roll out the remaining dough the size of the
baking pan, drape it over the rolling pin, and place it
over the filling. Press the dough edges together to
seal. Brush the pastry with the beaten egg. Cut a few
steam vents in the surface.

❧ Bake until golden brown, 45–60 minutes. Serve
warm or at room temperature.

serves 8

Catalonia

Albóndigas en Salsa de Almendra

meatballs in almond sauce

The proportion of bread to meat varies in albóndigas *depending upon the extravagance of the cook. These meatballs can be fried and served on toothpicks; cooked in a cazuela; fried and tossed in a sauce made of pan juices enriched with sherry and meat stock; or prepared as they are here, fried in olive oil, then briefly simmered in a wine sauce thickened by a signature Catalan almond picada.*

MEATBALLS

½ lb (250 g) ground (minced) beef

½ lb (250 g) ground (minced) pork

2 slices bread, about 2 oz (60 g) total, soaked in water to cover and squeezed dry

¼ cup (1½ oz/45 g) minced yellow onion (optional)

2 cloves garlic, finely minced

3 tablespoons finely minced fresh flat-leaf (Italian) parsley

1 egg, lightly beaten

1 teaspoon sweet paprika

½ teaspoon ground nutmeg or cinnamon

1 teaspoon salt

½ teaspoon freshly ground pepper

olive oil for deep-frying or sautéing

all-purpose (plain) flour for dusting

PICADA

2 cloves garlic, minced

3 tablespoons ground blanched almonds

2 tablespoons chopped fresh flat-leaf (Italian) parsley

½ teaspoon sweet paprika

a few saffron threads, crushed

salt and freshly ground pepper to taste

SAUCE

2 tablespoons olive oil

½ cup (3 oz/90 g) minced yellow onion

½ cup (4 fl oz/125 ml) dry white wine

⅔ cup (5 fl oz/160 ml) meat or chicken stock

♛ To make the meatballs, in a bowl, combine the beef, pork, soaked bread, onion (if using), garlic, parsley, egg, paprika, nutmeg or cinnamon, salt, and pepper. Knead with your hands until well mixed. Cover and refrigerate for 1 hour, as the mixture is easier to work with when cold.

♛ To make the *picada,* in a mini food processor or mortar, combine the garlic, almonds, parsley, paprika, and saffron and process or grind to a paste. Season with salt and pepper. Set aside.

♛ In a deep frying pan, pour in olive oil to a depth of 2 inches (5 cm) and heat to 375°F (190°C) on a deep-frying thermometer. While the oil is heating, form the meat mixture into 1-inch (2.5-cm) balls and dust them with flour, coating evenly.

♛ Working in batches, slip the balls into the hot oil and fry until golden, about 4 minutes. Using a slotted spoon, transfer to paper towels to drain. (Alternatively, in a large frying pan over medium heat, warm a little olive oil and sauté the meatballs until well browned on all sides, 8–10 minutes.)

♛ To make the sauce, in a large frying pan over medium heat, warm the olive oil. Add the onion and sauté until tender, 8–10 minutes. Add the wine, stock, and meatballs and simmer over low heat for 5 minutes. Add the *picada* and cook for a few minutes longer to blend the flavors. Taste and adjust the seasonings. Transfer to a serving dish and serve hot.

serves 6

Douro

Bolinhos de Bacalhau

salt cod fritters

Although they originated in northern Portugal, these golden fritters are now served throughout the country. Accompany with piri-piri *sauce (page 64) or a few lemon wedges.*

½ lb (250 g) boneless salt cod, soaked (see glossary, page 249)

2 boiling potatoes, about 10 oz (315 g) total

2 tablespoons olive oil

1 small yellow onion, minced

2 cloves garlic, finely minced

2 eggs, lightly beaten

3 tablespoons each chopped fresh flat-leaf (Italian) parsley and fresh cilantro (fresh coriander)

pinch of cayenne pepper

freshly ground black pepper to taste

milk, if needed

olive oil or vegetable oil for deep-frying

☙ Drain the cod and place in a saucepan with water to cover. Bring to a simmer over medium heat and cook until tender, 10–15 minutes. Drain and, when cool enough to handle, flake the cod, removing any bits of skin and small bones. Pulse in a food processor until finely shredded, then place in a bowl.

☙ Meanwhile, combine the potatoes with water to cover, bring to a boil, and boil until tender, 20–30 minutes. Drain and, when slightly cooled, peel and mash until smooth. Add to the salt cod.

☙ In a small sauté pan over medium heat, warm the oil. Add the onion and sauté until tender, about 8 minutes. Add the garlic and sauté for 2 minutes. Add the contents of the sauté pan to the cod mixture and mix well. Fold in the eggs, parsley, and cilantro. Season with cayenne pepper and black pepper. The mixture should be the consistency of firm mashed potatoes. If it is too stiff, beat in a little milk. Form into balls 1 inch (2.5 cm) in diameter.

☙ In a deep, heavy frying pan, pour in oil to a depth of 2 inches (5 cm) and heat to 375°F (190°C). Add the balls, a few at a time, and fry until golden, about 4 minutes. Using a slotted spoon, transfer to paper towels to drain. Serve at once.

serves 6–8

Sherry

The Andalusian towns of Jerez de la Frontera, Sanlúcar de Barrameda, and Puerto de Santa Maria lie at the three points of a triangle ribboned with vineyards. According to Spanish law, the Palomino Fino grapes harvested from these vines are the only ones that can be used to make the product labeled Spanish sherry. Jerez harbors most of the area's *bodegas,* the warehouses in which the legendary wines are fermented, aged, and bottled.

To make sherry, the pressed grapes are first allowed to ferment in open casks, then the wine is graded, fortified with brandy, and aged for a year or two. Finally, the critical *solera* process begins: Casks of sherry are arranged in a pyramid, with the oldest wines on the bottom and the youngest at the top. As the immature wines are slowly moved down the stack, they are blended with the older wines at each level, inheriting important characteristics as they age.

Fino and oloroso are the primary types of sherry. Both should be drunk from a tulip-shaped *copita,* its top just wide enough to appreciate the wine's heady aroma.

Salmorejo Cordobés

gazpacho cream dip

The word salmorejo *is used to describe a sauce made with water, vinegar, oil, salt, and pepper. Salmorejo cordobés adds tomato and garlic to this base, making it essentially a gazpacho without the water. It can be garnished with chopped hard-boiled eggs and diced ham, or with pieces of chopped orange. This purée is served in Córdoba and Seville, where it is used as a dip for fresh vegetables such as carrots, celery, pepper (capsicum) strips, and blanched green beans.*

½ lb (250 g) day-old coarse country bread, crusts removed and bread sliced

4 ripe tomatoes, peeled, seeded, and chopped

1 small green bell pepper (capsicum), seeded and coarsely chopped

3 cloves garlic, chopped

2 raw eggs

1 teaspoon salt, plus salt to taste

½ cup (4 fl oz / 125 ml) olive oil

¼ cup (2 fl oz / 60 ml) red or white wine vinegar

freshly ground pepper to taste

¼ lb (125 g) serrano ham, chopped (optional)

2 hard-boiled eggs, peeled and coarsely chopped (optional)

In a bowl, combine the bread with water to cover. Let soak for 15–20 minutes.

Squeeze the bread dry and place it in a blender or food processor along with the tomatoes, bell pepper, and garlic. Process until smooth. Add the raw eggs and 1 teaspoon salt and process to blend. Then, with the motor running, slowly drizzle in the olive oil, processing until it is incorporated and the mixture is emulsified. Mix in the vinegar and season with salt and pepper.

Spoon the purée into a shallow bowl. If desired, garnish with the chopped ham and hard-boiled eggs. Serve with a selection of raw and blanched vegetables for dipping.

serves 6

Catalonia

Empanadillas Rellenas de Espinacas

little spinach pies

Empanadillas, or "little pies," have been made in Spain since medieval times. This Catalan recipe is reminiscent of fatayeer sbanikh, *an Arabic spinach pie, except for the addition of the New World tomatoes. The spinach is cultivated in the region's extensive market gardens, which are located around the lower Ebro River delta, a fertile expanse that also produces grains, olives, and the grapes that go into making the well-regarded local red wines.*

Although these pies are baked, empanadillas *are sometimes deep-fried. Other popular fillings include tuna, chorizo, onion, or anchovy.*

PASTRY DOUGH

2 cups (10 oz/315 g) all-purpose (plain) flour

¼ cup (2 oz/60 ml) olive oil

2 tablespoons solid vegetable shortening

¼ cup (2 oz/60 ml) milk or water

1 teaspoon salt

½ teaspoon baking soda (bicarbonate of soda)

FILLING

⅓ cup (3 fl oz/80 ml) olive oil

4 cloves garlic, minced

1½ cups (9 oz/280 g) peeled, seeded, and chopped tomato

1½ lb (750 g) spinach, tough stems removed and chopped

½ cup (2 oz/60 g) pine nuts

2 hard-boiled eggs, peeled and coarsely chopped

salt and freshly ground pepper to taste

1 egg, beaten

To make the dough, put the flour into a bowl and make a well in the center. Add the oil, shortening, milk or water, salt, and baking soda to the well. Mix with a wooden spoon until the dough comes away from the sides of the bowl. Turn out onto a lightly floured work surface and knead briefly. Cover with a kitchen towel and let rest for 20–30 minutes.

Meanwhile, make the filling: In a frying pan over low heat, warm the olive oil. Add the garlic and sauté until softened, 2–3 minutes. Add the tomato and simmer, uncovered, until soft and some of the liquid has been absorbed, about 10 minutes. Add the spinach and pine nuts and cook until the spinach is wilted, 3–5 minutes longer. Remove from the heat. Pour off the excess oil from the filling, then fold in the chopped eggs and season with salt and pepper. Let cool to room temperature. Set aside.

Preheat an oven to 350°F (180°C). Lightly oil a baking sheet.

Divide the dough into 2 equal pieces. On a lightly floured work surface, and working with 1 piece at a time, roll out the dough about ⅛ inch (3 mm) thick or less. Cut out rounds 4–5 inches (10–13 cm) in diameter. You should have about 12 rounds in all. Place a tablespoon of filling in the center of each round, fold in half, and seal, turning up the edges to make a narrow rim. Place on the prepared baking sheet and brush with the beaten egg.

Bake until golden, 20–30 minutes. Serve warm or at room temperature.

serves 4–6

Andalusia

Ensalada Andaluza

green salad with serrano ham and tomato vinaigrette

As early as A.D. 500, lettuces, asparagus, leeks, garlic, and wild herbs and greens were used in salads around the Mediterranean. Vinegars were made from grapes, figs, or peaches and salt. During the years when the Moors planted the first market gardens and orchards in Spain, spring onions and citrus juices were added to the mix. With the discovery of the New World, tomatoes and peppers (capsicums) became salad standbys.

VINAIGRETTE

1 lb (500 g) ripe tomatoes, peeled, seeded, and coarsely chopped

3 cloves garlic, minced

1 tablespoon sweet paprika

1½ teaspoons ground cumin

1 teaspoon salt

½ cup (4 fl oz / 125 ml) extra-virgin olive oil

6–8 tablespoons (3–4 fl oz / 90–125 ml) red wine vinegar

2 heads romaine (cos) or butter (Boston) lettuce, leaves separated and torn into bite-sized pieces

2 hard-boiled eggs, peeled and sliced

2 or 3 green (spring) onions, thinly sliced

¼ lb (125 g) serrano ham, thinly sliced and cut into narrow strips

⅓ cup (2 oz / 60 g) mixed black and green olives

❀ To make the dressing, in a food processor or blender, combine the tomatoes, garlic, paprika, cumin, and salt and pulse to purée. With the motor running, slowly add the olive oil and vinegar, processing until fully incorporated.

❀ Place the lettuce in a bowl. Drizzle on just enough of the dressing to coat, toss well, and transfer to a platter. Top with the eggs, onions, ham, and olives. Spoon the rest of the dressing on top.

serves 4

Balearic Islands

Coca de Verduras

savory pie with greens

Most visitors to the Balearics arrive by overnight ferry from Barcelona or Valencia. The three largest islands of the chain, Majorca, Minorca, and Ibiza, each have a distinctive character and culture, but cooks on all of them are well known for their sweet rolls and savory pastries, including cocas. Similar to pizzas, cocas feature toppings as varied as caramelized onion, anchovies, and pine nuts or this simple combination of greens and onions.

DOUGH

1 tablespoon active dry yeast

½ cup (4 fl oz/125 ml) warm water

3½ cups (17½ oz/545 g) unbleached all-purpose (plain) flour

¾ cup (6 fl oz/180 ml) cold water

2 tablespoons olive oil

1½ teaspoons salt

cornmeal for dusting pan

TOPPING

1 lb (500 g) spinach

1 lb (500 g) Swiss chard

2–3 tablespoons olive oil

6 green (spring) onions, including tender green tops, chopped

salt to taste

sweet paprika to taste

1 large tomato, chopped

☙ To make the dough, in a large bowl, dissolve the yeast in the warm water. Add ½ cup (2½ oz/75 g) of the flour and stir to combine. Cover and let stand for about 30 minutes.

☙ Add the remaining 3 cups (15 oz/470 g) flour, the cold water, the olive oil, and the salt and stir with a wooden spoon until the dough comes away from the sides of the bowl. Turn out onto a lightly floured work surface and knead until smooth and elastic, about 10 minutes. (You can also make the dough in a stand mixer, mixing it with a paddle attachment and then kneading it on low speed with the dough hook for about 10 minutes.) Transfer the dough to an oiled bowl, cover the bowl with plastic wrap, and let stand in a warm place until the dough has doubled in size, about 1 hour.

☙ Turn out the dough onto a lightly floured work surface, punch down, and shape into 1 large ball or divide in half and shape into 2 balls. Place on a floured baking sheet, cover, and let rest in the refrigerator for about 30 minutes.

☙ Meanwhile, make the topping: Remove the tough stems from the spinach and Swiss chard leaves and cut the leaves into narrow strips. Set aside. In a large frying pan over medium heat, warm the olive oil. Add the green onions and sauté until softened, about 3 minutes. Add the spinach and chard and cook, stirring occasionally, until wilted, about 3 minutes. Transfer to a sieve and drain off any excess liquid. Season with salt and paprika. Set aside.

☙ If you are using a pizza stone, place it in an oven and preheat to 475°F (245°C) for at least 30 minutes.

☙ If making a single, rectangular crust, dust a baking sheet with cornmeal. On a lightly floured work surface, roll out and stretch the dough into a rectangle large enough to line the baking sheet. Transfer the rectangle to the baking sheet, top evenly with the greens mixture, and then scatter the tomato on top.

☙ If making 2 round crusts, roll out and stretch each ball into a 9-inch (23-cm) round, forming a slight rim at the edges. If using a pizza stone, place 1 round on a cornmeal-dusted baker's peel or rimless baking sheet. If not using a pizza stone, place the round on a cornmeal-dusted baking sheet. Top evenly with the greens mixture and then the tomato. Place the *coca*-topped baking sheet in the oven, or slide the *coca* from the baker's peel or sheet onto the stone.

☙ Bake until the crust is golden, about 15 minutes. Remove from the oven and let cool slightly. If making round *cocas,* slip the second one into the oven and bake in the same way. Cut the rectangular *coca* into squares or the round ones into wedges. Serve warm.

serves 8–10

Majorca is the most beautiful of the islands, with its aging olive trees and sandy coves bordering crystalline waters.

Olive Oil

The ancient Romans, responding to the felicitous climate, introduced the olive tree and the olive press to the Iberian Peninsula. The then-named Hispania (Spain) quickly became the principal supplier of olive oil (*aceite de oliva*, Spanish; *azeite de oliva* or simply *azeite*, Portuguese) to the empire. The Spanish oil, which traveled in earthenware amphorae, was even stocked in the pantries of the capital's senators: an 1872 archaeological dig centered on Mount Testaccio, a modest hill that rises alongside the Tiber, unearthed the shards of some 40 million Spanish oil containers.

Today in Spain, about four thousand square miles (10,360 sq km) are given over to olive cultivation, primarily in the Andalusian provinces of Jaén and Córdoba and in Catalonia. Despite little or no rainfall for months at a time, Andalusia alone produces one-fifth of the world's olive oil, much of it sold to Italy, where it is blended and bottled. Olive trees blanket stretches of Portugal as well, their silvery gray-green profiles standing alongside orchards of figs, almonds, and oranges in Algarve and with groves of cork-oaks and fields of wheat in Alentejo.

Spain's Ministry of Agriculture has established production zones for the country's best oils. In Catalonia, where the small, green Arbequina olive is crushed, Borjas Blancas and Siurana are protected by *denominaciones de origen*. In Andalusia, where the Picual, Picuda, and Hojiblanca are the most common oil olives, the zones are Baena, in the province of Córdoba, and Sierra de Segura, in the province of Seville. Notable extra-virgin oils are bottled in these areas, with Nuñez de Prado from Baena and Estornel and Siurana from Catalonia among the finest.

In general, Catalan oil is lighter and less sweet than its Andalusian counterpart and carries little spiciness and astringency. By contrast, Andalusian oil has fruity shadows, a richer color, and a more pronounced olive taste. Portuguese oil, although intensely colored and highly aromatic, is less distinguished. It is not, however, without its vocal partisans.

Basque Country

Gambas al Pil Pil

sizzling shrimp with garlic

You'll want to have plenty of bread on hand to capture the delicious pan juices from these garlicky crustaceans. This Basque tapa, called gambas al ajillo *in other parts of Spain, is traditionally served at the table sizzling—pil pileando—in a little metal pan. Sherry or lemon juice is not always used, but either one adds a nice contrast to the richness of the oil and garlic. You can easily substitute squid, cut into rings ½ inch (12 mm) wide, or sea or bay scallops for the shrimp. Gambas al-i-pebre, a variation with garlic and hot red pepper from the Albufera region of Valencia, has a more substantial sauce of rich fish stock thickened with fried bread, ground almonds, and pine nuts. It is quite filling and is thus usually served as a main course. This same peppery variation was originally made with eel.*

4–5 tablespoons (2–2½ fl oz/60–75 ml) olive oil

4 cloves garlic, finely minced

1 teaspoon red pepper flakes

1 teaspoon sweet paprika

1 lb (500 g) medium shrimp (prawns), peeled and deveined

1–2 tablespoons fresh lemon juice

1–2 tablespoons dry sherry

salt and freshly ground black pepper to taste

2 tablespoons chopped fresh flat-leaf (Italian) parsley

☙ In a sauté pan over medium heat, warm the olive oil. Add the garlic, red pepper flakes, and paprika and sauté for 1 minute until fragrant. Raise the heat to high, add the shrimp, lemon juice, and sherry, stir well, and sauté until the shrimp turn pink and are opaque throughout, about 3 minutes. Season with salt and pepper, sprinkle with parsley, and serve.

serves 4

Old Castile

Patatas a la Riojana

rioja-style potato and chorizo stew

Although patatas a la riojana *is very filling and could be a main course, it is more typically served as a tapa. It is common fare on the tables of the many wine makers of Rioja, whose fine, delightfully fruity reds are among the world's best enological bargains.*

¼ cup (2 fl oz/60 ml) extra-virgin olive oil, or as needed

4 large new potatoes, about 2 lb (1 kg) total weight, peeled and cut into slices 1 inch (2.5 cm) thick or into 1½-inch (4-cm) chunks

½ lb (250 g) chorizo

1 yellow onion, chopped

1 red bell or piquillo *pepper (capsicum), seeded and chopped*

2–4 cloves garlic, minced

2 teaspoons sweet paprika

1 small fresh red chile, seeded and minced

1 cup (8 fl oz/250 ml) water

salt and freshly ground black pepper to taste

2 tablespoons chopped flat-leaf (Italian) parsley

✤ In a large frying pan over medium heat, warm the ¼ cup (2 fl oz/60 ml) olive oil. Add the potatoes and sauté, stirring often, until pale gold, 10–15 minutes. Using a slotted spoon, transfer to a bowl. Add the chorizo to the oil remaining in the pan and fry, turning as needed, until crisp and golden, about 4 minutes, adding more oil if needed. Using tongs, transfer the chorizo to a cutting board. When cool enough to handle, cut into ½-inch (12-mm) pieces.

✤ Add the onion to the drippings in the pan and sauté over medium heat, stirring occasionally, until golden, about 15 minutes. Add the red pepper, garlic, paprika, and chile and sauté until the spices have been absorbed by the onion, about 5 minutes longer.

✤ Return the chorizo and potatoes to the pan and pour in the water. Cover tightly and simmer over low heat until the potatoes are tender, about 15 minutes. Season with salt and black pepper.

✤ Transfer to a serving dish, sprinkle with the parsley, and serve warm.

serves 8

Andalusia

Pinchos Morunos

moorish pork kabobs

Pincho, or pinchito, the diminutive, translates as "little thorn" or "little pointed stick," so pincho moruno *roughly means Moorish mouthfuls impaled on a thorn or skewer. Of course, the Moors were Muslims and did not eat pork, which means that Christian Spain took the Arab seasonings traditionally used on lamb kabobs (qodban) and applied them to their beloved meat.*

½ cup (4 fl oz/125 ml) olive oil

3 tablespoons ground cumin

2 tablespoons ground coriander

1 tablespoon sweet paprika

1½ teaspoons cayenne pepper

1 teaspoon ground turmeric

1 teaspoon dried oregano

1 teaspoon salt, plus salt to taste

½ teaspoon freshly ground black pepper

2 lb (1 kg) pork, cut into 1-inch (2.5-cm) cubes

2 tablespoons minced garlic

¼ cup (⅓ oz/10 g) chopped fresh flat-leaf (Italian) parsley

¼ cup (2 fl oz/60 ml) fresh lemon juice

lemon wedges

✤ In a small frying pan, combine the olive oil, cumin, coriander, paprika, cayenne pepper, turmeric, oregano, 1 teaspoon salt, and the black pepper. Place over low heat until warmed through and fragrant, about 3 minutes. Remove from the heat and let cool to room temperature.

✤ Place the pork pieces in a bowl and rub with the spice mixture. Add the garlic, parsley, and lemon juice and toss well. Cover and refrigerate overnight.

✤ The next day, preheat a broiler (griller), or prepare a fire in a grill. Thread the meat onto skewers and sprinkle with salt.

✤ Place on a broiler pan or a grill rack and broil or grill, turning once, until just cooked through, about 4 minutes on each side. Transfer to a platter and serve with lemon wedges.

serves 8

Andalusia

Rin Ran

salt cod and potato salad
with olives and peppers

*This salad originates in Jaén, a provincial capital
surrounded by vast olive groves. Another musical name
for the dish is* poti-poti, *or "a jumble."*

½ lb (250 g) boneless salt cod, soaked (see
glossary, page 249)

1 lb (500 g) small new potatoes

2 red bell peppers (capsicums), seeded and diced

½ cup (2½ oz/75 g) green olives, pitted

DRESSING

6 tablespoons (3 fl oz/90 ml) extra-virgin
olive oil

2 tablespoons red wine vinegar

1 teaspoon ground cumin

1 teaspoon sweet paprika

salt and freshly ground pepper to taste

¼ cup (⅓ oz/10 g) coarsely chopped fresh
flat-leaf (Italian) parsley

❧ Drain the cod and place in a saucepan with water
to cover. Bring to a gentle simmer over medium heat
and cook until tender, 10–15 minutes. Drain and,
when cool enough to handle, shred, removing any
bits of skin and small bones. Place in a large bowl.

❧ Meanwhile, combine the potatoes with water to
cover, bring to a boil, and boil until tender but still
firm enough to hold their shape when diced, about
20 minutes. Drain and, when cool enough to handle,
peel and cut into ½-inch (12-mm) dice. Add the
potatoes, bell peppers, and olives to the salt cod.

❧ To make the dressing, in a small bowl, whisk
together the olive oil, vinegar, cumin, and paprika.
Season with salt and pepper.

❧ Pour the dressing over the salt cod mixture and
toss well. Garnish with the parsley and serve.

serves 4

Catalonia

Escabeche

fish in a tart vinaigrette

While this is considered a signature dish of Lisbon and of the Estremadura and Ribatejo regions, escabeche is much beloved in Catalonia, too. One of the best renditions I've ever eaten was served in a tiny restaurant in La Boquería market in Barcelona. The centuries-old market, which is entered through a dramatic neo-Gothic arch off busy Las Ramblas, is where restaurateurs and home cooks shop for the finest meats, fish, fruits, vegetables, sausages, and cheeses the city has to offer. Bar Quim, with only six stools lined up along a counter, offers its space-limited clientele the opportunity to watch the owner-chef put together every plate.

The name escabeche comes from the Arabic sikbaj, or "vinegar stew." Originally it was made with meat and only rarely with fish, but today it is primarily a dish of pickled fish. Small, oily fish such as sardines or local Portuguese carapau (small mackerel) are traditionally used, as they take to the marinade particularly well, developing a smooth, velvety texture. Tuna is also an option. You can substitute fillets of a firm white fish, although they will not produce the same extraordinary texture. For maximum flavor, let the fish marinate for a couple of days before serving.

1½ lb (750 g) whole fresh sardines or
1 lb (500 g) tuna or white fish fillets

kosher salt

½ cup (4 fl oz/120 ml) olive oil

2 white onions, sliced paper-thin

2 carrots, peeled and grated (optional)

2 or 3 cloves garlic, smashed

2 small bay leaves, torn into pieces

⅔ cup (5 fl oz/160 ml) white vinegar

2 teaspoons salt

1 teaspoon sweet paprika (optional)

freshly ground pepper to taste

1 small lemon, sliced paper-thin

2 tablespoons chopped fresh cilantro
(fresh coriander)

☙ If using fresh sardines, lay the sardines on a plate, sprinkle with kosher salt, cover, and refrigerate overnight. The next day, slit each fish along its belly, gut it, and then remove its backbone and head. Rinse the sardines.

☙ Lay the sardines or fish fillets on a plate, sprinkle with kosher salt, and let stand for about 15 minutes.

☙ In a large frying pan over medium heat, warm 2 tablespoons of the olive oil. Add half of the fish and sauté, turning once, until golden on both sides and opaque throughout, 2–3 minutes total for the sardines or 4 minutes for the fish fillets. Transfer to a plate. Repeat with the remaining fish and 2 more tablespoons of the oil. Set the fish aside.

☙ Add the remaining ¼ cup (2 fl oz/60 ml) oil to the same pan over medium heat, add the onions, and sauté until limp, 8–10 minutes. Add the carrots (if using), garlic, bay leaves, vinegar, salt, paprika (if using), and pepper and let bubble for a minute or two. Remove from the heat and let cool. Toss in the lemon slices and cilantro.

☙ Arrange the fish on a deep platter, alternating layers of fish and the onion mixture. Cover, pouring any remaining liquid over the top, and refrigerate for 2 days before serving.

serves 6–8

Eels

One of the Basque region's most celebrated delicacies is *angulas,* or baby eels. These tiny freshwater denizens, each one the size of a tailor's needle, are cooked in small earthenware vessels, or *cazuelitas,* usually prepared *al pil pil,* that is, sizzling in a batch of garlic, chile, and olive oil. But their simple appearance belies the arduous journey their ancestors survived.

Eels spawned in the distant Sargasso Sea travel thousands of miles across the Atlantic in a three-year journey to Spain's northern waters. In the past, these tiny eels, or elvers, were so abundant that Basque farmers reportedly fed them to their hogs along with the usual ration of grain. But once their popularity in the Spanish kitchen was established, fishermen began netting them in numbers that threatened the eels with extinction.

Today, both wild and farmed elvers are served in the tapas bars of San Sebastián, Bilbao, and other Basque towns. Crusty bread and a glass of *txakolí,* the local wine, are the perfect accompaniments.

Camarão com Piri-Piri

shrimp with hot sauce

The hot sauce known as molho de piri-piri *is made all over Portugal, but the best version I have ever eaten was served in a seafood restaurant across from the fish market in Cascais on the Costa do Sol. The fiery sauce takes its name from the very hot* piri-piri *chile.*

PIRI-PIRI SAUCE

½ cup (2 oz/60 g) coarsely chopped fresh hot red chiles

4 cloves garlic, finely minced

1 teaspoon salt

1 cup (8 fl oz/250 ml) olive oil

¼ cup (2 fl oz/60 ml) white wine vinegar

2 cloves garlic, finely minced

2 small fresh red chiles, finely chopped, or 1 teaspoon cayenne pepper

½ cup (4 fl oz/125 ml) olive oil

2 lb (1 kg) jumbo shrimp (prawns), peeled and deveined

salt to taste

lemon wedges and coarse country bread

♛ To make the sauce, in a jar with a tight-fitting lid, combine the chiles, garlic, salt, olive oil, and vinegar. Cover, shake well, and let rest in the refrigerator for about 1 week before using. You should have about 1½ cups (12 fl oz/375 ml). (You will not use it all; store the remainder for up to 2 months.) Shake well before using.

♛ In a mortar, grind together the garlic and chiles or cayenne pepper to make a paste. Stir in the olive oil. Rub this mixture over the shrimp, place them in a bowl, cover, and refrigerate for 4 hours.

♛ Preheat a broiler (griller), or prepare a fire in a grill. Remove the shrimp from the marinade, reserving the marinade. Thread the shrimp onto skewers, piercing the shrimp twice, once near the tail and again near the head. Sprinkle with salt. Broil or grill, turning once and basting with the marinade, until opaque throughout, 5–6 minutes total.

♛ Arrange the skewers on a serving platter and garnish with the lemon wedges. Serve the bread and *piri-piri* sauce for dipping on the side.

serves 4–6

SOUPS AND STEWS

Iberia's soups are culinary kin to the hearty Spanish cocido and Portuguese cozido.

WHILE IT MAY SEEM ODD to open a chapter of soup recipes with a discussion about bread, it is actually quite appropriate, for it forms the basis of many Iberian soups. Bread has traditionally been a common means for extending meager rations, so it is not surprising that frugal cooks in Spain and Portugal have created a sizable repertoire of bread-thickened soups.

The Portuguese *açorda,* a dish little known outside Iberia, is a "dry" soup made by thickening broth with rustic bread and then enriching the mixture with egg. *Açorda de mariscos,* a classic of coastal Estremadura, and *açorda à alentejana,* a specialty of the sunny south, are the two most popular examples.

The earliest Spanish gazpacho called for bread as well, combining it with oil, vinegar, and garlic. These elements were mashed and thinned with water, then seasonings were added. The origin of the soup's name is debated. Many scholars believe it comes from the Latin *caspa,* meaning "fragment," referring perhaps to the crushed bread, but others insist it is derived from an Arabic or Hebrew word.

Today, gazpacho is at home in the Levante, La Mancha, and Catalonia, but Andalusia is the true capital of this summer soup, a central stronghold with over thirty distinctive versions. Probably one of the earliest recipes was *ajo blanco* made with garlic, bread, almonds, and grapes. But New World exploration dramatically expanded the Iberian pantry, and tomatoes and peppers (capsicums) were soon introduced into the basic mixture of bread and garlic, creating the memorable cold soup that most of us now associate with the name. Indeed, even the most jaded travelers cannot resist this Spanish classic, especially if they are seated in a tile-lined Andalusian courtyard under a full August moon, the air fragrant with jasmine blooms.

Portuguese cooks in Alentejo have their own version of this tomato-based soup. Called *gaspacho,* it sometimes includes ham or sausage and is ladled atop thick bread slices. On the hottest days, especially in busy Beja, a wheat-growing center that reputedly endures Portugal's highest summer temperatures, ice cubes are added to each bowl.

Bread also plays an important role in the rustic *sopa de ajo,* or "garlic soup," one of Spain's

Preceding spread: The glittering spectacle, elaborate rituals, and strict rules of the *corrida de toros,* little changed since the seventeenth century, are still taken seriously by Spanish aficionados. **Left:** Not even the mouthwatering display of fresh breads and cakes can bring a smile to these young patrons of Seville's Horno de San Buenaventura. **Above top:** *Piri-piri* sauce, a pungent mixture of fiery *piri-piri* chiles, olive oil, and garlic used as a kitchen seasoning and table condiment, is sold in markets all over Portugal. **Above bottom:** The Spanish wines of La Rioja, carefully aged in *barriques,* small oak barrels, are appreciated by oenophiles throughout the world.

Above top: Flowers festoon a balcony in San Sebastián, capital of Basque country and celebrated for the myriad tapas bars in the neighborhood known as La Parte Vieja. **Above bottom:** While most Spaniards take their midday meal and dinner at home, they visit cafés and tapas bars at other times of the day, pausing to enjoy a slice of Manchego or a plate of *patatas bravas*. **Right:** A local resident relaxes on a bench overlooking the blue waters of the Bay of Biscay.

most characteristic dishes. This soup, a mixture of bread, garlic, olive oil, and water, is not far removed from the original gazpacho and *açorda,* and, as with all traditional dishes, its style varies with the region. Most Spaniards agree, however, that the best versions are served in the south and southeast, where garlic is cultivated extensively and intricately woven strings of the pungent bulbs hang in every farmhouse and restaurant kitchen.

The *cocido* in Spain and the *cozido* in Portugal are closely related to the Iberian soup tradition. These are meals-in-a-bowl, simmered mixtures of meats or seafoods and vegetables. They are always welcome sights on a wintry evening in the dining room of a *parador* in Galicia or of a *taberna* on a cobblestoned *largo* in Tomar. They recall the pot-au-feu of France, the *bollito misto* of Italy, and the *adafina* of Morocco, with the last their likely origin.

The Jewish *adafina,* a dish of vegetables, beef and/or chicken, and eggs, was born out of two traditions, kosher law that proscribes cooking on the Sabbath and the Moorish preference for stewing. In Spain, this Jewish dish evolved into a Christian one with the advent of the Inquisition. Jews who did not

flee the Iberian Peninsula were forced to renounce Judaism and became Catholics. An important test of loyalty to the new faith was the consumption of pork or foods cooked with lard. Thus, to avoid being branded infidels, they added pork to their *adafinas,* often replacing the eggs and sometimes even the other meats. With that culinary innovation, the *cocido* and *cozido* were firmly established.

The simplest peasant versions of *cocido,* which are mostly beans and vegetables with little meat added—perhaps a piece of ham to flavor the broth—are eaten from a single bowl. In more elaborate presentations, the broth is strained and served with rice or fine noodles as a first course. Then the other ingredients are served, sometimes in two more courses, as is the case with the classic *cocido madrileño,* in which the vegetables are followed by the meats. In some regions, a *cocido* takes on the name of the pot in which it is served, such

as the *puchero* in La Mancha or the *olla* in Santander and Catalonia.

Geography defines the Spanish *cocido* as well. In far northern Cantabria, Spain's premier dairy region, *cocido montañés* is made with white beans, cabbage, potatoes, carrots, pork belly, blood sausage, chorizo, and pigs' snouts, ears, and shinbones. In central Spain, chickpeas (garbanzos) replace the white beans. *Cocido andaluz* calls for beef, pork, sausage, squash, green beans, and saffron, while the *olla* of Córdoba has only chickpeas, bacon, and cabbage. In Catalonia, the local *cocido, escudella i carn d'olla,* traditionally contains what seems like every conceivable starch, from white beans and chickpeas to noodles, rice, and potatoes, as well as ham, sausage, and chicken.

Although the Portuguese *cozido* does not achieve a similar complexity of styles and substance, it is nonetheless a respectable cousin to the Spanish *cocido.* Primarily a dish of the

Left: The Castelo de São Jorge, crowning a hilltop high above the roofs of Lisbon, offers breathtaking views of the city and the Tagus River. **Below top:** These young orange trees will soak up the warm Valencian sunshine to produce the sweet, juicy fruits that are exported to Spain's European partners and beyond. **Below bottom:** Cafés all over Spain are filled with the lively chatter of patrons enjoying a mid-day break.

north, of Minho and Trás-os-Montes, where brutal winters demand a hearty table, *cozido à portuguesa* is thick with meat, poultry, sausages, root vegetables, and cabbage but no beans. The broth is ladled up as a first course, and rice accompanies the meats and vegetables.

Because Iberia is surrounded on three sides by water, a large repertoire of fish and shellfish soups and stews grace coastal tables. In Spain, *zarzuela de mariscos* is an all-shellfish specialty of Catalonia, with the specific varieties depending upon what is available. Catalonia's prized *romesco* sauce of peppers, nuts, and olive oil is thinned with broth and loaded with the local fish and shellfish to produce Tarragona's celebrated *romesco de peix*. A classic of the Algarve, *amêijoas na cataplana* combines clams and sausage with a hint of chile in a dish named for the saucer-shaped pan in which it is cooked. The Catalonian *suquet de peix* and the northern Portuguese *caldeirada* are seafood soups hearty enough to be declared stews.

Unlike their cousins, *açordas* and gazpachos, these seafood stews are not made with bread. No Spanish or Portuguese diner would miss the chance to use a thick-crusted shard of rustic bread to mop up the last bit of broth at the bottom of the bowl.

Left: Spigots release freshly pressed olive oil into glass bottles at Nuestra Señora de la Oliva, an oil producer in Gibraleón, west of Seville. **Below top:** A woman carries an armful of fresh produce along a street in Ericeira, a Portuguese fishing village. **Below bottom:** In the bustling La Boquería market in Barcelona, savvy shoppers have a good eye for bargains and an appreciation for fresh seafood.

Catalonia

Zarzuela de Mariscos

shellfish stew

Zarzuela is both the name for this stew and Spanish for "operetta." This little shellfish mélange is so festive it resembles a lighthearted musical. Keeping the lobster in the shell and the tails on the shrimp makes for mildly messy eating, but shells add additional flavor to the dish and create a more dramatic presentation. Some versions of this recipe include crushed toasted almonds, and others a hint of chile. Some cooks add both.

2 small to medium live lobsters

¼ cup (2 fl oz/60 ml) olive oil

1½ cups (7½ oz/235 g) chopped yellow onion

1–2 tablespoons finely minced garlic

1 red bell pepper (capsicum), seeded and finely diced

1 green bell pepper (capsicum), seeded and finely diced

3 cups (18 oz/560 g) peeled, seeded and diced tomato (fresh or canned)

½ cup (2½ oz/75 g) almonds, toasted and ground (optional)

¼ teaspoon saffron threads, steeped in ¼ cup (2 fl oz/60 ml) dry white wine

1 bay leaf, torn into pieces

salt and freshly ground black pepper to taste

pinch of red pepper flakes (optional)

1½ cups (12 fl oz/375 ml) dry white wine

12–18 mussels, well scrubbed and debearded

12–18 clams, well scrubbed

12–18 large shrimp (prawns), peeled and deveined with tail fin shell intact

½–¾ lb (250–375 g) sea scallops, halved if large

1–2 tablespoons fresh lemon juice (optional)

romesco sauce (optional; page 184)

♛ Bring a large saucepan three-fourths full of salted water to a boil. Add the lobsters, immersing completely, and boil until the shells turn red, about 5 minutes. Using tongs, remove the lobsters and place under cold running water to cool. Working with 1 lobster at a time, and holding it over a sink, twist off the head and discard. Remove the claws and

separate at the knuckles. Lay the lobster, underside down, on a cutting board. Using a knife, cut the tail crosswise into 2-inch (5-cm) pieces. Crack the claws to expose the meat. Set the spindly legs aside for garnish. Repeat with the other lobster.

♛ In a large, heavy pot over medium heat, warm the olive oil. Add the onion and sauté until softened, about 5 minutes. Add the garlic and bell peppers and sauté until the vegetables are soft but not browned, about 5 minutes longer.

♛ Add the tomato, almonds (if using), saffron and wine, bay leaf, salt, black pepper, and the red pepper flakes, if desired. Raise the heat to high and bring to a boil. Cook until thickened, about 10 minutes.

♛ Add the wine, return to a boil and add the lobsters, the mussels, and the clams, discarding any mussels that fail to close to the touch and any open or broken clams. Cover and cook for about 5 minutes. Add the shrimp and scallops, re-cover, and cook until the lobsters, shrimp, and scallops are cooked and the clams and mussels have opened, 3–5 minutes more. Taste and adjust the seasoning as needed. Add the lemon juice, if desired, to balance the flavor.

♛ Ladle into warmed bowls, discarding any clams or mussels that failed to open, and accompany with the *romesco* sauce, if using. Serve immediately.

serves 6–8

Sunburned fishermen set sail from Catalonia's many ports in search of shrimp and langoustines in every color and size.

Andalusia

Gazpacho Blanco

cold almond soup with grapes

The texture of this chilled soup may seem a bit unusual at first, but it quickly begins to appeal. This gazpacho, as opposed to the more familiar tomato-based one laced with vegetables, is probably closest to the original version, which was nothing more than bread, water, oil, and vinegar. In bustling Málaga, where the harvest from nearby hillside vineyards is turned into a full-bodied, very sweet aperitif or dessert wine and sugary plump raisins, the soup is given an elegant and refreshing finish with the addition of peeled grapes. It is a cool antidote to the region's relentless summer heat.

1 cup (5½ oz/170 g) blanched almonds

4 small slices day-old coarse country bread, crusts removed, soaked in water to cover, and squeezed dry

2 cloves garlic

1 teaspoon salt, plus salt to taste

6 tablespoons (3 fl oz/90 ml) olive oil

3 tablespoons white wine vinegar

3 cups (24 fl oz/750 ml) ice water, or as needed

freshly ground pepper to taste

36 green seedless grapes, peeled and cut in half

☙ In a food processor or blender, combine the almonds, soaked bread, garlic, and the 1 teaspoon salt and pulse until the almonds are very finely ground. With the motor running, slowly add the olive oil, the vinegar, and 1 cup (8 fl oz/250 ml) of the ice water and process until you have a creamy white liquid. Transfer to a bowl.

☙ Stir in as much of the remaining 2 cups (16 fl oz/ 500 ml) ice water as needed to achieve the soup consistency you prefer. Season with salt and pepper. Cover and refrigerate until well chilled.

☙ Just before serving, stir in the grapes. Ladle into chilled bowls and serve.

serves 4

Nuts

Nuts are Iberian pantry staples. They are at the heart of many cakes and other sweets, particularly those made for centuries in the countries' convents and now sold in elegant shops such as Madrid's venerable Casa Mira. But nuts also turn up in the form of fried almonds sprinkled with salt and cayenne, in sauces such as *romesco,* and in soups such as *gazpacho blanco* (see facing page).

Many historians—although certainly not all—believe the Romans planted the first walnut trees in northern Spain and Portugal. Today the harvest is modest, but residents of the Douro are quick to extol the virtues of pairing a handful of freshly cracked walnuts with a glass of tawny port. This same area harbors the peninsula's primary chestnut orchards, the yield of which goes into such dishes as Galicia's *sopa de castañas* (page 97) and the olive oil–dressed boiled dried chest-nuts of Minho and Trás-os-Montes. The Greeks—or perhaps the Romans—may be responsible for the numerous hazelnut (filbert) orchards around the rampart-rimmed city of Tarragona, where many of the rich, spherical nuts go into the region's celebrated *romesco* sauces. Pine nuts still in the shell are sold in paper cones as snacks; once shelled, they turn up in exquisite desserts.

But the nut one most closely associates with Iberia is the almond. Introduced and popularized in cooking by the Moors, it is widely grown today in Andalusia, Alentejo, Algarve, and on the island of Majorca, where trees covered with thick, snowy blossoms carpet the countryside in spring. Almonds are used whole, chopped, or ground in savory soups and stews, and in cakes and confections from *turrón* to marzipan.

Estremadura

Sopa de Abóbora

butternut squash soup

Most squash soups are rich and filling, but the addition of lemon juice here contributes a welcome lightness. The use of cilantro as a garnish puts this recipe in the repertoire of cooks in Estremadura and farther south. Remember that once you have added the egg yolks, you cannot reheat the soup. If you like, you can omit the yolks and simply add the cream. For an extra flourish, garnish with toasted croutons.

¼ cup (2 oz/60 g) unsalted butter

2 yellow onions, chopped

1 butternut squash, about 1½ lb (750 g), halved, seeded, peeled, and cut into 1-inch (2.5-cm) pieces

5–7 cups (40–56 fl oz/1.25–1.75 l) chicken stock

salt and freshly ground pepper to taste

2 egg yolks

½ cup (4 fl oz/125 ml) heavy (double) cream

2 tablespoons fresh lemon juice

2 tablespoons chopped fresh cilantro (fresh coriander)

❧ In a heavy saucepan over medium heat, melt the butter. Add the onions and sauté until tender, 8–10 minutes. Add the squash pieces and 5 cups (40 fl oz/ 1.25 l) of the chicken stock. Raise the heat to high, bring to a boil, cover partially, reduce the heat to low, and simmer until the vegetables are very soft, about 30 minutes. Remove from the heat and let cool slightly.

❧ Working in batches, ladle the soup into a food processor or blender and purée until smooth. Return the purée to the saucepan. If it is too thick, add as much of the remaining stock as needed to correct the consistency. Bring to a simmer over medium-low heat and season with salt and pepper.

❧ In a small bowl, whisk together the egg yolks, cream, and lemon juice and swirl the mixture into the hot soup. Ladle immediately into warmed bowls. Garnish with the cilantro and serve at once.

serves 6

Ribatejo

Sopa de Pedra

stone soup

According to legend, a peasant couple told a hungry stranger their larder was bare. The visitor offered to show them how to make soup with only stones and water, but he suggested that adding a carrot and some bacon would be better. The peasants gradually "found" some food, and this hearty soup, in which kidney beans symbolize the stones, was born.

1 rounded cup (8 oz/250 g) dried red kidney beans, soaked (see glossary, page 246)

3 tablespoons olive oil

2 yellow onions, chopped

2 cloves garlic, minced

¼ lb (125 g) bacon, in one piece

¼ lb (125 g) chouriço or garlic sausage

4 boiling potatoes, peeled and diced

4 carrots, peeled and diced

2 turnips, peeled and diced

1 small head savoy cabbage or kale, shredded

2 cups (12 oz/375 g) diced canned plum (Roma) tomatoes

1 bay leaf

8 cups (64 fl oz/2 l) chicken stock

½ cup (¾ oz/20 g) chopped fresh cilantro (fresh coriander)

❧ Place the beans in a saucepan with water to cover, bring to a boil, reduce the heat to low, cover, and simmer until tender, about 1 hour. Drain.

❧ Meanwhile, in a saucepan over medium heat, warm the olive oil. Add the onions and garlic and sauté until tender, about 10 minutes. Add the bacon, sausage, potatoes, carrots, turnips, cabbage, tomatoes, bay leaf, and stock. Raise the heat to high, bring to a boil, reduce the heat to very low, and simmer until the vegetables are tender, about 30 minutes.

❧ Discard the bay leaf. Remove the meats and cut into ½-inch (12-mm) pieces. Return the meats and beans to the pan, add the cilantro, and simmer over medium heat for 5 minutes to warm through. Ladle into warmed bowls and serve immediately.

serves 6

Basque Country

Purrusalda

leek and potato soup

The name of this soup comes from puerro, *meaning "leek." In the Basque provinces, leeks are highly regarded, and this popular soup is considered the classic way to begin a meal.*

⅓ lb (5 oz/155 g) boneless salt cod (optional)

¼ cup (2 fl oz/60 ml) olive oil

2 cloves garlic

1½ lb (750 g) leeks (about 8 medium), including some tender green tops, halved lengthwise and sliced

1 lb (500 g) potatoes, peeled and diced

1 bay leaf

salt and freshly ground pepper to taste

3¾ cups (30 fl oz/940 ml) water or fish stock

1 teaspoon sweet paprika

꙰ If using salt cod, in a bowl, combine the salt cod with cold water to cover generously. Cover and refrigerate for 24–36 hours, changing the water at least 4 times. Drain the cod and break into small pieces, removing any bits of skin and any small bones. Set aside.

꙰ In a saucepan over medium heat, warm the olive oil. Add the garlic and sauté until golden, 4–5 minutes. Using a slotted spoon, transfer to a mortar.

꙰ Add the leeks to the oil remaining in the pan and sauté slowly over low heat until wilted, about 5 minutes. Add the potatoes, bay leaf, salt, pepper, and the cod, if using. Pour in the water or stock. Add the paprika to the garlic and crush with a pestle. Add to the leeks, bring to a boil over high heat, reduce the heat to low, and simmer until the leeks and the cod, if using, are very tender and the potatoes are falling apart, about 30 minutes.

꙰ Ladle into warmed bowls and serve immediately.

serves 4–6

Andalusia

Sopa de Albóndigas

meatball soup

This soup was probably of Jewish origin, initially made only with beef. After the Inquisition, however, pork was added to demonstrate one's conversion to Christianity. Today, the soup is included on many restaurant menus in Córdoba, a city that once was home to a large Jewish community and where one of the oldest synagogues in the country now stands in ruins. Tomatoes, saffron, and chopped hard-boiled eggs are added along with the tiny meatballs to a rich meat stock. Chickpeas and potatoes are part of the mix as well, making this soup almost hearty enough to be declared a stew.

MEATBALLS

¾ lb (375 g) ground (minced) beef, half beef and half pork, or lamb

⅓ cup (2 oz/60 g) grated yellow onion

½ cup (2 oz/60 g) dried bread crumbs

1 egg, lightly beaten

3 tablespoons chopped fresh flat-leaf (Italian) parsley

1 clove garlic, finely minced

½ teaspoon ground cinnamon (optional)

½ teaspoon ground cumin (optional)

1 teaspoon salt

½ teaspoon freshly ground pepper

2 tablespoons olive oil

1 yellow onion, chopped

¼ teaspoon saffron threads, crushed (optional)

1 cup (7 oz/220 g) drained cooked chickpeas (garbanzo beans)

1 cup (5 oz/155 g) peeled and diced boiling potatoes

6 cups (48 fl oz/1.5 l) flavorful meat stock

2 cups (12 oz/375 g) peeled, seeded, and diced tomato (fresh or canned; optional)

salt and freshly ground pepper to taste

¼ cup (⅓ oz/10 g) chopped fresh flat-leaf (Italian) parsley

2 hard-boiled eggs, peeled and chopped (optional)

To make the meatballs, in a bowl, combine the meat, onion, bread crumbs, egg, parsley, garlic, the cinnamon and cumin (if using), salt, and pepper. Knead with your hands until all the ingredients are fully incorporated and evenly distributed throughout the mixture. (If you have time, cover and refrigerate the mixture for 1 hour to make forming the meatballs easier.) Using your hands, shape the mixture into tiny meatballs and set aside.

In a large saucepan over medium heat, warm the olive oil. Add the onion and sauté until tender, about 10 minutes. Add the saffron, if using, the chickpeas, potatoes, stock, and the tomato, if using. Raise the heat to high and bring to a boil. Reduce the heat to low and simmer, uncovered, to blend the flavors and partially cook the potatoes, about 10 minutes.

Slip the uncooked meatballs into the broth and simmer gently until cooked through, about 20 minutes. Season with salt and pepper.

Using a slotted spoon, transfer the meatballs to warmed soup bowls, dividing evenly. Ladle the hot soup stock and an equal amount of the vegetables over the meatballs. Sprinkle with the parsley and chopped eggs, if using, and serve immediately.

serves 6

Cazuela and Tacho de Barro

Every cook in Spain and Portugal has at least one—and more likely several—earthenware cooking vessels on the kitchen shelf. In Spain, these invaluable dishes are called *cazuelas,* from the Arabic *qas'ah,* or bowl, while in Portugal they are known as *tachos de barro.* They come in all colors, shapes, and sizes, from small enough to contain a tapa of *champiñones al ajillo* to large enough to handle a *caldeirada* served to a dozen friends. They retain heat magnificently and can be used in the oven and carefully over a direct flame.

New earthenware dishes must be seasoned before they are used, or you risk them cracking when they come in contact with direct heat. An excellent Spanish cook advised me on the intricacies of the curing process: first, rub the unglazed base of the *cazuela* with three cloves of garlic, then allow it to stand for a bit until the garlic juices are absorbed, and finally fill it with hot water and bring the water slowly to a boil. Once it boils, discard the water, and the *cazuela*—or *tacho de barro*—is ready to use. I suspect the garlic rub may be simply folklore, but I am not one to ignore the advice of a fine cook. To

avoid future cracking, remember to never pour boiling liquid into a cold *cazuela* nor put a hot *cazuela* onto a cold surface.

Sopa de Ajo

garlic soup

Sopa de ajo was probably the inspiration for the original gazpacho. Traditionally, it was a mixture of chopped garlic, crumbled stale bread, olive oil, and water, the pantry staples of the poor. But it has evolved to have many regional variations. In Málaga, cooks might use fish stock, and in Galicia, rye bread is used.

The addition of paprika earmarks this recipe as the Madrid version. Sometimes the eggs are beaten and then whisked into the soup. In every case, however, the garlicky creation is believed to be a surefire cure for hangovers.

6 tablespoons (3 fl oz / 90 ml) olive oil

12 cloves garlic

12 thin slices coarse country bread, crusts removed

2 teaspoons sweet paprika

6 cups (48 fl oz / 1.5 l) chicken stock or water

salt and freshly ground pepper to taste

6 eggs

chopped fresh flat-leaf (Italian) parsley

❦ Preheat an oven to 350°F (180°C).

❦ In a large saucepan over medium heat, warm the oil. Add the garlic cloves and sauté until golden and fragrant, 3–4 minutes. Using a slotted spoon, remove and discard the garlic. Working in batches, add the bread to the garlic-flavored oil and sauté, turning as needed, until pale gold and crisp, 4–5 minutes. Using the slotted spoon, transfer the bread to 6 ovenproof individual bowls or *cazuelas,* placing 2 slices in each bowl. Put the bowls on a baking sheet. Add the paprika to the pan over medium heat, stir once, and then add the stock or water and bring to a boil. Season with salt and pepper.

❦ Break 1 egg into each bowl and ladle the boiling stock or water over the eggs, dividing it evenly. Slip the baking sheet into the oven and bake until the egg whites have set up but the yolks are still runny, about 10 minutes.

❦ Garnish each bowl with parsley and serve at once.

---

serves 6

Algarve

Amêijoas na Cataplana

clams with sausage and tomatoes

A cataplana *is a clam-shaped hinged pan typical of the Algarve. It is used on the stove top and can be turned over to ensure even cooking of its contents. You can buy a* cataplana *in a specialty cookware store, or you can make this dish in a deep frying pan with a tight-fitting lid. Serve the clams in shallow bowls, either spooned over wedges of boiled potatoes or accompanied with lots of coarse country bread.*

2 tablespoons olive oil

3 yellow onions, thinly sliced

4 cloves garlic, finely minced

1–2 teaspoons red pepper flakes or 2 fresh chiles, finely minced

1 bay leaf, torn into pieces

¼ lb (125 g) presunto or prosciutto, diced

¼ lb (125 g) linguiça or chouriço, *casings removed and crumbled*

1 cup (8 fl oz/250 ml) dry white wine

2–3 cups (12–18 oz/375–560 g) diced canned tomato with the juices

3 lb (1.5 kg) small clams such as Manila, well scrubbed

½ cup (¾ oz/20 g) chopped fresh flat-leaf (Italian) parsley

freshly ground black pepper to taste

lemon wedges (optional)

❦ In a large sauté pan over medium heat, warm the olive oil. Add the onions and sauté until tender, about 8 minutes. Add the garlic and the red pepper flakes, if using, and sauté until softened, about 3 minutes more. Add the bay leaf, ham, sausage, wine, tomato, and the fresh chiles, if using. Simmer for 10 minutes. Add the clams, hinge side down, discarding any that are open or broken. Cover and cook until the clams open, 3–5 minutes.

❦ Spoon the clams and juices into warmed bowls, discarding any clams that failed to open. Sprinkle with the parsley and a liberal grinding of black pepper. Serve with lemon wedges, if desired.

serves 4

Sofrito, Refogado, and Picada

A trinity of mixtures, the *sofrito,* the *refogado,* and the *picada,* is what contributes distinctive character to countless Spanish and Portuguese dishes.

Spanish cooks use the *sofrito,* a kind of base sauce, to give body and richness to soups, stews, braises, and fricassees. At its most basic, a *sofrito* is onions and garlic cooked slowly in olive oil until soft and golden. Tomatoes are usually added, and sometimes chiles, peppers (capsicums), and herbs broaden the palate of flavors.

The Portuguese *refogado,* also known as a *cebolada,* is a close cousin to the *sofrito.* Cooks from Oporto to Faro begin a myriad of dishes with a splash of olive oil and a shower of onions. The onions are cooked until they form a thick, sweet golden purée, then garlic and tomatoes may be added.

The *picada* is a traditional Catalan preparation. Commonly made from nuts, fried bread, garlic, and perhaps spices, ground together to a paste, the fragrant mixture is added during the final stages of cooking to thicken a sauce and heighten its bouquet.

Potaje de Garbanzos y Espinacas

chickpea and spinach soup

This is a Lenten dish, served on Good Friday and other fast days in Madrid, where chickpeas are popular additions to soups and cocidos. Salt cod is typically added to round out the flavors. The calendar of the Catholic Church traditionally includes many such holy days on which believers are required to abstain from eating meat—indeed, nearly one-third of the days of the year—thus, meatless soups such as this one are not unusual in the Spanish kitchen. The fact that until relatively recent times only those of privilege have been able to afford meat has also contributed to a roster of meat-free recipes. Yet this soup has a non-Lenten life as well, with cooks stirring diced ham or a ham hock into the pot in place of the salt cod.

A picada of fried bread and garlic (see sidebar, left) is added to enrich the soup, producing a fairly thick result. If you want a soupier dish, thin it with a little vegetable stock or water. Minus the fish, the thick soup appears on tapas tables in Seville.

In Portugal, a similar soup is called sopa de grão com espinafres. *The picada is missing, of course. Instead, Portuguese cooks purée half of the cooked chickpeas and stir the purée back into the soup pot. A garnish of fresh cilantro (fresh coriander) is added before serving.*

2 cups (14 oz/440 g) dried chickpeas (garbanzos)

7 cloves garlic

2 yellow onions

1 bay leaf

2 teaspoons salt, plus salt to taste

½ lb (250 g) boneless salt cod, soaked (optional; see glossary, page 249)

1½ lb (750 g) spinach, stemmed

3 tablespoons olive oil

2 slices coarse country bread, crusts removed

pinch of saffron threads

water or vegetable stock, if needed

freshly ground pepper to taste

½–1 cup (3–6 oz/90–185 g) diced cooked ham (optional)

2 hard-boiled eggs, peeled and chopped (optional)

⚜ Pick over the chickpeas and discard any stones or misshapen beans. Rinse well and place in a bowl with water to cover generously. Let soak overnight in the refrigerator.

⚜ The next day, drain the chickpeas and place them in a saucepan with water to cover. Add 4 cloves of the garlic, the onions, and the bay leaf and bring the mixture to a boil over high heat. Reduce the heat to low, cover, and simmer, adding the 2 teaspoons salt after the first 15 minutes of cooking, until the chickpeas are tender, about 1 hour.

⚜ Meanwhile, drain the cod, if using, and place in a saucepan with water to cover. Bring to a gentle simmer over medium heat and cook until tender, 10–15 minutes. Drain well and, when cool enough to handle, using your fingers, break the cod into bite-sized pieces, removing and discarding any bits of skin and any small bones. Set the pieces of fish aside.

⚜ When the chickpeas are done, using a slotted spoon, remove the onions and garlic cloves and set aside. Remove and discard the bay leaf. Leave the chickpeas in their liquid off the heat.

⚜ Place the spinach in a sauté pan with just the rinsing water clinging to the leaves. Place over medium heat and cook, turning occasionally, until wilted, 3–4 minutes. Remove the pan from the heat, drain the spinach well, pressing out excess moisture, and drain and chop the spinach coarsely. Set aside.

⚜ In a small sauté pan over medium heat, warm the olive oil. Add the bread and the remaining 3 garlic cloves and sauté until the bread and garlic are golden, 5–6 minutes. Transfer to a food processor or blender and add the saffron, the reserved cooked onions and garlic, and 1 cup (8 fl oz/250 ml) of the chickpea liquid. Process until the mixture is a smooth purée. This is the *picada*.

⚜ Pour the *picada* into the chickpeas and add the wilted spinach. Stir well and bring to a simmer over medium heat. If the mixture is too thick, thin with water or vegetable stock. Season to taste with salt and lots of pepper. Add the salt cod or ham, if using, and heat through.

⚜ To serve, ladle the soup into warmed bowls. Garnish each serving with the chopped eggs, if using, then serve immediately.

serves 6–8

Andalusia

Cachorrenas

bitter orange soup with fish and clams

Cádiz is a port city on the Atlantic that dates back to the time of the Phoenicians. Bitter Seville oranges traditionally flavor this local soup of clams and fish, but because they are rarely found outside of Spain, a mixture of orange and lime juices makes a respectable substitute. A similar soup is called caldo de perro.

1 lb (500 g) firm white fish fillets such as monkfish, flounder, or cod

kosher salt for sprinkling

3 tablespoons olive oil

1 large yellow onion, chopped

2 cloves garlic, minced

1 teaspoon ground cumin

2 teaspoons sweet paprika

4 cups (32 fl oz/1 l) fish stock or water

½ lb (250 g) small clams such as Manila, well scrubbed

⅓ cup (3 fl oz/80 ml) fresh orange juice

2 tablespoons fresh lime juice

salt and freshly ground pepper to taste

chopped fresh mint or fresh flat-leaf (Italian) parsley (optional)

❧ Cut the fish fillets into strips 1½ inches (4 cm) long and ½ inch (12 mm) wide and place on a plate. Sprinkle lightly with kosher salt, cover, and refrigerate until ready to cook.

❧ In a saucepan over medium heat, warm the olive oil. Add the onion and sauté until tender, 8–10 minutes. Add the garlic, cumin, and paprika, reduce the heat to low, and cook, stirring occasionally, until the garlic is tender, about 5 minutes. Add the fish stock or water, raise the heat to medium, and bring to a boil. Reduce the heat to low and simmer for 15 minutes to blend the flavors. Add the fish pieces and the clams (discard any clams that are open) and cook until the fish is opaque throughout and the clams have opened, 7–10 minutes. Discard any clams that do not open. Stir in the orange and lime juices and season with salt and pepper.

❧ Ladle into warmed bowls and garnish with mint or parsley, if desired. Serve immediately.

serves 4–6

Andalusia

Sopa de Almejas con Piñones

clam and pine nut soup

The birthplace of this hearty soup is the clam-rich marshlands of the Guadalquivir River in Andalusia.

2½ lb (1.25 kg) small clams, well scrubbed

3½ cups (28 fl oz/875 ml) water

2 cups (8 oz/250 g) pine nuts

¼ cup (2 fl oz/60 ml) olive oil

5 cloves garlic, thinly sliced

1 tablespoon all-purpose (plain) flour

2 cups (16 fl oz/500 ml) fish stock or water

⅓ cup (3 fl oz/80 ml) dry sherry

6 slices coarse country bread, crusts removed and toasted

3 eggs, beaten

❧ Put the clams in a wide saucepan, discarding any that are open. Add the water and bring to a boil over high heat. Cover and cook just until the clams open, 5–7 minutes. Remove from the heat. Using a slotted spoon, transfer the clams to a bowl, discarding any that failed to open. Reserve the liquid. Remove all but 12 clams from their shells. Set aside.

❧ In a frying pan over medium heat, toast the pine nuts, shaking the pan often, until golden, about 5 minutes. Let the nuts cool, then grind to a paste in a mortar or food processor.

❧ In a saucepan over medium heat, warm the olive oil. Add the garlic and sauté until fragrant, 2–3 minutes. Add the flour and cook, stirring, until blended, 1–2 minutes. Add the ground nuts, the stock or water, the sherry, and the reserved clam liquid. Simmer over low heat, uncovered, for 15 minutes. Meanwhile, preheat an oven to 425°F (220°C).

❧ Add the shelled clams to the soup and heat through. Place 6 ovenproof soup bowls on a baking sheet and ladle the soup into them. Top with the reserved clams in the shell. Place a slice of bread on top of each soup bowl. Distribute the beaten eggs evenly among the bowls.

❧ Bake until the tops are golden and slightly set, 5–8 minutes. Serve immediately.

serves 6

Andalusia

Gazpacho Andaluz

cold tomato soup

After the Spaniards returned from the New World with tomatoes and peppers, the original bread, oil, and water gazpacho evolved into this refreshing summer soup. Countless variations exist on this specialty of Andalusia. Some gazpachos have bread crumbs incorporated into the mix; others use bread in the form of a garnish of garlic croutons. In some recipes, all the vegetables are puréed. In others, only half the vegetables are puréed and finely chopped vegetables are served as a garnish. Some soups have herbs, while others have none. But all of these gazpachos have one common element: ripe and flavorful tomatoes. This soup can be made the day before serving.

2 slices day-old coarse country bread, crusts removed, soaked in water just to cover, and squeezed dry

2 small cucumbers, peeled, seeded, and coarsely chopped

1 small yellow or red (Spanish) onion, chopped

2 cloves garlic, minced

2½ lb (1.25 kg) ripe tomatoes, peeled, seeded, and coarsely chopped

2 small green bell peppers (capsicums), seeded and coarsely chopped

6 tablespoons (3 fl oz/90 ml) extra-virgin olive oil

3 tablespoons red wine vinegar, or to taste

salt and freshly ground pepper to taste

ice water or tomato juice (optional)

GARNISHES

4–6 tablespoons (2–3 fl oz/60–90 ml) extra-virgin olive oil

2 tablespoons minced garlic

2 slices coarse country bread, cut into ½-inch (12-mm) cubes

2 cups (12 oz/375 g) diced, peeled ripe tomato

½ cup (2½ oz/75 g) diced, peeled, and seeded cucumber

½ cup (2½ oz/75 g) minced green bell pepper (capsicum)

¼ cup (1½ oz/45 g) finely minced red (Spanish) onion

♛ Put the soaked bread, cucumbers, onion, garlic, most of the chopped tomatoes, and 1 of the bell peppers in a food processor or blender. Purée until smooth and pour into a large bowl.

♛ Finely chop the rest of the chopped tomatoes and the remaining bell pepper and add to the soup. Stir in the olive oil and vinegar and season with salt and pepper. If the soup is too thick, add a little ice water, or if the tomatoes are not perfect, add a little tomato juice. Cover and refrigerate until well chilled.

♛ To prepare the garnishes, in a frying pan over medium heat, warm the olive oil. Add the garlic and sauté briefly until fragrant. Add the bread cubes and fry, turning as needed, until golden brown on all sides, 4–5 minutes. Transfer to paper towels to drain.

♛ Put the croutons, tomato, cucumber, bell pepper, and onion in small separate bowls and set on the table. Ladle the gazpacho into chilled bowls and let diners add garnishes as desired.

serves 6–8

Andalusia's clear blue waters, white villages, and bountiful tables have long seduced sculptors and painters, composers and poets.

Minho

Caldo Verde

"green" soup

A specialty of Minho, caldo verde is served all over
Portugal. It calls for couve, *a dark green cabbage*
rarely found beyond the Iberian Peninsula, so you will
need to substitute kale or collard greens. If you choose
to purchase a dry sausage, you may skip the first step.

½ *lb (250 g)* linguiça *or* chouriço

¼ *cup (2 fl oz / 60 ml) olive oil, plus*
4 teaspoons

1 large yellow onion, chopped

3 potatoes, about 1 lb (500 g) total weight,
peeled and cut into slices ¼ inch (6 mm) thick

2 cloves garlic, finely minced

6 cups (48 fl oz / 1.5 l) water

2 teaspoons salt, plus salt to taste

¾ *lb (375 g) kale or collard greens, tough stems*
removed and very finely shredded

freshly ground pepper to taste

♨ If using fresh sausages (see note), preheat an oven
to 375°F (190°C). Prick with a fork and place on a
baking sheet. Bake until firm, about 25 minutes.
Remove from the oven, let cool slightly, then slice
¼ inch (6 mm) thick; set aside.

♨ In a large saucepan over medium heat, warm the
¼ cup (2 fl oz/60 ml) olive oil. Add the onion and
sauté until tender, about 8 minutes. Add the potatoes
and garlic and sauté for a few minutes, stirring often.
Add the water and the 2 teaspoons salt, cover, reduce
the heat to low, and simmer until the potatoes are
very soft, about 20 minutes.

♨ Mash the potatoes to a purée with a wooden
spoon or potato masher. Add the sausage and cook
over low heat for 5 minutes longer to warm through.
Add the greens, stir well, and simmer, uncovered, for
3–5 minutes. Do not overcook. The greens should
stay bright green and slightly crunchy. Season with
salt and pepper.

♨ Ladle the soup into bowls, drizzle each serving
with 1 teaspoon olive oil, and serve at once.

serves 4

Estremadura

Caldeirada

fisherman's soup

Caldeirada, *the Portuguese fisherman's hearty soup, is prepared with an unchanging list of basic ingredients: onions, garlic, tomatoes, chiles, bell peppers, and, of course, white wine. Beyond those, however, there is much variation. In Lisbon, the soup features white fish, clams, fried bread triangles, and sometimes boiled potatoes. In the Algarve, there are no potatoes but lots of local shellfish. This recipe draws on inspiration and the day's catch, so feel free to improvise, adding clams, shrimp (prawns), scallops, or squid during the last few minutes of simmering. In Galicia, the similarly named* caldereta *is a paprika-tinged fish stew traditionally made on board a fishing vessel. The potatoes that go into the pot are typically cooked in seawater—thereby guaranteeing the stew's marine credentials. In the Balearics,* caldereta de langosta, *flavored with thyme and garlic, showcases the islands' succulent lobsters.*

2 lb (1 kg) assorted white fish fillets such as cod, halibut, snapper, flounder, and sea bass, cut into 2-inch (5-cm) pieces

kosher salt for sprinkling

3 tablespoons olive oil, plus extra for frying bread

2 yellow onions, chopped

2 green bell peppers (capsicums), seeded and chopped

4 tomatoes, peeled, seeded, and chopped

3 large cloves garlic, minced

1 cup (8 fl oz/250 ml) dry white wine, plus about ¼ cup (2 fl oz/60 ml) if steaming clams separately

freshly ground pepper to taste

2 lb (1 kg) clams, well scrubbed

6 slices coarse country bread, crusts removed

6 tablespoons (3 oz/90 g) unsalted butter

chopped fresh flat-leaf (Italian) parsley

❧ Sprinkle the fish fillets with kosher salt, cover, and refrigerate for at least 1 hour or as long as 2 hours.

❧ In a large saucepan over medium heat, warm the 3 tablespoons olive oil. Add the onions and bell peppers and sauté until softened, about 10 minutes.

❧ Add the tomatoes, garlic, and the 1 cup (8 fl oz/250 ml) wine and season with salt and some grindings of pepper. Add the fish, raise the heat to high, and bring to a boil. Reduce the heat to low, cover, and simmer gently for about 10 minutes. If the pan is large enough, add the clams (discard any that are open or broken), cover, and steam until they open, about 5 minutes. By then, the fish should test done. If the pan is too small to accommodate the clams, steam them in the ¼ cup (2 fl oz/60 ml) white wine in a separate pan for about 5 minutes and then add them to the stew, discarding any that failed to open.

❧ In a large sauté pan over medium heat, warm about 4 tablespoons olive oil. In batches, add the bread and fry, turning as needed, until golden, 5–6 minutes. Using tongs, transfer to paper towels to drain. Add more oil to the pan for each batch. Cut each slice on the diagonal and place 2 triangles on the bottom of each of 6 large soup bowls.

❧ When the soup is ready, add the butter and swirl the pan a few times to thicken the juices. Ladle the soup and the fish over the bread. Sprinkle with parsley and serve immediately.

serves 6

Galicia

Sopa de Castañas

chestnut soup

Until the eighteenth century, chestnuts played a significant role in the Galician diet. But then disease wiped out the region's vast stands of chestnut trees, and potatoes quickly replaced the once-abundant nuts in everyday cooking.

1 lb (500 g) fresh chestnuts or about 10 oz (315 g) canned or vacuum-packed chestnuts, without sugar

6 cups (48 fl oz / 1.5 l) water

1 yellow onion, chopped, plus 3 tablespoons chopped

1 clove garlic, chopped

¼ lb (125 g) serrano ham, chopped

3 oz (90 g) salt pork, chopped

1 teaspoon salt, plus salt to taste

3 tablespoons olive oil

freshly ground pepper to taste

3 tablespoons fresh lemon juice

6 thin slices coarse country bread, cut in half and toasted

❧ If using fresh chestnuts, cut a deep cross in the flat side of each nut. Bring a saucepan three-fourths full of water to a boil, add the chestnuts, and boil for 15 minutes. Drain and, while the nuts are still warm, remove the thin shell and the furry inner lining. Cut the nuts in half and return them to the saucepan. If using canned chestnuts, drain them; if using vacuum-packed chestnuts, unwrap. Halve the nuts and place in a saucepan.

❧ Add the water, the 1 chopped onion, garlic, ham, salt pork, and 1 teaspoon salt to the chestnuts and bring to a boil over high heat. Cover partially, reduce the heat to low, and simmer until the nuts are very soft, about 1½ hours.

❧ In a small frying pan over medium heat, warm the oil. Add the 3 tablespoons onion and sauté until tender, about 8 minutes. Stir the onion into the soup. Season with salt and pepper, then stir in the lemon juice. To serve, ladle the hot soup into warmed soup bowls and top with the toasted bread.

serves 6

Paradores and Pousadas

Most travelers feel a journey is incomplete unless they experience a country's true regional dishes. The Spanish system of *paradores*, government-operated hotels, ensures that visitors can do just that. These hostelries are primarily housed in landmark buildings such as former convents, monasteries, manor houses, palaces, and, in the case of the lovely Parador El Molino Viejo, the ruins of an Asturian cider mill. Guests are invariably treated to an exquisite table of local dishes, whether it be the roast suckling pig at the fifteenth-century Parador de Avila or the *caldereta extremeña* (goat stew) at the richly landscaped Parador de Trujillo.

The Portuguese, seeing the value of the *parador* system, borrowed the concept and established their own chain of accommodations called *pousadas*. As with their Spanish counterparts, these operations tend to be housed in historic structures, such as the Pousada do Castelo in Obidos, once a medieval castle, or the Pousada de Santa Marinha in Guimarães, where today sixteenth-century monks' cells shelter a steady stream of guests.

Alentejo

Açorda à Alentejana

bread soup with coriander, garlic, and egg

Each serving of this well-known Portuguese soup is crowned with a poached egg that the diner swirls into the soup.

3 tablespoons finely minced garlic, plus 1 whole clove

1 teaspoon kosher or sea salt

1 cup (1½ oz/45 g) chopped fresh cilantro (fresh coriander)

¾ cup (6 fl oz/180 ml) extra-virgin olive oil

6 thick slices coarse country bread, each about 1 inch (2.5 cm) thick, crusts removed

6 eggs

5–6 cups (40–48 fl oz/1.25–1.5 l) chicken stock or water

❦ In a mortar, combine the minced garlic, salt, and half of the cilantro and mash to a coarse paste. Add ¼ cup (2 fl oz/60 ml) of the olive oil, 1 tablespoon at a time, mixing until well blended. Spoon into 6 warmed ovenproof soup bowls and keep warm.

❦ In a large frying pan over medium heat, warm about ¼ cup (2 fl oz/60 ml) of the remaining oil. Add as many of the bread slices as will fit comfortably and sauté, turning as needed, until golden, 5–6 minutes total. Using tongs, transfer to paper towels to drain. Repeat with the remaining bread slices and oil. While the bread is still hot, rub on both sides with the whole garlic clove, then cut into 1½-inch (4-cm) cubes. Distribute the cubes evenly among the bowls and toss with the garlic mixture.

❦ In a large sauté pan, pour in water to a depth of 1½ inches (4 cm). Bring the liquid to just under a boil. One at a time, break the eggs and carefully slip into the water. Cook until the whites are barely firm and the yolks are just glazed, 3–5 minutes. Using a slotted spoon, transfer them to a bowl of cold water.

❦ In a saucepan, bring the stock or water to a boil and then ladle most of it over the bread mixture in the bowls. Using the slotted spoon, place 1 egg on top of the bread mixture in each bowl. Gently ladle on the remaining hot stock or water. Sprinkle with the remaining chopped cilantro and serve at once.

serves 6

Beira Alta

Sopa de Feijão Verde à moda da Beira

green bean soup

In the spring, young fava (broad) beans may be used instead of green beans in this popular soup from the largely rural, mountainous Beira Alta. If possible, use vegetable stock, as it allows the flavors of the vegetables to be more distinct than if you use poultry stock. Like most peasant soups in Portugal, however, the soup is traditionally made with water.

5 tablespoons (2½ fl oz/75 ml) extra-virgin olive oil

2 yellow onions, chopped

1 lb (500 g) tomatoes, peeled, seeded, and chopped

1 lb (500 g) boiling potatoes, peeled and diced

4 cups (32 fl oz/1 l) vegetable or chicken stock

1 lb (500 g) green beans, trimmed and cut on the diagonal into 1-inch (2.5-cm) pieces

salt and freshly ground pepper to taste

3 tablespoons chopped fresh mint (optional)

❦ In a large saucepan over medium heat, warm the olive oil. Add the onions and sauté until tender, 8–10 minutes. Add the tomatoes and potatoes and sauté, stirring, until well combined, 3–5 minutes. Add the stock, raise the heat to high, and bring to a boil. Reduce the heat to low and simmer, uncovered, until the potatoes are very tender, about 20 minutes. Remove from the heat and let cool slightly.

❦ Working in batches, ladle the soup into a food processor or blender and purée until smooth. Return the purée to the saucepan.

❦ Bring a saucepan three-fourths full of salted water to a boil. Add the green beans and cook until crisp-tender, about 5 minutes. Drain, reserving a bit of the cooking water to add to the purée if it is too thick.

❦ Reheat the purée and season with salt and pepper. Add the green beans and simmer over medium heat until heated through, about 5 minutes. Thin with the reserved cooking water if needed.

❦ Ladle into warmed soup bowls and garnish with the chopped mint, if desired. Serve at once.

serves 4–6

Andalusia

Olla Gitana

gypsy stew

Andalusia is the home of Spain's Gypsies. This stew, a favorite of the Gypsy table, is traditionally made in a round pot called an olla. Earthenware or iron, the olla is narrower at the top than at the bottom and has handles for easy maneuvering. Without the meat, this stew is a rich soup of neighboring Levante, but with the addition of pork ribs, it becomes an Andalusian meal-in-a-bowl. The use of the almond picada belies a strong Moorish influence, while the pear is the Gypsy touch. Some recipes replace the pork ribs with tripe and assorted sausages.

1 cup (7 oz/220 g) dried chickpeas
(garbanzo beans)

1½ lb (750 g) meaty pork spareribs

½ lb (250 g) green beans, trimmed and cut into
2-inch (5-cm) lengths

1½ cups (7½ oz/235 g) diced or coarsely
chopped peeled pumpkin

2 or 3 pears, peeled, halved, cored, and cut into
chunks

1 bunch Swiss chard, coarsely chopped

½ cup (4 fl oz/125 ml) olive oil

10 almonds, toasted

1 slice coarse country bread, crusts removed

1 clove garlic

2 tablespoons red or white wine vinegar

1 yellow onion, diced

1 tablespoon sweet paprika

2 tomatoes, peeled, seeded, and diced

pinch of saffron threads steeped in ¼ cup
(2 fl oz/60 ml) hot chicken stock

☙ Pick over the chickpeas, discarding any stones or misshapen beans. Rinse well and place in a bowl with water to cover generously. Let soak overnight in the refrigerator.

☙ The next day, drain the chickpeas and place in a deep saucepan. Add the pork ribs and cold water to cover. Bring to a boil over high heat, reduce the heat to low, and skim off any foam. Simmer until almost tender, about 1 hour. Add the green beans, pumpkin, pears, and Swiss chard and simmer for 10 minutes.

☙ Meanwhile, in a sauté pan over medium heat, warm the olive oil. Add the almonds, bread, and garlic and cook, stirring the almonds and garlic and turning the bread as needed, until golden, about 5 minutes. Using a slotted spoon, transfer the bread, almonds, and garlic to a mortar and grind with a pestle. Add the vinegar and mix well. This is the *picada*.

☙ Add the onion to the oil remaining in the pan and sauté until pale gold, 10–12 minutes. Stir in the paprika and then the tomatoes. Cook for 10 minutes to soften the tomatoes, then add the saffron and stock and mix well.

☙ Add the *picada* and the tomato mixture to the soup and simmer over low heat for 10 minutes to blend the flavors. Taste and adjust the seasonings.

☙ Ladle into warmed bowls and serve hot.

serves 6–8

Minho

Canja

chicken soup with rice, lemon, and mint

Along with caldo verde *(page 94), this is the best-known Portuguese soup and is served all over the country. As far back as the fifteenth century, it was recommended as a curative to anyone suffering from consumption. It is comforting and nourishing and quite simple to prepare. The stock must be rich and flavorful, which is best accomplished by reducing regular stock over high heat to concentrate the flavor. In Alentejo province, cooks sometimes add* linguiça *instead of chicken, and many cooks now use tiny rice-shaped pasta instead of rice. The generous addition of mint contributes a signature flavor of the northern Portuguese provinces.*

5 cups (40 fl oz/1.25 l) reduced chicken stock (see note)

1 cup (8 fl oz/250 ml) water

1 cup (7 oz/220 g) long-grain white rice

1 whole chicken breast, about 1 lb (500 g), boned, skinned, and cut into strips 1 inch (2.5 cm) long and ½ inch (12 mm) wide

¼ cup (2 fl oz/60 ml) fresh lemon juice

salt and freshly ground pepper to taste

6 tablespoons (⅓ oz/10 g) chopped fresh mint

✾ In a small, heavy saucepan, combine 1 cup (8 fl oz/ 250 ml) of the chicken stock and the water. Bring to a boil over high heat, stir in the rice, reduce the heat to low, cover, and simmer until all the liquid is absorbed, 20–25 minutes. Remove from the heat.

✾ Pour the remaining 4 cups (32 fl oz/1 l) chicken stock into a heavy saucepan and bring to a simmer over medium heat. Add the chicken pieces, reduce the heat to low, and cook very gently until tender and cooked through, 15–20 minutes.

✾ Add the rice and lemon juice and season with salt and pepper. Heat briefly, then stir in the mint, ladle into warmed bowls, and serve at once.

serves 4–6

New Castile

Cocido Madrileño

madrid hotpot

Cocido madrileño *is the classic Spanish one-pot meal, cooked in an* olla *for hours. In Catalonia, a similar dish is called* escudella de Pagès *and includes both white beans and chickpeas, while the broth has both rice and noodles. The version from La Mancha is known as* olla podrida, *or "rotting pot," a dish that Cervantes memorialized in* Don Quixote.

Versions of this bean-and-meat stew appear all over Spain and Portugal, and in Spain, the chickpea, introduced by the Carthaginians via Cádiz or Málaga, is always used. In Portugal, however, the famous cozido à portuguesa *does not contain any beans, although it does include meats, poultry, sausages, cabbage, potatoes, carrots, and turnips. The broth is served first, then the rice is heaped on a platter and the sliced meats and vegetables are placed on top.*

1½ cups (10½ oz/330 g) dried chickpeas (garbanzo beans)

6 oz (185 g) bacon, cut into 3 equal pieces

1 pig's foot

1 lb (500 g) beef or veal shank, in one piece

1 stewing chicken, about 4 lb (2 kg)

1 bouquet garni of 3 thyme sprigs, 3 parsley sprigs, 1 bay leaf, 2 or 3 cloves, and a few peppercorns

¼ lb (125 g) serrano ham, in one piece

¼ lb (125 g) blood sausage

3 qt (3 l) water, plus ½ cup (4 fl oz/125 ml)

4 boiling potatoes such as Yukon gold, peeled and diced

3 leeks, including the tender green part, sliced

3 carrots, peeled and cut into thick slices

2 medium turnips, peeled and cut into eighths

½ cup (3½ oz/105 g) short-grain white rice or (1½ oz/45 g) broken egg noodles

salt and freshly ground pepper to taste

⅔ lb (10 oz/315 g) chorizo

1–2 tablespoons olive oil

3 cups (9 oz/280 g) coarsely chopped green cabbage

❧ Pick over the chickpeas, discarding any stones or misshapen beans. Rinse well and place in a bowl with water to cover generously. Let soak overnight in the refrigerator.

❧ The next day, drain the chickpeas and place in a large, deep pot. Add the bacon.

❧ Bring another large pot three-fourths full of water to a boil. Add the pig's foot, beef or veal shank, and chicken and blanch for 5 minutes. Lift them out of the water and add to the pot holding the chickpeas.

❧ Place the ingredients for the bouquet garni on a piece of cheesecloth (muslin), bring together the corners, and tie securely with kitchen string. Add to the pot holding the chickpeas along with the ham, blood sausage, and the 3 qt (3 l) water. Bring to a boil over high heat, reduce the heat to low, and skim off any foam. Cover and simmer gently until the meats are tender and falling off the bone, about 2½ hours.

❧ Add the potatoes, leeks, carrots, and turnips and continue to simmer until the vegetables are tender, about 35 minutes longer.

❧ Remove the meats from the pot and cut into bite-sized pieces. Set aside.

❧ Scoop out 6 cups (48 fl oz/1.5 l) of the cooking liquid into another pan. Bring to a boil, add the rice or noodles, and cook until tender, just a few minutes for the noodles or 20 minutes for the rice. Season with salt and pepper.

❧ Prick the chorizo in a few places with a fork. In a large sauté pan over medium-high heat, brown the chorizo in the olive oil for a few minutes, turning as needed. Add the cabbage and the ½ cup (4 fl oz/ 125 ml) water and simmer until the cabbage is tender and the chorizo is warmed through, about 8 minutes. Remove the chorizo and cut into pieces.

❧ To serve, using a large skimmer, scoop out the chickpeas and vegetables and mound them in the center of a large deep platter. Pile the meats on top, discarding any bones. Pour on enough of the remaining cooking liquids to moisten lightly. Serve the rice or noodle broth for the first course, then the sausage and cabbage, and finally the chickpeas, vegetables, and meat.

serves 8–10

Estremadura

Açorda de Mariscos

shellfish and bread soup

Typical of Lisbon, this soup is so well regarded that a local restaurant has been named for it: the venerable Pap' Açorda, located in the city's sixteenth-century Bairro Alto district, serves countless bowls of the flavorful dish daily. But tascas all over the picturesque cobblestoned capital offer açorda de mariscos, *from tiny dozen-seat dining rooms in the Moorish-built Alfama district to more ample spaces in the eighteenth-century Baixa and Chiado areas.*

The soup sometimes includes chunks of fish to stretch it when economy is a concern. Occasionally, it uses only shrimp (prawns) and a stock made from the shells, with a bit of chopped tomato added, along with a garnish of chopped hard-boiled eggs. Be sure the bowls are piping hot so that the stock will not cool down too quickly. It needs to remain hot enough to cook the eggs partially.

12–18 slices coarse country bread, about 1 inch (2.5 cm) thick

1 clove garlic, plus 4 tablespoons (1½ oz / 45 g) finely minced garlic

½ teaspoon salt

6 cups (48 fl oz / 1.5 l) fish stock or a mixture of fish stock and shrimp stock

¾ cup (6 fl oz / 180 ml) extra-virgin olive oil

2 yellow onions, chopped

1–2 teaspoons red pepper flakes

12 mussels, well scrubbed and debearded

18 clams (or more if tiny), well scrubbed

⅓ cup (3 fl oz / 80 ml) dry white wine

18 shrimp (prawns), peeled and deveined

¼ cup (⅓ oz / 10 g) finely chopped fresh flat-leaf (Italian) parsley

½ cup (¾ oz / 20 g) finely chopped fresh cilantro (fresh coriander)

6 eggs, at room temperature

❧ Preheat a broiler (griller). Arrange the bread slices on a baking sheet and slip under the broiler. Toast, turning once, until golden. Remove from the broiler. While the slices are still warm, rub them on both sides with the whole garlic clove and then cut them into 1-inch (2.5-cm) cubes. Set aside.

❧ In a mortar, combine 2 tablespoons of the minced garlic and the salt and mash to a paste with a pestle.

❧ In a saucepan, bring the stock to a boil. Adjust the heat so that it remains at a simmer.

❧ In another saucepan over low heat, warm 2 tablespoons of the olive oil. Add the onions and sauté until tender, 8–10 minutes. Add the remaining 2 tablespoons minced garlic and the red pepper flakes and sauté until the garlic is fragrant, about 3 minutes. Add the hot stock and simmer for 3–5 minutes to allow the flavors to marry.

❧ In a large sauté pan, combine the mussels and clams, discarding any mussels that fail to close to the touch and any clams that are open or broken. Pour in the wine, place over high heat, cover, and cook until the shellfish open, 3–6 minutes. Using a slotted spoon, transfer the mussels and clams to a bowl, discarding any that failed to open; cover and keep warm. Add the liquid in the pan to the stock.

❧ Add the shrimp to the hot stock and poach until opaque throughout, about 3 minutes.

❧ Divide the bread, parsley, cilantro, and garlic paste evenly among warmed soup bowls. Divide the remaining 10 tablespoons (5 fl oz/160 ml) olive oil evenly among the bowls. Now distribute the cooked shrimp, clams, and mussels among the bowls. Break 1 egg in each bowl. Bring the remaining stock to a boil and ladle into the bowls.

❧ Serve at once.

serves 6

Açorda, Miga, and Sopa Seca

The breads of Portugal are generally dark-crusted beauties, and generations of Portuguese cooks have been reluctant to waste even a crumb. This has led to a trio of *escudo*-saving dishes made with the unfinished loaves left from family meals.

The best-known of the three is the *açorda,* a soup in which bread and eggs are added to simmering broth or water. *Açorda de mariscos* (see facing page), which features the sweet, pink shrimp caught off Portugal's long seacoast, is a specialty of Lisbon, while *açorda à alentejana* (page 98), served in farmhouses and *tascas* throughout the Alentejo, is a more frugal concoction of bread, water, eggs, olive oil, and garlic.

Migas are commonly thicker, meatier preparations. They are cooked and served in a *tacho de barro* (page 84), with the moistened, seasoned bread cubes on the bottom and pork or other meats on top.

The last of the trio is the *sopa seca,* a specialty of northern Portugal. This hearty concoction is made by layering cooked meat or poultry and vegetables alternately with bread slices in an earthenware dish and topping it off with boiling stock—a perfect dish for the rugged, verdant north.

Catalonia

Estofado de Buey
a la Catalana

beef stew with vegetables and spices

While beef is not widely served in Spain and Portugal, this hearty stew is a superb member of the relatively small repertoire of beef recipes. In Asturias, baby turnips and pearl onions are added to a similar dish. The use of unsweetened chocolate might seem a bit unusual to many observers, but the Spaniards quickly took to this food from the New World. Indeed, even some Catalan picadas include a dose of bitter chocolate called xocolata a la pedra, *"chocolate on the stone," which contains cinnamon and sugar, somewhat like the well-known Ybarra brand from Mexico. I have added cinnamon along with the unsweetened chocolate to replicate this taste. Although not traditional, marinating the meat overnight in some of the spice and wine results in maximum flavor and tenderness.*

4 cups (32 fl oz/1 l) dry red wine

2 teaspoons freshly ground pepper, plus pepper to taste

1 teaspoon ground cinnamon

½ teaspoon ground cloves

3 lb (1.5 kg) beef chuck or other stewing beef, cut into 2-inch (5-cm) cubes

½ cup (4 fl oz/125 ml) olive oil or ½ cup (4 oz/125 g) lard

¼ lb (125 g) bacon, cut into ¼-inch (6-mm) dice

4 large yellow onions, chopped

salt to taste

2 tablespoons finely minced garlic

3 bay leaves, crumbled

1 large tomato, peeled and diced (optional)

1 cup (8 fl oz/250 ml) veal or beef stock

24 baby carrots or carrot chunks, peeled (optional)

24 small new potatoes, peeled

½ cup (4 fl oz/125 ml) dry sherry

1 oz (30 g) unsweetened chocolate, grated

6 tablespoons (½ oz/15 g) chopped fresh flat-leaf (Italian) parsley

☙ In a nonaluminum pan, combine 2 cups (16 fl oz/ 500 ml) of the wine, 1 teaspoon of the pepper, ½ teaspoon of the cinnamon, and the cloves. Add the beef cubes, mix well, cover, and refrigerate overnight.

☙ The next day, bring the meat to room temperature. Using a slotted spoon, lift the meat from the marinade and discard the marinade. In a large frying pan over high heat, warm half of the olive oil or melt half of the lard. Working in batches, brown the meat on all sides, 8–10 minutes. Using the slotted spoon, transfer the meat to a plate.

☙ When all the meat is browned, add the remaining olive oil or lard to the pan over medium heat. Add the bacon and cook, stirring, until lightly browned, about 5 minutes. Add the onions and a sprinkling of salt and sauté until tender, about 10 minutes. Add the garlic, the remaining 1 teaspoon pepper and ½ teaspoon cinnamon, the bay leaves, the tomato (if using), the remaining 2 cups (16 fl oz/500 ml) wine, and the stock. Return the meat to the pan, raise the heat to high, and bring to a boil. Reduce the heat to low, cover, and cook until the meat is tender but not falling apart, about 2 hours.

☙ Meanwhile, if using the carrots, bring a large saucepan two-thirds full of salted water to a boil. Add the carrots and parboil for about 10 minutes, then drain and set aside. Place the potatoes in the same saucepan with salted water to cover generously, bring to a boil, and boil until nearly tender, about 15 minutes. Drain and set aside.

☙ When the beef is ready, using a slotted spoon, transfer it to a large *cazuela* or heavy pot. Using a large spoon, skim the fat off the top of the stewing liquids and discard. Pass the contents of the frying pan through a food mill or sieve placed over a bowl. Add the sherry and the chocolate and mix well. Pour this sauce over the beef and add the cooked potatoes and the carrots, if using. Place over medium heat and bring to a simmer. Adjust the heat to maintain a gentle simmer and cook, uncovered, for about 15 minutes to blend the flavors.

☙ Taste and adjust the seasonings. Sprinkle with the parsley and serve.

serves 6–8

MAIN DISHES

The centerpiece of the meal offers an elaborate mosaic of foods and cooking styles.

ON A SPANISH OR PORTUGUESE restaurant menu, main dishes are usually listed under two no-frills categories: fish and shellfish, and meats and poultry. Yet these simple divisions belie the rich variety that characterizes the centerpiece of the Iberian meal—a course that offers a wealth of possibilities in both the style of cooking and the choice of foods.

Historically, Spanish cooking styles have been divided into three geographical zones, with the center the zone of roasting, the south the zone of frying, and the colder north the zone of braising. Over time, of course, these methods migrated, spilling easily over their culinary borders. Two additional signature methods for meats and fish are *a la plancha* and

a la parrilla, cooking on a heavy metal griddle and grilling on a grid over a charcoal fire, respectively. The same cooking techniques prevail in neighboring Portugal, where geography similarly defines their popularity, with fried seafoods traditionally found along the warm southern coast and braised meats sustaining residents of the cold rural north.

An amazing array of fish and shellfish is pulled from the Iberian coastline of the Mediterranean and the Atlantic. In terms of both its consumption of fish and the size of its fishing fleet, Spain holds second place in the world, after the Japanese. Some of the best seafood comes from the cold Atlantic waters of the Basque provinces, where fishermen catch *quisquillas* (tiny shrimp/prawns), *camarones* (small shrimp), *langostas* (spiny lobsters), and *centollos* (spider crabs). Squid cooked in their ink are a specialty of the region, as are eels prepared with garlic, chile, and saffron and small, flavorful sardines, called *bokartas,* either batter-fried or doused with cider.

Preceding spread: Portugal's long west coast offers dramatic cliffs, bracing Atlantic waves, and fine, deep-colored sand. **Above:** The milk that goes into nutty, full-flavored Manchego cheese comes from sheep that graze on the high, dry plains of La Mancha. **Right:** This elaborately decorated window in the Alhambra, the exquisite fortified palace of the Nasrid kings, looks out onto a beautiful garden.

Of course, not only northerners love fish. Tuna is enjoyed all over Spain, and in Andalusia, sardines, sole, mullets, squid, anchovies, shark, and hake are dusted with flour and dropped into hot oil to make the region's popular *fritura de pescados*.

Fish and shellfish are abundant in Portugal as well, and account for some 40 percent of the population's protein consumption. Sesimbra, a lovely fishing village on the Arrábida Peninsula, is known for its fine swordfish, and Setúbal and the Algarve's small Quartiera are ports recognized for mullet. Tuna, sea bass, skate, sole, whiting, and squid are served throughout the country, as are clams from Faro and Portimão, shrimp from the resort town of Monte Gordo, eel from lagoon-locked Aveiro, and lobster from Sagres, the promontory-sited village from which Henry the Navigator charted the seas. Fried or grilled sardines are staples on nearly every menu.

With this bounty of fresh seafood, it may seem at first surprising to discover the Portuguese passion for salted fish. But Portugal has long been a great seafaring nation, and by the sixteenth century, Portuguese sailors fishing the Grand Bank southeast of Newfoundland had perfected the salting of cod at sea to preserve it for the long voyage home, where it was dried under the hot coastal sun. Today, the most popular of all the country's fish dishes still revolve around *bacalhau,* or salt cod, an ingredient that the Portuguese fondly call *o fiel amigo*—"the faithful friend"—and for which they claim a repertoire so extensive that a different recipe can be prepared for every day of the year.

The Spaniards, particularly the Basques, began cooking salt cod *(bacalao)* perhaps a century later, creating such memorable dishes as *bacalao a la vizcaína* (with peppers and pork) and *bacalao a pil pil* (simmered in olive oil and garlic). Although the Spanish enthusiasm for the preserved fish never reached that of the Portuguese, they did make it an important part of their Catholic dietary regimen, incorporating it into countless Lenten meals and Friday suppers. Today the Great Bank is nearly fished out and most of the salt cod sold in markets in Portugal and Spain comes from processors in

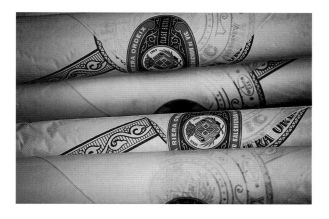

Left: The tables of both Spain and Portugal have been influenced by the abundant seafood pulled from the surrounding waters. **Above top:** Various cured sausages are typical tapas bar fare, served in cubes or slices and usually eaten with a piece of crusty bread. **Above middle:** The Alfama, Lisbon's oldest and most atmospheric quarter, gives visitors a striking—and romantic—view of the Tagus River. **Above bottom:** Spanish cooks have devised recipes for using every part of the ubiquitous pig.

Norway. Sadly, this integral part of the Iberian diet that once fed the rich and poor alike has now become a pricey import.

There is an old Portuguese saying that "fish does not pull a cart," that is, it does not give enough strength. So despite the abundance from the sea and a wealth of grains and vegetables, meat is central to the Portuguese diet. Although Iberia is not known for its beef, and what is produced is of limited quantity and inconsistent quality, the Portuguese are addicted to steak, usually frying it and smothering it with onions or topping it with a fried egg or a slice of *presunto*.

Above: The emerald green landscapes of northern Spain stand in bold contrast to the familiar straw-colored plains of Old and New Castile. **Right top:** A Basque couple enjoys a roadside picnic lunch built around the local foods and wine. **Right bottom:** In a plaza in the heart of Seville, flamenco dancers spin smoothly, their graceful hand movements contributing to the passion of the dance.

In Spain, the finest beef is raised on pasturelands around Avila, in the Basque country, in Galicia, and in Andalusia. The Galician provinces of Lugo and Orense, where rugged *vaqueiros* tend their herds on horseback, are renowned for their particularly flavorful beef. Each August the village of San Isidoro, in Lugo, hosts a lively fiesta that includes a blessing of the local cattle. This high-quality meat is usually marinated and spit-roasted, while the balance is braised.

Both Muslims and Jews are prohibited from eating pork, so sheep have been raised in Portugal and Spain for centuries, especially in Trás-os-Montes and on the plains of Castile. Baby lamb is usually cooked whole on a spit, and more mature meat is braised in various styles, including *al chilindrón* (with peppers) or *cochifrito* (with lemon) in Spain and *chanfana* (in red wine) in Portugal. The Portuguese are especially fond of stuffing lamb legs or chops with mint and garlic, nuts and olives, or sausage. Kid or goat is popular in the three Beiras and in Ribatejo, where it is usually spit-roasted or braised.

But above all, Iberian cooks revere the pig. In Portugal, aficionados of *leitão assado* (roast suckling pig) travel to the modest town of Mealhada, in Beira Litoral, where restaurants specializing in crisp-skinned piglets spit-roasted over hardwood fires line both sides of the road. In rural Spain, *la matanza,* the pig slaughter, is held every November 11, a venerable ritual that commemorates the beast's culinary versatility and puts food on the table in countless forms. The meat is used not only for grilling, roasting, or braising, but also for salted or smoked hams and sausages. Every part of the animal is eaten—ears, snout, feet, tail, and blood, and the fat is rendered for lard.

Hundreds of companies, both large and small, fashion Spanish sausages from the prized pig, many of which are used in main dishes in the form of stuffings or seasonings or sometimes cooked together with other meats or vegetables. The mildly spicy chorizo is the most common Spanish cured sausage (see sidebar, page 133), while the closely related Portuguese *chouriço* is very garlicky, with a rich

red-brown hue from the addition of pepper. Spanish blood sausage, *morcilla,* or *morcela* in Portuguese, mixes pork blood and onions with rice. Lightly smoked Portuguese *paio,* made from pieces of pork tenderloin, is popular in the Algarve and Alentejo.

Alheira, a highly seasoned Portuguese sausage, has an interesting history. Created by the Marranos, or Portuguese Jews, who wished to demonstrate their loyalty to their newly adopted Christianity, the sausages were originally made from a mixture of poultry and bread, which was then disguised with paprika, garlic, and chiles to resemble the popular pork products of the day. Today, these same sausages usually contain pork.

Chicken does not enjoy the same breadth of preparation that seafoods or meats do. This is not because Spaniards and Portuguese don't like chicken, but rather because in the past the birds were so highly valued for their eggs. The result was a great repertoire of egg dishes, from *tortillas* to *huevos rellenos* to the Moorish-inspired egg sweets of both countries, and far

fewer chicken dishes, with spit-roasted whole birds and cut-up hens cooked with tomatoes and peppers in earthenware pans among the most common. On Christmas Eve, however, most Spanish cooks make chicken the center-piece of the meal, often stuffing it with fruits and nuts and serving it on a silver platter.

Today, of course, highly industrialized poultry production has made chickens more available, although discriminating shoppers in both countries still seek out the free-range fowl sold in open markets. In Spain, savvy locals look for the capons raised on grain and chestnuts around the small town of Vilalba, in the province of Lugo, where a community of dedicated farmers are celebrated for their top-flight birds. Because Spain and Portugal are on the migratory routes of fowl flying south in the winter, game birds such as quail and partridge, pheasant and goose, woodcock and pigeon also land in cooking pots, as do duck, turkey, rabbit, and myriad other fowl, illustrating yet again that a rich variety is at the heart of the Iberian meal.

Left: Near Barcelona's Port Vell, a Mediterranean sun sets on the Monument a Colom, which honors Christopher Columbus—the admiral stands atop a tall stone column, his arm pointing out to sea—for his successful return voyage from the New World. **Below top:** Barcelona's history as a cosmopolitan seaport is evident everywhere you turn. **Below bottom:** The meat counters in Spanish markets are stocked with various fresh cuts of beef, pork, and lamb, while most shoppers look to specialty purveyors for a full range of fresh and cured sausages and the prized *jamón serrano*.

Catalonia

Lomo de Cerdo con Higos

pork with figs

The Moors loved to combine fruit and meat, and Catalan cooks readily embraced the idea. Pork and figs—dried or fresh—make a particularly delicious pairing. If you like, the figs can be cooked the day before, and the sauce can be made several hours ahead of serving and reheated.

FIGS

1 lb (500 g) dried black figs or 12–16 fresh figs

1 cup (8 fl oz/250 ml) oloroso or amontillado sherry

2 lemon slices

1 cinnamon stick

2 whole cloves

PORK AND BASTING MIXTURE

1 boneless pork loin, about 3 lb (1.5 kg), tied

tiny garlic slivers (optional)

salt and freshly ground pepper to taste

pinch of ground cinnamon

½ cup (4 fl oz/125 ml) oloroso or amontillado sherry

½ cup (4 fl oz/125 ml) fresh orange juice

¼ cup (3 oz/90 g) honey

SAUCE

3 tablespoons unsalted butter

1 large yellow onion, chopped

3 cloves garlic, minced

1 cup (8 fl oz/250 ml) oloroso or amontillado sherry

1 cup (6 oz/185 g) peeled, seeded, and diced tomato (optional)

1 cup (8 fl oz/250 ml) chicken stock

¼ cup (1 oz/30 g) ground toasted almonds

1 tablespoon grated orange zest

½ teaspoon ground cinnamon

salt and freshly ground pepper to taste

❦ If using dried figs, place them in a saucepan with the sherry, lemon slices, cinnamon stick, and cloves. Add water as needed to cover and place over medium heat. Bring to a simmer and cook until tender, 10–15 minutes. Remove from the heat and set aside

to steep for an hour or two. Using a slotted spoon, transfer the figs to a cutting board. Remove and discard the lemon slices, cinnamon stick, and cloves from the cooking liquid and reserve the liquid. Cut the figs in half and set aside. If using fresh figs, proceed as directed but poach them in the sherry mixture for only 3–5 minutes.

❦ Preheat an oven to 400°F (200°C).

❦ To prepare the pork, trim away any excess fat. If desired, cut a series of evenly spaced slits into the surface of the loin with the tip of a sharp knife and slip a garlic sliver into each slit. Then rub the roast all over with salt, pepper, and cinnamon. Place the pork on a rack in a roasting pan. In a small bowl, stir together the sherry, orange juice, and honey.

❦ Roast the pork, basting every 15 minutes with the sherry mixture, until an instant-read thermometer inserted into the thickest part registers 147°F (64°C), 40–45 minutes. Let rest for 10 minutes. Alternatively, test the roast by cutting into it with a sharp knife; the meat should be lightly pink at the center.

❦ About 30 minutes before the roast is ready, begin making the sauce: In a frying pan over medium heat, melt the butter. Add the onion and sauté until tender, about 8 minutes. Add the garlic and cook until tender, about 3 minutes longer. Add the sherry, tomato (if using), stock, almonds, orange zest, cinnamon, and reserved fig liquid, raise the heat to high, and cook until thickened, 8–10 minutes. Spoon half of the sauce into a blender and purée, then return to the saucepan. Add the figs and heat through. Season with salt and pepper.

❦ Snip the strings on the roast and slice the pork. Arrange the pork slices on a warmed platter and spoon the sauce over them. Surround the slices with the figs. Serve at once.

serves 4

Catalan goatherders believe that the heady fragrance of figs ripening on the tree makes their animals jittery.

Costeletas de Carneiro Escondidinho

lamb chops with port, mustard, and cream

This flavorful dish comes from Oporto, the commercial heart of northern Portugal and the center of the port wine trade. The contrast of the nuttiness of the wine, the heat of the mustard, and the richness of the cream works well with lamb chops or lamb loin. Serve with fried potatoes and sautéed carrots with mint.

12 loin lamb chops, each about 1½ inches (4 cm) thick

salt and freshly ground pepper to taste

2 tablespoons olive oil or unsalted butter

1 cup (8 fl oz/250 ml) dry port

3 tablespoons Dijon mustard

1 cup (8 fl oz/250 ml) heavy (double) cream

☙ Sprinkle the lamb chops with salt and pepper. In a large, heavy frying pan over medium-high heat, warm the olive oil or melt the butter. Add the chops and cook, turning once, until well seared and cooked to desired doneness, about 10 minutes for rare and 14 minutes for medium-rare. Transfer to a warmed platter and keep warm.

☙ Remove the pan from the heat, add the port, and deglaze the pan, stirring to dislodge any browned bits from the pan bottom. Return the pan to medium heat and simmer the port for a minute or so to burn off the alcohol. Whisk in the mustard and cream and continue to simmer until thickened, about 5 minutes. Season with salt and pepper.

☙ Return the chops to the pan and swirl them in the sauce. Transfer to warmed individual plates, spooning the sauce over the top, and serve at once.

serves 6

Basque Country

Bacalao a la Vizcaína

salt cod, bay of biscay style

The color of this famous Basque dish of salt cod with onions and peppers comes from choricero *peppers, dried sweet red peppers that impart a smoky quality to the sauce. Dried ancho chiles and* pimentón de La Vera, *the preferred sweet paprika, produce a similar effect. During Lent, the lard is omitted.*

1½ lb (750 g) salt cod, preferably a single thick, solid piece or 2 thick pieces, soaked (see glossary, page 249)

1 large red bell pepper (capsicum)

4 ancho chiles

1 cup (8 fl oz/250 ml) olive oil

4 yellow onions, chopped

4 cloves garlic, minced

¼ cup (⅓ oz/10 g) chopped fresh flat-leaf (Italian) parsley

1 tablespoon sweet paprika

½ teaspoon hot paprika (optional)

salt and freshly ground pepper to taste

1 cup (4 oz/125 g) dried bread crumbs or crushed soda crackers

2 hard-boiled egg yolks

salt and ground pepper to taste

4 tablespoons (2 oz/60 g) lard, melted

Drain the cod, reserving a little of the soaking water, and place the cod in a saucepan with water to cover. Bring to a gentle simmer over medium heat and cook until tender, 10–15 minutes. Drain well. Cut into 4 equal pieces, removing any bits of skin and any small bones.

Preheat an oven to 400°F (200°C).

Bring a saucepan three-fourths full of water to a boil. Add the bell pepper and blanch for 3–4 minutes. Drain and, when cool enough to handle, peel away the skin. Remove the stem and seeds and chop finely; set aside. Place the ancho chiles in a small saucepan, add water to cover, and bring to a boil. Drain immediately, re-cover with fresh water, and bring to a boil again. Drain and repeat one more time. Then drain the chiles, cut them open, and remove the seeds. Scrape the pulp from the skins and reserve. You should have about ¼ cup (2 oz/60 g).

In a large frying pan over medium heat, warm the olive oil. Add the onions, garlic, and parsley and sauté until the onions are tender, about 10 minutes. Stir in the sweet paprika and the hot paprika, if using, and cook for a minute or two. Add the bell pepper and the ancho pulp and sauté until soft, about 15 minutes. Remove from the heat.

Meanwhile, in a mortar, pound the bread crumbs or crackers with some of the cod soaking liquid until a paste forms. Add the hard-boiled egg yolks, mixing well. Add this mixture to the onion mixture and transfer to a blender. Purée until smooth, then pass through a sieve to strain out any lumps. Season to taste with salt and pepper. Pour 2 tablespoons of the melted lard into a *cazuela* or baking dish in which the fish will fit in a single layer. Tip the dish to coat evenly. Add a few ladlefuls of the sauce. Place the fish on top, then ladle the remaining sauce on top. Drizzle with the remaining 2 tablespoons lard.

Bake until the cod is heated through, about 15 minutes. Serve hot directly from the dish.

serves 4

Estremadura

Espadarte à Lisboeta

swordfish with tomatoes and anchovies

The little resort and fishing village of Sesimbra, renowned for its swordfish, is a center for sportfishing. When the fleet comes in, the day's catch is auctioned off at the picturesque harbor. If you cannot get swordfish, thick fillets of cod or sea bass will do. And if fresh tomatoes are not full of flavor, use canned for this dish.

6 swordfish steaks, about 7 oz (220 g) each

salt and freshly ground pepper to taste

5 tablespoons (3 fl oz / 80 ml) olive oil

1 yellow onion, chopped

2 cups (12 oz / 375 g) peeled, seeded, and chopped plum (Roma) tomato

1 tablespoon finely minced anchovy

2 tablespoons tomato paste dissolved in ¼ cup (2 fl oz / 60 ml) dry white wine

20 black olives, pitted and coarsely chopped

¼ cup (⅓ oz / 10 g) chopped fresh flat-leaf (Italian) parsley, plus extra parsley for garnish

lemon wedges

☙ Preheat an oven to 400°F (200°C). Oil a baking dish in which the fish steaks will fit in a single layer.

☙ Sprinkle the fish with salt and pepper and refrigerate until ready to cook. In a large frying pan over medium heat, warm the olive oil. Add the onion and sauté until tender, about 8 minutes. Add the tomato, anchovy, tomato paste dissolved in white wine, olives, and parsley and simmer until thickened, about 5 minutes.

☙ Place the fish steaks in the prepared baking dish. Spoon the tomato sauce over the fish. Bake until the fish is opaque throughout, about 15 minutes.

☙ Remove from the oven and sprinkle with additional parsley. Serve immediately directly from the dish. Accompany with lemon wedges.

serves 6

Basque Country

Marmitako

tuna with peppers and potatoes

Marmitako comes from marmita, a large, concave earthenware cooking utensil. The dish is usually made with tuna, although some recipes call for mackerel. Many cooks favor green peppers only, while others like red ones or a mix of green and red. The dish can be simmered on top of the stove or baked in a moderate oven. In other words, marmitako, a rich blend of potatoes and fish bound with a sauce of peppers, has as many interpretations as there are Basque cooks. Serve the hearty dish with grilled coarse country bread.

1½ lb (750 g) albacore tuna fillet, cut into 2-inch (5-cm) pieces

salt to taste

3 tablespoons olive oil

1 yellow onion, chopped

2 cloves garlic, minced

2 red or green bell peppers (capsicums), seeded and finely chopped

2 lb (1 kg) boiling potatoes, peeled and cut into 2-inch (5-cm) chunks

½ cup (4 fl oz / 125 ml) tomato sauce

¼ teaspoon hot paprika, or to taste (optional)

freshly ground pepper to taste

☙ Sprinkle the fish lightly with salt and refrigerate until ready to cook. In a large frying pan over medium heat, warm the olive oil. Add the onion and sauté until tender, about 8 minutes. Add the garlic and peppers and sauté for a few minutes longer until the peppers begin to soften. Add the potatoes and enough water just to cover. Simmer, uncovered, until the potatoes are tender, about 20 minutes.

☙ Add the tuna, the tomato sauce, and the paprika, if using, and mix well. Cover and simmer until the fish is opaque throughout, about 10 minutes longer. Season with salt, pepper, and paprika (if using). Transfer to a warmed platter and serve at once.

serves 4

Alentejo

Salmonete Setubalense

mullet with orange-wine sauce

Orange groves surround the fishing port of Setúbal, which is known for its bitter oranges. The traditional sauce for this fish is a wine-and-orange-flavored butter accented by the fish's liver. I like to heighten the flavor by rubbing the fish with orange zest, salt, and sugar before cooking. Red mullet is the star of this dish, but salmon or snapper can be used with delicious results.

¼ cup (2 oz/60 g) sugar

2 tablespoons grated orange zest

2 tablespoons kosher salt

1 teaspoon freshly ground pepper

6 small, whole red mullet, salmon trout, or red snapper, about 1 lb (500 g) each, cleaned with heads intact, or 6 salmon fillets, 6–7 oz (185–220 g) each

1 cup (8 fl oz/250 ml) dry white wine

½ cup (4 fl oz/125 ml) fresh orange juice

6 tablespoons (3 oz/90 g) unsalted butter, melted, plus extra butter as needed

2 small oranges, sliced

¼ cup (⅓ oz/10 g) chopped fresh mint or flat-leaf (Italian) parsley

❀ In a small bowl, stir together the sugar, orange zest, salt, and pepper. Rub this mixture on the fish, place the fish in a covered container, and refrigerate for about 3 hours.

❀ Preheat an oven to 450°F (230°C). Butter a baking dish in which the fish will fit in a single layer.

❀ Place the fish in the prepared dish and drizzle evenly with the wine, orange juice, and melted butter. Bake until the fish is opaque throughout when a knife is inserted at the thickest point, 8–10 minutes. Transfer the fish to a warmed platter. Add more butter to the pan juices as needed to thicken it into a sauce, then spoon over the fish.

❀ Garnish the fish with the orange slices and sprinkle with the mint or parsley. Serve immediately.

serves 6

Spanish Wines

Thanks to the Phoenicians and Greeks, the Spanish were drinking wine long before the ancient Romans arrived and replanted existing vines with Italian varieties. Today, thirty carefully drawn areas, called *denominaciones de origen,* fall under the watchful eye of a national institute whose sole job is to maintain the high standards of the country's wines.

Many of the best bottlings come from the Old Castile regions of Rueda, Ribera del Duero, and Rioja. Rueda is famous for its modestly complex whites made from the Verdejo grape. Not far from the bustling, rather homely city of Valladolid, in an area known as Tierra de Vino, Vega Sicilia, one of the rarest and most sought-after Spanish reds, is produced. Its label carries the Ribera del Duero *denominación,* as do a pair of other superb red wines of the area, Tinto Pesquera and Vina Pedrosa.

The wines of Rioja have long enjoyed a higher profile that those of their fellow Castilian cousins. Production from these rugged foothills was poured at countless feasts in ancient Rome, and the area's historic monasteries, which lay along the popular pilgrimage route to Santiago de Compostela, made wines to quench the thirst of the constant stream of travelers. Today, the same area is home to Spain's most familiar red table wines, at home and abroad, as well as a few light and fruity whites.

Next door, Navarre, a rich stretch of oak forests, snow-capped mountains, clear rivers, and fertile valleys, is the source of some well-regarded reds made from the same varieties used in Rioja. The most celebrated wines of Aragon, to the south, are the big, bold, dark reds from the Cariñena *denominación*. Farther south still, Catalonia, with six designated areas, produces respectable wines of every kind: red, white, sweet dessert, and the country's best *cava,* or sparkling wine.

Estremadura

Frango no Espeto

grilled chicken on a spit

Portuguese who have worked in Brazil and eaten at the local churrascarias *usually return to their home-land with a taste for meat cooked on a spit or grill, and many eateries have opened to cater to them. This recipe is a specialty of Bonjardein, a popular, rustic restaurant in Lisbon. While it would be nice to have a rotisserie at home, you can achieve a piquant and crisp bird by marinating it in a little piri-piri sauce and then cooking it on a charcoal grill. Traditionally, the meat is basted with a mixture of one part melted butter and two parts piri-piri sauce, accented with extra garlic. For those who do not have a supply of the fiery chile condiment in their pantry, I have included a recipe for an instant hot marinade that can be substi-tuted with great success. You may also eliminate the marinating and simply baste the chicken with the piri-piri–butter mixture.*

If using poussins or Cornish hens, butterfly them or ask the butcher to do it for you. Serve the grilled chicken with thick French fries and sliced tomatoes sprinkled with chopped mint.

QUICK PIRI-PIRI MARINADE

2 cups (16 fl oz/500 ml) olive oil

1 tablespoon red pepper flakes

½ cup (4 fl oz/125 ml) fresh lemon juice

3 cloves garlic, smashed

4 poussins, Cornish hens, or broiler chicken halves, about 1 lb (500 g) each

3 tablespoons unsalted butter

1 tablespoon minced garlic

salt and freshly ground black pepper to taste

☙ To make the quick *piri-piri* marinade, in a saucepan over medium heat, heat the olive oil until it is very hot but not boiling. Drop in a red pepper flake. If it skips to the surface of the oil and bubbles but doesn't turn brown or black, add all of the pep-per flakes. If the oil is too hot, the flakes will burn and you will have to start all over, as you don't want the oil to taste bitter. If the oil is not hot enough, the pepper flake will sink but not bubble. Keep heating and testing with a few random flakes. They should sizzle and bubble and stay on the surface of the oil

for a few minutes. Then the action will subside and the oil will become a pale orange. Remove from the heat. Add the lemon juice and garlic, then let the marinade cool completely. Pour off 6 tablespoons (3 fl oz/90 ml) and reserve for basting.

☙ If using poussins or Cornish hens, first butterfly them: Rinse the birds. Insert a sharp knife through the cavity of a bird and split the bird down the back. Then carefully cut along the backbone to remove it entirely. Bend the bird until it lies flat. Tuck the wings under. Remove the excess neck skin. The bird will have the shape of a butterfly. Repeat with the remaining birds. Place the birds in a shallow con-tainer and pour the cooled marinade over them. If you are using broiler halves, simply combine them with the marinade. Cover and refrigerate overnight.

☙ The next day, prepare a fire in a charcoal grill. Bring the birds to room temperature.

☙ To make the basting sauce, in a small frying pan, melt the butter. Add the reserved *piri-piri* marinade and the minced garlic and simmer for 2–3 minutes. Season with salt and black pepper.

☙ Remove the birds from the marinade and sprin-kle them with salt and black pepper. Place on the grill rack, skin side up, and grill, basting with the *piri-piri*–butter mixture, 5–6 minutes. Turn and cook, continuing to baste, until the juices run clear when a thigh is pierced, about 5 minutes longer. The timing will depend upon the intensity of the fire.

☙ Transfer to a warmed platter and serve.

serves 4

The tastiest Spanish chickens are fattened on a diet of grain and chestnuts spiked with local wine or brandy.

Carneiro à Transmontana

lamb with mint and garlic

There are two ways to prepare this recipe from Trás-os-Montes, a rough mountain terrain where goats and sheep are raised. Some cooks use a bone-in leg of lamb and rub the herb paste over the exterior. Others stuff the mint-garlic mixture into a boneless leg, where the flavors can permeate the meat more intensely, as is done here. Garnish with fresh mint leaves.

1 leg of lamb, 5–6 lb (2.5–3 kg), boned

¾ cup (1 oz/30 g) chopped fresh mint

¼ cup (1½ oz/45 g) finely minced bacon

2 tablespoons finely minced garlic

1 tablespoon paprika

1 teaspoon salt, plus salt to taste

½ teaspoon freshly ground pepper, plus pepper to taste

5 tablespoons (2½ fl oz/75 ml) red wine vinegar

½ cup (4 fl oz/125 ml) olive oil

☙ Unroll the leg of lamb, fat side down, and trim away all excess fat and sinews. In a mortar or small bowl, combine the mint, bacon, garlic, paprika, 1 teaspoon salt, ½ teaspoon pepper, and 2 tablespoons of the vinegar and mix to form a paste. Rub the paste evenly over the inside of the lamb leg. Roll up the leg and tie securely with kitchen string. Wrap the lamb in plastic wrap and refrigerate for 12–24 hours.

☙ Preheat an oven to 400°F (200°C). Unwrap the lamb and bring to room temperature.

☙ Put the lamb on a rack in a roasting pan. In a small bowl, stir together the olive oil and the remaining 3 tablespoons vinegar. Brush the lamb lightly with some of the mixture. Sprinkle with salt and pepper.

☙ Roast, basting with the oil-vinegar mixture every 8–10 minutes, until an instant-read thermometer inserted into the thickest part registers 120°F (49°C) for rare, 45–50 minutes, or 130°–135°F (54°–57°C) for medium, 55–60 minutes. Alternatively, test by cutting into the leg with a sharp knife; the meat should be rosy or done to your liking.

☙ Transfer the lamb to a warmed platter and let rest for 10 minutes. Snip the strings and slice to serve.

serves 6–8

Estremadura

Iscas à Portuguesa

sautéed liver, portuguese style

Traditionally, this dish, a specialty of Lisbon, is prepared with pork or lamb liver, which is not always easy to find at the butcher shop. But more readily available calf's liver works well. Ask the butcher to cut the liver into thin slices.

1 lb (500 g) calf's liver, thinly sliced horizontally

¾ cup (6 fl oz / 180 ml) dry white wine

2 tablespoons white wine vinegar

5 or 6 cloves garlic, minced

1 bay leaf

2 whole cloves

3–4 tablespoons lard or olive oil

2–3 oz (60–90 g) bacon, chopped

꙼ Trim the liver into uniform pieces so that the pieces will cook at the same time. In a shallow non-aluminum dish, combine the wine, vinegar, garlic, bay leaf, and cloves. Add the liver and turn to coat evenly. Cover and refrigerate for 4–8 hours.

꙼ Lift the liver pieces from the marinade and pat dry with paper towels. Discard the bay leaf and cloves from the marinade and set the marinade aside.

꙼ In a large sauté pan over medium-high heat, melt the lard or warm the olive oil. Add the bacon and cook until crisp, about 5 minutes. Add the liver and cook quickly, turning once, until cooked but still pink at the center, 1½–2 minutes on each side. Using a slotted spatula, transfer the liver and bacon to a warmed platter and keep warm.

꙼ Add the reserved marinade to the pan, raise the heat to high, bring to a boil, and deglaze the pan, stirring to dislodge any browned bits from the pan bottom. Boil for a few minutes until the liquid is reduced by half. Spoon the pan sauce over the liver and serve immediately.

serves 3 or 4

Douro

Tripas à Moda do Porto

tripe, oporto style

Oporto is known for its repertoire of tripe dishes, and for centuries the locals have been called tripeiros, *a name that, according to legend, was born out of war. During the fifteenth-century battle of Ceuta in North Africa, Henry the Navigator commandeered the best of Oporto's provisions, including the finest beef, to feed his troops. He left the tripe behind, and the rest is culinary history. In Oporto this classic tripe dish is called* tripas, *but in the south it is known as* dobrado *and is cooked with chickpeas (garbanzo beans) instead of white beans. Serve with rice.*

1 cup (7 oz/220 g) dried small white beans

1 calf's foot, pig's foot, or ham hock

dry red wine (optional)

1 lb (500 g) honeycomb tripe, cut into 1-inch (2.5-cm) squares

4 tablespoons (2 fl oz/60 ml) olive oil or lard

2 yellow onions, chopped

2 carrots, peeled and chopped

2 cloves garlic, minced

2 tablespoons sweet paprika

1 tablespoon ground cumin

1 tablespoon curry powder (optional)

½ cup (¾ oz/20 g) chopped fresh flat-leaf (Italian) parsley

1 bay leaf

2 cups (12 oz/375 g) canned plum (Roma) tomato, chopped, with the juices

¼ lb (125 g) chouriço, *sliced*

3–4 oz (90–125 g) presunto *or prosciutto,* chopped

freshly ground pepper to taste

☙ Pick over the beans, removing any stones or misshapen beans. Rinse well, place in a bowl with water to cover, and let soak overnight.

☙ The next day, put the calf's or pig's foot or ham hock in a saucepan with lightly salted water, with red wine, or with a mixture to cover. Bring to a simmer over medium heat, reduce the heat to low, cover, and simmer, skimming occasionally, until the meat softens a bit, 2–2½ hours. Add the tripe and continue to simmer until tender, 1½–2 hours longer.

☙ Meanwhile, drain the beans and place in a large saucepan with water to cover by 3 inches (7.5 cm). Bring to a boil over high heat, reduce the heat to low, cover, and simmer until tender, 1–1½ hours.

☙ Remove the saucepan holding the meat from the heat. Using a slotted spoon or tongs, lift out the foot or hock and let cool until the meat can be cut from the bones. Add the meat and the tripe to the cooked beans along with a bit of the cooking liquid.

☙ In a large saucepan over medium heat, warm the olive oil or melt the lard. Add the onions, carrots, and garlic, and sauté until the onions are tender, 10–15 minutes. Add the paprika, cumin, curry powder (if using), parsley, and bay leaf and stir well. Then add the tomato, sausage, and ham and cook, stirring occasionally, about 5 minutes longer.

☙ Add the onion mixture to the beans and tripe. This dish should not be too soupy, so remove any excess liquid. Bring to a boil over high heat, reduce the heat to low, and simmer, uncovered, for 30 minutes to marry the flavors. The consistency should be almost dry. Season with pepper. Transfer to a warmed serving dish and serve.

serves 4

Catalonia

Perdiz con Coles

partridge with cabbage

The combination of partridge and cabbage is popular throughout both Spain and Portugal. In Portugal, where the dish is called perdizes com repolho, a mixture of tawny port and beef stock might be used in place of the red wine. Instead of making meat-stuffed cabbage packets, cooks sometimes use the cabbage to wrap the well-browned birds, and the sausage is cooked, crumbled, and then sprinkled all around the birds in the baking dish. Other cooks roll the cabbage leaves into packets without stuffing them, dip them in flour and then in egg, and fry them before adding them to the baking dish.

In the absence of partridges, poussins or Cornish hens can be used. To give the stuffed packets in this Catalan version a heartier filling, mix in ½ pound (250 g) ground (minced) pork with the soaked bread. Serve with simple roasted or mashed potatoes.

4 partridges, about 1 lb (500 g) each

¾ cup (6 fl oz / 180 ml) olive oil or lard

1 lb (500 g) butifarra or other cured pork sausage

4 slices bacon, chopped

2 large yellow onions, chopped

12 cloves garlic, minced

1 lb (500 g) tomatoes, peeled, seeded, and diced

2 carrots, peeled and sliced

1 teaspoon each chopped fresh thyme and marjoram

pinch of ground cinnamon or cloves

1 strip orange zest

1 cup (8 fl oz / 250 ml) dry red wine

¼ cup (2 fl oz / 60 ml) brandy

salt and freshly ground pepper to taste

1 head savoy cabbage

½ teaspoon freshly grated nutmeg, or more to taste

3 slices white bread, soaked in milk to cover and squeezed dry

1 cup (5 oz/155 g) all-purpose (plain) flour

1 egg

❦ Preheat an oven to 375°F (190°C).

❦ Rinse the birds and pat dry. In a large roasting pan placed over medium-high heat on the stove top, warm half of the olive oil or lard. Add the birds and turn to brown on all sides, about 10 minutes. Add the sausage and bacon and cook for a few minutes to color. Add the onions, garlic, tomatoes, carrots, thyme, marjoram, cinnamon or cloves, and orange zest. Mix together the wine and brandy in a cup and baste the birds with the mixture. Transfer the pan to the oven and roast until the birds are tender and cooked through, about 1 hour. Transfer the birds and sausages to a large *cazuela* or other large baking dish, cover, and set aside. Taste the sauce remaining in the pan and adjust with salt and pepper. Reserve.

❦ Meanwhile, bring a large pot two-thirds full of salted water to a boil. Add the cabbage and parboil for 10 minutes. Drain well and let cool.

❦ When the cabbage is cool enough to handle, carefully separate the leaves, reserving 8 perfect large outer leaves. Chop the rest of the cabbage, discarding the tough core and any tough ribs. Lay the 8 leaves out on a work surface. Sprinkle with salt, pepper, and the nutmeg. In a bowl, combine the soaked bread and about 2 cups (6 oz/185 g) of the chopped cabbage. Divide the mixture evenly among the cabbage leaves, placing it in the middle of each leaf. Working with 1 leaf at a time, fold the top end over the filling, fold in the sides, and then fold in the stem end and roll up into a cylindrical packet.

❦ Spread the flour on a plate, and lightly beat the egg in a shallow bowl. In a large frying pan over high heat, warm the remaining oil or lard. Dip each packet first in the flour, tapping off the excess, and then in the egg and slip them into the hot oil or lard. Fry, turning once, until golden and crusty on both sides, 3–5 minutes. Transfer to paper towels to drain briefly.

❦ Slice the pork sausages. Place the cabbage packets between the birds and evenly distribute the sausage slices between the birds and the packets. Spoon the sauce over the packets and sausages.

❦ Cover the *cazuela* and place it in the oven. Roast, basting one more time with the sauce, for 15–20 minutes. Serve hot directly from the dish.

serves 4

Sausages

Two reasons to visit Vich, a Catalan town perched in the foothills of the Pyrenees, are its neoclassical cathedral's golden murals by Josep María Sért and its large, twice-weekly market, a tradition since the tenth century. Perhaps the best reason to stop at Vich, however, is to sample the locally made *butifarra,* a cooked and dried sausage of pork, pork blood, and seasonings that is produced all over Catalonia but is arguably at its finest in this mountain town.

But the *butifarra* is a bit player in Spain, a country whose citizenry is crazy for sausages. The chorizo, in contrast, is the star. At its simplest it is a cured pork sausage flavored with garlic and paprika. But every region has its own version of this ubiquitous *salchicha:* sometimes the meat is coarsely ground, sometimes fine; some mixtures include heavy doses of chile, some are sweetened with cinnamon or nutmeg. They are all tucked into natural pig casings, however, and can turn up thinly sliced as a tapa or tucked in among other ingredients in their common role as assertive seasonings.

The Portuguese make a similar pork sausage, which they call *chouriço.* Hefty and deep, rich red, it too carries a sizable measure of paprika and garlic, as does its slimmer cousin, the *linguiça. Piri-piri* and red wine usually flavor both sausages, which are standard bar fare—generally grilled and sliced—as well as flavorful additions to *cozidos* and other dishes.

Catalonia

Rape en Salsa de Piñones

monkfish with pine nut sauce

Many Spanish fish dishes include sauces made with nuts. Here, a sauce made from pine nuts, the best of which are harvested in Old Castile, cloaks monkfish pulled from the coastal waters of Catalonia.

SAUCE

2 tablespoons olive oil

1 large yellow onion, finely chopped

¼ cup (1 oz/30 g) pine nuts, toasted and ground

¼ cup (½ oz/15 g) fresh bread crumbs

1 tablespoon finely minced garlic

1 teaspoon sweet paprika

1½ cups (9 oz/280 g) peeled, seeded, and chopped tomatoes

1 cup (8 fl oz/250 ml) fish stock or white wine

salt and freshly ground pepper to taste

1½ lb (750 g) monkfish fillet, cut into slices 1 inch (2.5 cm) thick

salt and freshly ground pepper to taste

2 tablespoons olive oil

1 cup (5 oz/155 g) English peas, parboiled 2 minutes and drained (optional)

¼ cup (1 oz/30 g) pine nuts, toasted

¼ cup (⅓ oz/10 g) finely chopped fresh flat-leaf (Italian) parsley or mint

♕ For the sauce, in a frying pan over medium heat, warm the oil. Add the onion and sauté until tender, 8–10 minutes. Add the ground pine nuts, bread crumbs, garlic, and paprika; cook for 3 minutes. Add the tomatoes and stock or wine and cook until thickened, 5–8 minutes. Season with salt and pepper.

♕ Sprinkle the fish with salt and pepper. In a large frying pan over medium heat, warm the olive oil. Add the fish and sauté, turning once, for about 3 minutes on each side. Pour the sauce over the fish, add the peas, if desired, and simmer until the fish is opaque throughout, about 5 minutes longer.

♕ Transfer the fish and sauce to a platter, garnish with pine nuts and parsley or mint, and serve.

serves 4

Trás-os-Montes

Truta à Moda de Bragança

trout in the style of bragança

Trout in great numbers swim in the many freshwater streams of Trás-os-Montes. In Bragança, the main town of the province, local cooks prepare the fish in the same manner as cooks do in Navarre, in Spain, wrapping the trout in ham and sautéing them until golden. But even the simplest recipes develop variations over time. Some cooks tuck the ham inside the trout, while others chop it and add it to the pan juices. Unless you've just gone fishing, use farm-raised trout for this dish.

4 whole freshwater trout, cleaned with heads intact, about ¾ lb (375 g) each

salt and freshly ground pepper to taste

8 thin slices presunto or prosciutto

about ¾ cup (4 oz/125 g) all-purpose (plain) flour

⅓ cup (3 fl oz/80 ml) olive oil

½ cup (4 fl oz/125 ml) dry white wine (optional)

lemon wedges

♕ Sprinkle the trout inside and out with salt and pepper. Stuff 1 ham slice inside each trout, and then wrap 1 ham slice around each fish, leaving the head and the tail exposed. Skewer closed with toothpicks or tie with kitchen string.

♕ Spread the flour on a large plate. One at a time, dip each trout in the flour, tapping off the excess.

♕ In a large frying pan over medium heat, warm the olive oil. Add the trout and fry, turning once, until golden on both sides, about 4 minutes on each side. Transfer the fish to a warmed platter. Discard the toothpicks or string.

♕ If desired, pour the wine into the pan, raise the heat to high, and deglaze the pan, stirring to scrape up any browned bits from the pan bottom. Remove from the heat and pour over the fish.

♕ Serve at once with the lemon wedges.

serves 4

Minho

Rojões à Cominho

pork with cumin, lemon, and cilantro

Lemon and cumin temper the richness of the meat in this traditional pork dish from Minho. Accompany with sautéed greens topped with toasted bread crumbs.

2 tablespoons ground cumin

1½ tablespoons finely minced garlic

2 teaspoons freshly ground pepper, plus pepper to taste

1 teaspoon salt, plus salt to taste

7 tablespoons (¾ oz/20 g) chopped fresh cilantro (fresh coriander)

2 tablespoons fresh lemon juice

grated zest of 1 lemon

1 cup (8 fl oz/250 ml) dry white wine

2 lb (1 kg) pork shoulder or butt, cut into 1½-inch (4-cm) cubes

2 tablespoons lard or olive oil

chicken stock, as needed to cover

4 paper-thin lemon slices, cut into quarters

❧ In a small bowl, stir together the cumin, garlic, 2 teaspoons pepper, 1 teaspoon salt, 4 tablespoons (⅓ oz/10 g) of the cilantro, the lemon juice and zest, and the wine. Place the pork in a nonaluminum container, and rub the cumin mixture into the meat. Cover and refrigerate overnight.

❧ The next day, drain the pork, reserving the marinade. Pat the meat dry. In a heavy saucepan over high heat, melt the lard or warm the olive oil. Add the pork and sauté until golden, 8–10 minutes. Add the reserved marinade and enough chicken stock just to cover the meat. Raise the heat to high and bring to a boil. Reduce the heat to low, cover, and simmer until very tender, about 45 minutes, adding the lemon slices during the last 10 minutes of cooking.

❧ Season with salt and pepper and transfer to a warmed serving bowl. Sprinkle with the remaining 3 tablespoons cilantro and serve immediately.

serves 6

New Castile

Lomo de Cerdo Adobado

pork with paprika and garlic

The term adobado is used for a traditional method of cooking in which the meat is left to marinate for up to three days in a mixture of garlic, paprika, cumin, herbs, olive oil, and vinegar or wine. I first tasted this fabulous pork dish when Madrid-based Tomás Herranz came to cook as a guest-chef at my San Francisco restaurant, Square One. Like many talented cooks, Tomás didn't measure anything, nor did he work from a written recipe. But I paid close attention, and this is his version of lomo de cerdo adobado. Here, I have cooked the pork on a grill, as he did at the restaurant, but you may also roast it in a 350°F (180°C) oven, allowing 45–60 minutes for the loin or about 25 minutes for the tenderloins.

1 boneless pork loin, 2–3 lb (1–1.5 kg), tied, or 2 pork tenderloins, about 1 lb (500 g) each

2 tablespoons olive oil

1½ tablespoons finely minced garlic

2 teaspoons dried oregano

2 tablespoons sweet paprika

1 tablespoon ground cumin

2 teaspoons fresh thyme leaves

1 bay leaf, crumbled

1 teaspoon salt, plus salt to taste

½ teaspoon freshly ground pepper, plus pepper to taste

½ cup (4 fl oz/125 ml) dry sherry or dry white wine

☸ Trim off any excess fat from the pork and place the meat in a shallow nonaluminum container.

☸ In a small frying pan over low heat, combine the olive oil, garlic, and oregano and heat for 2 minutes to release their aromas. Whisk in the paprika, cumin, thyme, bay leaf, 1 teaspoon salt, ½ teaspoon pepper, and the wine and cook for 1 minute over low heat.

Remove from the heat and set aside to cool to room temperature. When fully cooled, pour the marinade over the meat and rub it in well. Cover and refrigerate for at least overnight or for as long as 2–3 days.

☸ Prepare a fire in a charcoal grill, or preheat a broiler (griller).

☸ Lift the pork from the marinade and pat dry. Sprinkle the pork lightly with salt and pepper. Place on the grill rack or on a broiler pan slipped under the broiler and grill or broil, turning as needed to brown well on all sides, until an instant-read thermometer inserted into the thickest part registers 147°F (64°C), about 10 minutes for the tenderloins and 20 minutes for the loin. Alternatively, test the pork by cutting into it with a sharp knife; the meat should be lightly pink at the center.

☸ Transfer the pork to a cutting board and let rest for a few minutes. Slice and then arrange the slices on a warmed platter. Serve at once.

serves 4–6

Minho

Santola no Carro

crab in a cart

In Portugal, fishermen pull small, hard-shell crabs from cold coastal waters. For this dish, Portuguese cooks extract the meat from the crabs, season it and add corn-bread crumbs for body, and then stuff the mixture back into the shells. As these small crabs are not available everywhere, ramekins or scallop shells can be used in place of the shells for baking. If you have purchased fresh crabs and picked the crabmeat from them, reserve some of the tomalley and use instead of mayonnaise.

8 tablespoons (4 oz/125 g) unsalted butter

1 large or 2 small yellow onions, minced

3 cups (18 oz/560 g) crabmeat, picked over for shell fragments

1 cup (2 oz/60 g) fresh bread crumbs, preferably from corn bread

2 tablespoons chopped fresh flat-leaf (Italian) parsley

½ cup (2½ fl oz/75 g) sliced brine-cured black olives

¼ cup (2 fl oz/60 ml) mayonnaise

piri-piri *sauce (page 64) to taste*

salt and freshly ground pepper to taste

lemon wedges

❧ Preheat an oven to 450°F (230°C). Generously butter 4 ramekins or large scallop shells.

❧ In a frying pan over medium heat, melt 6 table-spoons (3 oz/90 g) of the butter. Add the onion and sauté until golden, about 15 minutes. Remove from the heat and place in a bowl.

❧ Add the crabmeat, bread crumbs, parsley, olives, and mayonnaise and mix well. Season with the *piri-piri* sauce, salt, and pepper. Spoon the crab mixture into the prepared ramekins or scallop shells. Cut the remaining 2 tablespoons butter into bits and use to dot the surface.

❧ Bake until golden and heated through, 8–10 minutes. Garnish with lemon wedges and serve.

serves 4

Algarve

Atum à Portuguesa

tuna with garlic and chile

Although the Portuguese use piri-piri, *the favorite chile of cooks in their former African colonies, other easier-to-find hot red chiles can replace it here. As this marinade is quite intense, rub it on the fish no more than two hours before cooking. If you don't add the chiles and cilantro, this recipe is very much like the Spanish* atún adobado, *essentially tuna with garlic and paprika.*

3 or 4 fresh hot red chiles, finely minced (see note)

1 cup (1½ oz/45 g) finely chopped fresh cilantro (fresh coriander)

2 tablespoons finely minced garlic

1 tablespoon sweet paprika

1 tablespoon freshly ground pepper

½ cup (4 fl oz/125 ml) olive oil

¼ cup (2 fl oz/60 ml) fresh lemon juice

1½ lb (750 g) tuna fillet, cut into 4 equal pieces

salt to taste

❧ In a nonaluminum container, stir together the chiles, half of the cilantro, the garlic, paprika, and pepper. Stir in the olive oil and lemon juice. Add the tuna and rub the mixture into the fish. Cover and refrigerate for 2 hours.

❧ Prepare a fire in a charcoal grill, or preheat a broiler (griller).

❧ Sprinkle the fish with salt. Place on an oiled grill rack or broiler pan and slip under the broiler. Grill or broil, turning once, for about 3 minutes on each side for medium-rare, or until done to your liking.

❧ Transfer to a warmed platter or individual plates. Garnish with the remaining cilantro and serve.

serves 4

Estremadura

Bife à Cebolada

onion-smothered steak

Bife *means "steak" in Portuguese, and the preferred way of cooking it is frying. For the prestigious* bife à portuguesa, *a filet mignon is rubbed with crushed garlic, salt, and pepper and fried in a mixture of butter and olive oil. Thin slices of* presunto *are placed on top, and the steak is garnished with lemon wedges. Not everyone can afford filet mignon, however, and much of the Portuguese beef is not very tender. That is how the very popular* bife à cebolada *evolved.*

Traditionally, the onions are cooked along with the steak until they become a melting purée and the steak is tender. If instead an excellent-quality steak is used, such as the rib-eye called for here, the onions are prepared separately, the steak is panfried to the desired degree of doneness, and the onion mixture, which is known as a refogado *(see sidebar, page 88), is spooned on top. Tuna steaks prepared the same way but without the addition of port are known as* bifes de atum à cebolada. *Fried potatoes are the customary side dish in either case.*

2 tablespoons red wine vinegar

2 teaspoons minced garlic

1½ teaspoons sweet paprika

½ teaspoon salt, plus salt to taste

½ teaspoon freshly ground pepper, plus pepper to taste

4 rib-eye steaks, about ½ lb (250 g) each

¼ cup (2 fl oz/60 ml) olive oil

2 cups (10 oz/315 g) chopped yellow onion

½ cup (3 oz/90 g) diced canned plum (Roma) tomato

1 small bay leaf (optional)

¼ cup (2 fl oz/60 ml) tawny port (optional)

3 tablespoons chopped fresh flat-leaf (Italian) parsley

❦ In a mortar or small bowl, combine 1 tablespoon of the vinegar, 1 teaspoon of the garlic, the paprika, and ½ teaspoon each salt and pepper and mix together to form a paste. Rub the paste on both sides of the steaks and set aside at room temperature to marinate for about 1 hour.

❦ In a frying pan over medium heat, warm the olive oil. Add the onion and cook, stirring often, until golden, about 25 minutes. Add the remaining 1 tea-spoon garlic, the tomato, the remaining 1 tablespoon vinegar, and the bay leaf and port, if using, and sim-mer, uncovered, over medium heat for 10 minutes to blend the flavors. Season with salt and pepper and stir in the parsley. Remove from the heat and set aside.

❦ Place 2 large, heavy frying pans over high heat and sprinkle them both with salt. When the pans are very hot, add the steaks and cook over high heat, turning once, 3–5 minutes on each side for rare, or to desired doneness. Add the onion sauce and heat through, turning the steaks in the sauce to coat.

❦ Transfer the steaks to warmed individual plates or a platter and spoon the onion sauce on top. Serve immediately.

serves 4

Basque Country

Codornices en Hoja de Parra

quail in grape leaves

Game birds—quail, partridge, pheasant—are much prized in Spain, and in the fall local hunters as well as hunting enthusiasts from elsewhere can be seen slowly making their way over the hills and across the tablelands in pursuit of their prey. Spanish cooks prefer these wild birds to their tamer-tasting farm-raised kin, and plump, meaty charcoal-grilled wild quail are regular fare from Andalusia to La Mancha to the Basque provinces. In this recipe, the tiny birds are stuffed with fragrant thyme sprigs and lemon zest, then wrapped in grape leaves and grilled, but Basque cooks also serve the succulent birds with haricot beans, braise them and douse them with a simple white wine sauce, or stuff them with halved fresh figs and cook them on the grill. Serve these leaf-wrapped quail with coarse country bread fried in olive oil.

12 quail, preferably boneless

salt and freshly ground pepper to taste

12 fresh thyme sprigs

12 lemon zest strips

12 jarred grape leaves, rinsed of brine and stems removed

12 long slices bacon

olive oil for brushing

☙ Prepare a fire in a charcoal grill.

☙ Rinse the quail and pat dry. Rub inside and out with salt and pepper. Stuff a thyme sprig and a lemon zest strip inside each bird. Wrap each bird in a grape leaf and then in a slice of bacon. Secure in place with kitchen string or skewer with a toothpick. Brush the birds with olive oil.

☙ Place the birds on an oiled grill rack and grill, turning once, until tender and well browned, 5–8 minutes on each side. Transfer to a warmed platter, remove the strings or toothpicks, and serve at once.

serves 6

Navarre

Cordero Cochifrito

lamb with lemon and paprika

From the earliest days in Spain and Portugal, lamb played a significant role in the diets of the Jews and Muslims who lived alongside the Christians. The result is a large repertoire of lamb recipes in the cuisine of both countries. Cochifrito, one of the simplest and best dishes of this legacy, is a specialty of Navarre, a region known for its high-quality milk-fed lamb. Some versions of this dish call for puréeing a canned pimiento and a bit of chile and adding it along with a bread-and-garlic picada to thicken the pan juices.

2 lb (1 kg) boneless lamb shoulder, cut into 1-inch (2.5-cm) pieces

salt and freshly ground pepper to taste

¼ cup (2 fl oz/60 ml) olive oil

2 yellow onions, chopped

4 cloves garlic, minced

1 tablespoon sweet paprika

4 tablespoons (⅓ oz/10 g) chopped fresh flat-leaf (Italian) parsley

¼ cup (2 fl oz/60 ml) fresh lemon juice

lemon wedges

❦ Sprinkle the lamb with salt and pepper. In a heavy frying pan over high heat, warm the olive oil. Working in batches, add the lamb and brown well on all sides, 5–8 minutes. Using a slotted spoon, transfer the lamb to a heavy pot.

❦ Add the onions and garlic to the fat remaining in the frying pan over medium heat and sauté until tender, 8–10 minutes. Add the paprika and sauté for 1 minute longer. Transfer the onions, garlic, and all the pan juices to the pot holding the lamb. Then add 2 tablespoons of the parsley and all of the lemon juice to the lamb and bring to a boil over high heat. Reduce the heat to low, cover, and simmer until the lamb is tender, about 1 hour.

❦ Taste and adjust the seasonings. Transfer to a warmed serving dish and sprinkle with the remaining 2 tablespoons parsley. Serve with lemon wedges.

serves 6

Beira Baixa

Carneiro Recheado à Portuguesa

lamb chops stuffed with almonds, olives, and bread crumbs

With the exception of the cilantro, the filling used to stuff these lamb chops resembles a Catalan picada, a mixture typically used for enriching and thickening a sauce. If you like, pair with sautéed carrots with mint and boiled or fried potatoes.

2 tablespoons unsalted butter or olive oil

1 cup (5 oz/155 g) chopped yellow onion

3 cloves garlic, minced

1 cup (2 oz/60 g) fresh bread crumbs

¼ cup (⅓ oz/10 g) chopped fresh cilantro (fresh coriander)

6 tablespoons (1½ oz/45 g) sliced (flaked) almonds, toasted and coarsely chopped

3 tablespoons pitted green olives, coarsely chopped

1 egg, lightly beaten

salt and freshly ground pepper to taste

12 loin lamb chops, each about 1½ inches (4 cm) thick

❦ Prepare a fire in a charcoal grill, or preheat a broiler (griller).

❦ In a small frying pan over medium heat, melt the butter or warm the olive oil. Add the onion and sauté until tender, 8–10 minutes. Add the garlic and sauté until fragrant, a few minutes longer. Transfer to a bowl and add the bread crumbs, cilantro, almonds, olives, egg, salt, and pepper.

❦ Using a small, sharp knife, cut a pocket in each lamb chop as wide and deep as you can before hitting the bone. Spoon the filling into the pockets, dividing it evenly. Skewer closed with toothpicks.

❦ Place the chops on an oiled grill rack, or arrange on a broiler pan and slip under the broiler. Grill or broil, turning once, until browned on both sides and cooked to medium-rare when cut into with a knife, 4–5 minutes on each side.

❦ Transfer the chops to warmed individual plates and serve immediately.

serves 6

Cider

While the rest of Spain makes and sips wine, many Asturians and Basques prefer lightly fermented *sidra,* or cider. They have been quaffing the amber-gold beverage since the time of the ancient Greeks, and, not surprisingly, considerable ritual has grown up around the making and the consumption of this favorite spritzy drink.

The cider is made in cider houses called *sidrerías.* Apples are harvested in the autumn, fed into a press, and crushed to a pulp. The juices from the pulp slowly drip through mesh into vats, where the first fermentation occurs within a few hours and a second one follows shortly after. For the next three months or so, the fermentation and aging continue and the cider eventually reaches about five percent alcohol. In January, it is tasted to judge its progress, and some four months later it is ready to drink.

In days gone by, the cider was left in its natural state in the barrels in which it was aged. Today, however, most of it is very lightly aerated and bottled for sale in shops. Despite this nod to modernization, strict rituals still

surround the serving and drinking of cider, as one can see on a visit to the sawdust-strewn bar of a cider house or to a *chigre* (tavern) in the ancient Asturian capital of Oviedo and other area towns.

The bars, no-frills establishments, their air thick with the pungent aroma of cider, are primarily male bastions, places to gather, visit, and drink. The pouring of the cider is startlingly showy and utterly practical: With one fully extended arm, the barman grasps a bottle above his head. In his other hand he holds a large, widemouthed glass as close to the floor as possible. The liquid travels from the bottle in a narrow, continuously flowing stream and strikes the side of the glass, the pressure producing a lovely, light, lacy golden foam. This is the source of the faint effervescence that marks every good Spanish cider. It traditionally is poured to a depth of only two fingers, and because the foam lasts only briefly, the nicely tart cider is drunk immediately, usually in a single gulp.

The pleasantly musky beverage is used in the local cooking as well, in such dishes as hake with cider (see recipe at right) or clams steamed in cider.

Asturias

Merluza a la Sidra

hake with cider

As grapes are hard to cultivate in Galicia and Asturias and apple trees thrive, it's not surprising to find that hard cider, instead of wine, is used in the local cooking, just as it is in the apple-orchard-rich French regions of Normandy and Brittany. This dish is usually made with hake or sea bass (lubina), but you may use cod, flounder, or another mild white fish. Not every version of the recipe calls for apples, but they do heighten the flavor of the cider.

8 tablespoons (4 fl oz/125 ml) olive oil

1 yellow onion, finely chopped

2 cloves garlic, minced

about ¾ cup (4 oz/125 g) all-purpose (plain) flour

1 dried chile, soaked in lukewarm water for 30 minutes to soften, drained, and stem removed

2 tomatoes, peeled, seeded, and chopped

2 small apples, peeled, cored, and chopped

1 cup (8 fl oz/250 ml) hard apple cider

2 large boiling potatoes, peeled and sliced ½ inch (12 mm) thick

1½ lb (750 g) hake or other white fish fillet, cut into 4 equal pieces (see note)

salt and freshly ground pepper to taste

16 clams, well scrubbed

3 tablespoons chopped fresh flat-leaf (Italian) parsley

☙ In a frying pan over medium heat, warm 2 table-spoons of the olive oil. Add the onion and garlic and sauté until the onion is tender, about 8 minutes. Add 1 tablespoon of the flour, the soaked chile, the toma-toes, and the apples. Stir well and pour in the cider. Bring to a boil over medium heat, adjust the heat to maintain a simmer, and simmer until the apples are soft, 8–10 minutes. Remove from the heat and pass the mixture through a food mill or purée in a blender or food processor. Set the sauce aside.

☙ Preheat an oven to 450°F (230°C).

☙ Bring a pot of water to a boil over high heat. Add the potato slices and boil until about half-cooked, about 5 minutes. Drain and set aside.

☙ Spread the remaining flour on a plate. Sprinkle the fish pieces with salt and pepper and then dip them in the flour, tapping off the excess. In a large frying pan over high heat, warm the remaining 6 tablespoons (3 fl oz/90 ml) oil. Add the fish and fry, turning once, to brown lightly on both sides. Transfer to a *cazuela* or other baking dish and set aside.

☙ Add the potatoes to the same oil over high heat and fry, turning once, until golden on both sides. Transfer to the *cazuela* and add the clams, discarding any that are open or broken, and the cider sauce.

☙ Place in the oven and bake until the clams open and the fish is heated through, about 15 minutes. (If you prefer, you can finish cooking this dish on the stove top, using a deep frying pan and covering it with a lid.)

☙ Remove from the oven and discard any clams that failed to open. Sprinkle with the parsley and serve directly from the dish.

serves 4

Galicia

Rape con Grelos

monkfish with greens

Plump, meaty monkfish, also known as angler, is popular in Spanish fish cookery, especially with cooks who live along the Galician coastline, the most important fishing region in the country. Here, it is prepared simply with greens, and some cooks add a few handfuls of tiny local clams to the pan as well. If you like, pass a bowl of alioli *(page 194) at the table.*

about ¼ cup (2 fl oz/60 ml) olive oil

2 yellow onions, chopped

3 cloves garlic, finely minced

½ teaspoon red pepper flakes (optional)

1 bay leaf

4 cups (32 fl oz/1 l) fish stock

salt and freshly ground pepper to taste

2 tablespoons fresh lemon juice (optional)

2 lb (1 kg) monkfish, rock fish, or sea bass fillet, cut into pieces about 2 by 3 inches (5 by 7.5 cm)

1½ lb (750 g) small clams such as Manila, well scrubbed (optional)

1 lb (500 g) Swiss chard, tough stems removed, cut into fine strips

6 slices coarse country bread, ½ inch (12 mm) thick, grilled or toasted

In a saucepan over medium heat, warm enough olive oil to form a film on the pan bottom. Add the onions and garlic and sauté until softened, 3–4 minutes. Add the red pepper flakes, if using, and the bay leaf and sauté until the onions are tender, 8–10 minutes. Do not allow the garlic to brown. Add the stock and simmer, uncovered, for 15 minutes. Season with salt, pepper, and the lemon juice, if using.

Transfer the onion sauce to a wide saucepan. Add the fish, the clams, if using (discard any clams that are open or broken), and the Swiss chard. Place over medium-high heat, cover, and simmer until the clams have opened and the fish is cooked, about 5 minutes. (Discard any clams that failed to open.)

Transfer the fish, clams (if used), and sauce to warmed individual bowls. Accompany each serving with a piece of the bread cut into thirds.

serves 6

Galicia

Vieiras a la Gallega

scallops baked in white wine

The Galician town of Santiago de la Compostela has been an important Christian center since the early ninth century, when the remains of Saint James the Apostle were discovered and enshrined there. From the beginning, pilgrims traveled great distances to visit the site. Upon arriving, they would stop to buy and eat a scallop and then pin the empty shell on their hats. The story behind how the scallop shell came to symbolize the journey varies, although it always includes a man rising from the sea covered in a cloak of white shells. In any case, today shops near the cathedral are filled with scallop-shaped curios, and dishes based on scallops appear on the local menus.

16 large scallops, preferably dry-pack dayboat

1 lemon, halved

6 tablespoons (3 fl oz/90 ml) olive oil

1 large yellow onion, finely chopped

2 oz (60 g) ham or bacon, chopped (optional)

1 cup (8 fl oz/250 ml) dry white wine

2 teaspoons sweet paprika

pinch of cayenne pepper

salt and freshly ground black pepper to taste

¼ cup (⅓ oz/10 g) chopped fresh flat-leaf (Italian) parsley

½ cup (2 oz/60 g) dried bread crumbs

Preheat an oven to 400°F (200°C).

Oil a *cazuela* or baking dish or 2 individual ramekins. Place the scallops in the prepared dish(es) and squeeze a bit of lemon juice over them. Cover and refrigerate until the sauce is ready.

In a frying pan over medium heat, warm the olive oil. Add the onion and the ham or bacon, if using, and sauté until the onion is very soft, about 15 minutes. Add the wine and deglaze the pan, scraping up the browned bits on the pan bottom, then cook until reduced by half, 5–8 minutes. Stir in the paprika, cayenne, salt, black pepper, and parsley, and spoon over the scallops. Top evenly with the bread crumbs. Bake until golden and bubbling, about 15 minutes. Remove from the oven and serve immediately.

serves 2

Andalusia

Pato a la Sevillana

duck with orange and olives

The Moors brought bitter oranges to southern Spain, and today they are grown in Andalusia and primarily used for marinades and for cooking down into a thick, tangy marmalade. Centuries later, the Portuguese traders who opened a sea route to the Far East returned to the Iberian Peninsula with sweet oranges from China, which the Spanish soon planted in vast groves in Levante.

Ducks, which are eaten in many parts of Spain, from the warm south to the cool northern reaches of Galicia, here are paired with olives and bitter Seville oranges, to produce a wonderful dish of sharp, pleasing flavors. This is a rich concoction, however, and you may prefer to roast the whole ducks in a 400°F (200°C) oven for about an hour (prick them first with a fork so they release their fat during cooking) and make the sauce separately, then carve the ducks and spoon the sauce over them. If you cannot find bitter oranges, sweet oranges will still produce a satisfying dish—just add a squeeze of lime juice to replicate the flavor.

2 tablespoons olive oil

2 ducks, about 5 lb (2.5 kg) each, cut into serving pieces

1 large yellow onion, chopped

2 tablespoons all-purpose (plain) flour

2 cups (16 fl oz/500 ml) dry white wine or fino sherry

3 carrots, peeled and thickly sliced

2 oranges, cut into slices ¼ inch (6 mm) thick

2 fresh flat-leaf (Italian) parsley sprigs

1 fresh thyme sprig

1 bay leaf

salt and freshly ground pepper to taste

cornstarch (cornflour) for thickening pan juices, if needed

1 cup (5 oz/155 g) green olives, pitted and coarsely chopped

☙ In a large, heavy frying pan over high heat, warm the olive oil. Working in batches, sauté the duck pieces until golden brown on all sides, about 10 minutes. Transfer to a plate and keep warm. Drain off all but 3 tablespoons of the fat from the pan.

☙ Add the onion to the fat remaining in the pan over medium heat and sauté until golden brown, about 15 minutes. Add the flour and cook, stirring, for a few minutes to thicken. Add the wine and deglaze the pan, stirring to dislodge any browned bits on the pan bottom. Return the duck to the pan along with the carrots, oranges, parsley, thyme, and bay leaf. Season with salt and pepper, add just enough water to cover, cover the pan, and cook over low heat until the duck is tender, 45–60 minutes.

☙ Transfer the duck to a warmed platter and keep warm. Using a large spoon, skim off the fat from the pan and purée the remaining sauce in a blender. Pour the puréed sauce into a saucepan and bring to a simmer over medium heat. If it is too thin, mix together a little cornstarch and water to form a thin paste and stir it into the sauce. Add the olives, heat through, and taste and adjust the seasonings.

☙ Spoon the olive-and-orange sauce over the duck and serve immediately.

serves 4–6

Estremadura

Meia Desfeita de Bacalhau

salt cod with chickpeas

The cooks of Estremadura specialize in creative dishes made with chickpeas, combining them here with Portugal's ubiquitous salt cod.

1½ lb (750 g) salt cod, soaked (see glossary, page 249)

4 hard-boiled eggs, peeled

¾ cup (6 fl oz / 180 ml) olive oil

3 yellow onions, chopped

3–5 cloves garlic, minced

1 teaspoon sweet paprika

2 cups (14 oz / 440 g) drained, cooked chickpeas (garbanzo beans)

½ cup (4 fl oz / 125 ml) white wine vinegar

1 cup (1½ oz / 45 g) chopped fresh flat-leaf (Italian) parsley

few drops of piri-piri sauce (page 64)

salt to taste

18 oil-cured black olives

olive oil and white wine vinegar for serving

♛ Drain the salt cod and place in a saucepan with water to cover. Bring to a gentle simmer over medium heat and cook until tender, 10–15 minutes. Drain well and, when cool enough to handle, flake the cod, removing any bits of skin and any small bones. Set aside. Slice 3 of the hard-boiled eggs, then chop the remaining egg. Set aside separately.

♛ In a large frying pan over medium heat, warm the olive oil. Add the onions and sauté until tender, 8–10 minutes. Add the garlic and paprika and sauté until the garlic is translucent, about 2 minutes longer. Add the cod, chickpeas, sliced eggs, vinegar, half of the parsley, and the *piri-piri* sauce and cook, stirring, until heated through, a few minutes. Season with salt.

♛ Transfer to a warmed platter and garnish with the chopped egg and olives and the remaining parsley. Pass olive oil and vinegar at the table.

serves 6

Frango à Beira Alta

roast chicken with ham and curd cheese

*In sparsely populated Beira Alta, with its granite hills,
superb Dão wines, and excellent local cheeses, cooks
tuck* presunto *under the skin of a roasting chicken to
add flavor, along with a bit of salt, and then they stuff
the cavity with a rich blend of soft cheese mixed with
butter and ground pepper. Basting the bird with butter
results in a beautiful golden brown skin.*

1 roasting chicken, 4 lb (2 kg)

2 slices presunto *or* prosciutto

*¾ cup (6 oz / 185 g) cottage cheese or soft,
fresh sheep's or cow's milk cheese*

*6 tablespoons (3 oz / 90 g) unsalted butter, at
room temperature*

freshly ground pepper to taste

salt to taste

1½ lb (750 g) small new potatoes, peeled

☙ Preheat an oven to 350°F (180°C).

☙ Rinse the chicken and pat dry. Using your fingers,
ease the skin away from the breast meat of the
chicken, being careful not to tear the skin. Slip
the ham under the skin, covering the breast, and press
the skin back into place. Place the cheese in a small
bowl. Cut 2 tablespoons of the butter into small
pieces and mix with the cheese. Season with pepper.
Spoon the cheese mixture into the chicken cavity
and skewer or sew closed with kitchen string.

☙ In a small pan, melt the remaining 4 tablespoons
(2 oz / 60 g) butter and season with salt and pepper.
Set aside to use for basting.

☙ Place the chicken, breast side up, on a rack in a
roasting pan and place the potatoes in the pan, surrounding the bird. Roast, basting the chicken and the
potatoes with the seasoned butter every 8–10 minutes, until the juices run clear when a thigh joint is
pierced or until an instant-read thermometer
inserted into the thickest part of the thigh without
touching the bone registers 160°F (71°C), about
1½ hours.

☙ Transfer the chicken and potatoes to a warmed
platter. To serve, using a large spoon, scoop out the
cheese and place in a bowl to pass at the table.

serves 4

Asturias

Entrecó al Cabrales

steak with cabrales cheese

Queso Cabrales, *a rich, blue-veined cheese that Spaniards consider the equal of French Roquefort or English Stilton, is a specialty of Asturias, where its production remains a farmhouse industry carried on in isolated mountain-lined valleys. The unique flavor of the cheese depends on the use of three kinds of milk— goat, cow, and sheep—and age-old procedures that call for pressing the curds into a wheel, salting and drying, and then aging in limestone caves for a few months until the distinctive mold has formed. Much of the output is eaten locally, and the rest shows up in fancy cheese shops from Madrid to Málaga. Cabrales is primarily an eating cheese, but it also makes a rich and creamy sauce for steak.*

1½ lb (750 g) veal or beef fillet, cut into 4 steaks, each about 1½ inches (4 cm) thick

salt and freshly ground pepper to taste

¼ cup (2 oz/60 g) unsalted butter

3 oz (90 g) Cabrales or Roquefort cheese, crumbled

1 cup (8 fl oz/250 ml) half-and-half (half cream) or light (single) cream

½ cup (4 fl oz/125 ml) beef stock

2 tablespoons brandy

❧ Sprinkle the steaks on both sides with salt and pepper. In a large frying pan over medium heat, melt the butter. Add the steaks and cook, turning once, 3–4 minutes on each side for rare, or as desired. Transfer the steaks to a platter; keep warm.

❧ Add the cheese, cream, stock, and brandy to the frying pan. Cook over high heat until reduced by half, about 8 minutes. Spoon over the steaks and serve at once.

serves 4

Alentejo

Porco com Amêijoas à Alentejana

pork with clams

The combination of pork and clams is a signature dish of Alentejo, and the kitchen at the Pousada dos Lóios, in the unspoiled provincial walled capital of Evora, makes a particularly memorable version. The pigs of the province dine on acorns, making the pork especially sweet, and the salty clams provide a nice contrast to the rich meat. Massa de pimentão (a paste of roasted red peppers, garlic, and olive oil) diluted with wine is sometimes used in place of the marinade presented here. Serve this popular dish with boiled potatoes. Sometimes a squeeze of lemon is added at the table.

2 lb (1 kg) boneless pork shoulder or butt, cut into 1-inch (2.5-cm) cubes

1 cup (8 fl oz/250 ml) dry white wine, or as needed

3 tablespoons sweet paprika

1 bay leaf

2 whole cloves

5 cloves garlic, chopped

4 tablespoons (2 oz/60 g) lard or (2 fl oz/ 60 ml) olive oil

2 yellow onions, chopped

4 tomatoes, peeled, seeded, and diced

2 lb (1 kg) small clams such as Manila, well scrubbed

3 tablespoons chopped fresh cilantro (fresh coriander)

2 tablespoons chopped fresh flat-leaf (Italian) parsley

☙ Place the pork in a nonaluminum container and add the 1 cup (8 fl oz/250 ml) wine, paprika, bay leaf, cloves, and 3 of the garlic cloves. Toss well to mix evenly, cover, and refrigerate overnight.

☙ The next day, drain the pork, reserving the marinade. Pat the meat dry.

☙ In a large frying pan over medium heat, melt 2 tablespoons of the lard or warm 2 tablespoons of the olive oil. Working in batches, brown the pork cubes on all sides until golden brown, about 5 minutes. Using a slotted spoon, transfer to a plate.

☙ In a large saucepan over medium heat, melt the remaining 2 tablespoons lard or warm the remaining 2 tablespoons oil. Add the onions and sauté until soft, 8–10 minutes. Add the remaining 2 cloves garlic and the tomatoes and cook, stirring occasionally, until the tomatoes are soft, about 5 minutes. Add the browned pork to the onion mixture along with the reserved marinade, cover, reduce the heat to low, and cook until the pork is tender, about 1 hour. Check from time to time and add more wine if the pork threatens to scorch.

☙ Add the clams, discarding any that are open or have broken shells, cover, raise the heat to high, and cook until the clams open, about 5 minutes. (Discard any clams that failed to open.)

☙ Transfer the pork and clams to a warmed serving dish and sprinkle with the cilantro and parsley. Serve immediately.

serves 6–8

Gastronomic Societies

Basque men are clever, industrious souls who seem to excel at whatever they attempt, whether they be fishermen or farmers, astronomers or artists. Not surprisingly, these same men are also fine cooks. Indeed, the Basque kitchen has long been considered the province of men, and the *sociedades gastronómicas*, men-only eating societies, are the product of that tradition.

Membership is limited in these clubs, where men come together to drink, socialize, cook, and eat. In cities such as San Sebastián and Bilbao, they are often rather elaborate establishments, outfitted with an efficient kitchen, a well-stocked bar, and a piano for the inevitable singing of Basque songs. In towns and villages, the trappings may be simpler, but the playful carousing is no less spirited and the food no less wonderful.

Each evening, a few members will cook the dinner and the expenses will be paid by everyone at the table, bolstered by a donation from the society's coffers. Members can brings guests, but they must be men. Women, alas, are permitted to enter only on a handful of occasions each year—and they must never go near the kitchen.

Beira Litoral

Leitão Assado à Bairrada

roast suckling pig, beira style

Roast suckling pig is served throughout Spain and Portugal for special feasts. Old Castile, especially the town of Segovia, is known for young, tender suckling pig scented with thyme, but this recipe is from the town of Coimbra, in Beira Litoral, where many Portuguese pigs are raised. The pig is traditionally roasted in a wood-burning oven or on a spit over an open fire, but a conventional home oven will work well, too. You will need to ask your butcher to special-order the suckling pig. Then, when you go to pick it up, request that he or she open the cavity from the belly side and clean out the innards, saving the liver. You'll also need a large roasting pan with a rack to elevate the pig, to ensure the skin will be crisp. Stuff it or not, but serve it with fried potatoes, greens drizzled with piri-piri sauce (page 64), and a plate of orange segments. Pour a dry red wine.

1 suckling pig, 7–10 lb (3½–5 kg), cleaned

OPTIONAL STUFFING

2 tablespoons unsalted butter

1 pig's liver, about ½ lb (250 g), coarsely chopped

2 yellow onions, chopped

2 tomatoes, peeled and chopped

1 piece ham, about 1 lb (500 g), chopped

¾ cup (4 oz/125 g) pitted oil-cured black olives, coarsely chopped

2 tablespoons all-purpose (plain) flour mixed with about 2 tablespoons water to form a paste

2 egg yolks or 1 whole egg, lightly beaten

salt and freshly ground pepper to taste

PASTE

½ lb (250 g) lard, melted and cooled, or 1 cup (8 fl oz/250 ml) olive oil

2 oz (60 g) bacon, finely chopped

4 cloves garlic, minced

¼ cup (⅓ oz/10 g) chopped fresh flat-leaf (Italian) parsley

1 tablespoon salt

2 teaspoons freshly ground pepper

1 cup (8 fl oz/250 ml) dry white wine

☙ Wash the pig well inside and out.

☙ If you are making the stuffing, melt the butter in a frying pan over medium heat. Add the liver and sauté until lightly browned, about 5 minutes. Using a slotted spoon, transfer to a plate and set aside. Add the onions to the butter remaining in the pan and sauté until golden, about 15 minutes. Add the tomatoes and cook, stirring often, for 5 minutes. Return the liver to the pan along with the ham and olives. Stir in the flour-water paste and cook for about 5 minutes to thicken and cook the flour. Stir in the egg yolks or whole egg to bind, reduce the heat to very low, and cook for about 5 minutes longer until thick. Season with salt and pepper. Remove from the heat and let cool. Spoon the filling into the pig's cavity and sew closed with kitchen string.

☙ To make the paste, in a small bowl, stir together the lard or olive oil, bacon, garlic, parsley, salt, and pepper. Rub this mixture all over the outside of the pig. If you have not stuffed the pig, rub the cavity with it as well. Let marinate at room temperature for 2 hours.

☙ Preheat an oven to 425°F (220°C).

☙ Cover the ears and tail of the pig with aluminum foil. Place the pig upside down on a rack in a roasting pan and roast for 20 minutes. Reduce the temperature to 350°F (180°C) and roast, basting every 15 minutes with the white wine, for 1 hour. Turn the pig over and continue to roast until an instant-read thermometer inserted into the thickest part of the thigh registers 147°F (64°C), about 1 hour longer.

☙ Carefully transfer the pig to a carving board. Cut off the head and scoop out the stuffing. Remove the crispy skin, then quarter the pig. Carve the meat from the shoulders and haunches. Separate the ribs. Place the meat on a large platter and serve.

serves 6–8

Douro

Bacalhau à Gomes de Sá

salt cod and potato gratin

Gomes de Sá, a well-regarded nineteenth-century Oporto restaurateur, created this hearty gratin, which is now a national dish.

1 lb (500 g) boneless salt cod, soaked (see glossary, page 249)

milk to cover, if needed

1½ lb (750 g) boiling potatoes (3 large), peeled

6 tablespoons (3 fl oz/90 ml) olive oil

2 yellow onions, thinly sliced

2 cloves garlic, minced

½ cup (¾ oz/20 g) chopped fresh flat-leaf (Italian) parsley

1 teaspoon freshly ground pepper

20 oil-cured black olives

2 hard-boiled eggs, peeled and sliced

❧ Drain the cod and place in a saucepan with water to cover. Bring to a gentle simmer over medium heat and cook until tender, 10–15 minutes. Drain, let cool slightly, then break up with your fingers, removing any bits of skin and small bones. Taste the cod. If too salty, cover with milk and let rest for 30 minutes, then drain and set aside. At the same time, combine the potatoes with water to cover, bring to a boil, and boil until tender but firm, 20–25 minutes. Drain and slice ¼ inch (6 mm) thick. Set aside.

❧ In a frying pan over medium heat, warm 2 tablespoons of the oil. Add the onions and sauté until just tender, 7–8 minutes. Add the garlic and cook for 2 minutes. Transfer to a bowl. In the same pan, warm 3 tablespoons of the oil over medium heat. Add the potatoes and sauté until golden, about 5 minutes.

❧ Preheat an oven to 400°F (200°C). Oil a large gratin dish or 4 individual dishes. Layer half of the potatoes in the bottom(s), top with half of the cod, and then half of the onions. Sprinkle with a little of the parsley and pepper. Repeat the layers, then drizzle the top(s) with the remaining oil.

❧ Bake until golden, about 25 minutes. Garnish with the olives and hard-boiled eggs and sprinkle with the remaining parsley. Serve at once.

serves 4

Alentejo

Lulas Recheadas

stuffed squid

Squid are greatly enjoyed in Portugal. At their simplest, they are grilled and dressed with olive oil and lemon. Other times they are stuffed and grilled or braised in a sauce of stock and wine.

12 medium or 16 small squid, cleaned (see glossary, page 250)

¼ cup (2 fl oz/60 ml) olive oil, plus olive oil for brushing

1½ cups (7½ oz/235 g) chopped yellow onion

4 cloves garlic, minced

½ cup (3 oz/90 g) chopped presunto or prosciutto

1½ cups (3 oz/90 g) fresh bread crumbs

¼ cup (2 fl oz/60 ml) fresh lemon juice

6 tablespoons (½ oz/15 g) chopped fresh flat-leaf (Italian) parsley

salt and freshly ground pepper to taste

1 egg, lightly beaten

⅓ cup (3 fl oz/80 ml) olive oil

3–4 tablespoons fresh lemon juice

2 tablespoons dried oregano

❧ Leave the squid bodies whole and chop the tentacles. Set aside. In a frying pan over medium heat, warm the ¼ cup (2 fl oz/60 ml) olive oil. Add the onion and sauté until tender, 8–10 minutes. Add the garlic, ham, tentacles, and bread crumbs and sauté, stirring often, until blended, about 2 minutes. Add the lemon juice, parsley, salt, and pepper. Stir in the egg, remove from the heat, and let cool.

❧ Prepare a fire in a grill. Stuff the squid bodies with the cooled filling and skewer closed with toothpicks. Thread the squid onto metal skewers, placing 3 on each. Brush with olive oil and sprinkle with salt and pepper. Grill, turning once, until firm and light grill marks appear, about 3 minutes on each side.

❧ Meanwhile, in a bowl, stir together the olive oil, lemon juice, and oregano. When the squid are ready, slip them onto a warmed platter and spoon the olive oil mixture over them. Serve at once.

serves 4

Catalonia

Pollo en Samfaina

chicken with eggplant, peppers, and tomatoes

Catalan samfaina, like Provençal ratatouille, is a mixture of onions, garlic, eggplant, peppers, and tomatoes, cooked down to a fragrant and unctuous stew.

1 chicken, about 4 lb (2 kg), cut into pieces

salt and freshly ground pepper to taste

¼ cup (2 fl oz / 60 ml) olive oil

¼ lb (125 g) diced serrano ham (optional)

2 large yellow onions, sliced or coarsely chopped

3 cloves garlic, minced

1 lb (500 g) Asian (slender) eggplants (aubergines), cut into 1-inch (2.5-cm) pieces

¾ lb (375 g) zucchini (courgettes), cut into ½-inch (12-mm) chunks

2 green or red bell peppers (capsicums), seeded and cut into large dice

1½ lb (750 g) tomatoes, peeled, seeded, and chopped

1 bay leaf

2 tablespoons chopped fresh thyme or marjoram

½ cup (4 fl oz / 125 ml) dry white wine

❦ Rinse the chicken pieces, pat dry, and sprinkle with salt and pepper. In a large, heavy frying pan over high heat, warm the oil. Working in batches, brown the chicken pieces on all sides, 8–10 minutes. Using tongs, transfer to a plate. Add the ham, if using, to the oil remaining in the pan over medium heat and sauté for 1 minute. Add the onions and sauté until soft, about 10 minutes. Add the garlic, eggplants, zucchini, and peppers and cook, stirring often, until the mixture begins to soften, about 5 minutes.

❦ Add the tomatoes, bay leaf, thyme or marjoram, and wine, then return the chicken to the pan and toss well with the vegetables. Cover and simmer over low heat until the chicken is tender, 25–35 minutes. Season with salt and pepper and serve immediately.

serves 4

Old Castile

Pollo en Pepitoria

fried chicken with almond and egg sauce

This is an old Castilian recipe. It is described in Hispano-Arab documents as far back as the thirteenth century and in texts by the scholars Diego Granado in 1599, Martinez Montiño in 1611, and Juan de Altamiras in 1745. In Spanish, a pepita *is a seed. Pine nuts were used in the original Moorish-inspired recipe, and the mashed yolks of hard-boiled eggs were added to thicken the sauce. Today, almonds are used in place of the pine nuts, but you could use a combination of the two. A pinch of ground cinnamon and cloves may be used instead of the nutmeg.*

½ cup (4 fl oz / 125 ml) olive oil

½ cup (2½ oz / 75 g) blanched almonds

3 cloves garlic, chopped

1 slice coarse country bread, crust removed

1 chicken, 3–4 lb (1.5–2 kg), cut into serving pieces

salt and freshly ground pepper to taste

¾ cup (6 fl oz / 180 ml) chicken stock

¼ teaspoon saffron threads, crushed

½ cup (4 fl oz / 125 ml) fino sherry

1 bay leaf

1 teaspoon chopped fresh thyme

2 hard-boiled egg yolks, mashed

freshly grated nutmeg to taste

3 tablespoons finely minced fresh flat-leaf (Italian) parsley

☙ In a frying pan over medium heat, warm a few tablespoons of the oil. Add the almonds and sauté until pale gold, 3–5 minutes. Using a slotted spoon, transfer the almonds to a blender, food processor, or mortar. Add the garlic to the oil remaining in the pan and sauté over medium heat for a minute or two until lightly browned. Using the slotted spoon, add the garlic to the almonds. Now fry the bread in the same oil, turning as necessary, until golden, about 5 minutes. Remove from the pan, break up into several pieces, and add to the almonds.

☙ Rinse the chicken pieces, pat dry with paper towels, and sprinkle with salt and pepper.

☙ In a large, heavy frying pan over high heat, warm the remaining oil. Add the chicken pieces and sauté, turning often, until golden, 8–10 minutes. Using tongs or the slotted spoon, transfer to a plate.

☙ Measure out 2 tablespoons of the chicken stock and place in a small pan. Add the saffron, heat gently, and set aside. Add the remaining stock to the frying pan used for the chicken along with the sherry. Bring to a boil over high heat and deglaze the pan, stirring to dislodge any browned bits from the pan bottom. Return the chicken to the pan, add the bay leaf and thyme, reduce the heat to low, cover, and simmer gently until the juices run clear when a chicken thigh is pierced, about 10 minutes longer.

☙ Meanwhile, add the saffron and its liquid to the almond mixture along with the egg yolks and grind finely to form a *picada*. When the chicken is ready, add the *picada*, stir well, and simmer for a few minutes to thicken the pan sauce.

☙ Season with salt, pepper, and nutmeg and transfer to a warmed deep platter. Sprinkle with the parsley and serve immediately.

serves 4

Catalonia

Conejo con Peras y Nabos

rabbit with pears and turnips

When the Romans first arrived on the Iberian Peninsula around 200 B.C., they found a land over-run with rabbits. Hispania means "land of the rabbits," and thus it comes as no surprise that Spanish cooks use the rabbit in countless dishes. The simplest preparation is to grill it and serve it with alioli (page 194). It can also be cooked al chilindrón (with peppers), en samfaina (with onions, garlic, eggplant, peppers, and tomatoes), or en pepitoria (with an almond picada). As has been noted, the theme of meat and fruit is a signature of Catalan cooking. Some versions pair prunes and pine nuts, but in this recipe, pears and turnips are the sweet accompaniment for the lean, mild taste of rabbit.

2 leeks, chopped

1 yellow onion, chopped

1 carrot, peeled and chopped

1 ripe tomato, peeled and chopped

2 cloves garlic, chopped

3–4 cups (24–32 fl oz/750 ml–1 l) chicken or vegetable stock

8 small turnips, peeled

all-purpose (plain) flour for dusting turnips

olive oil for frying

2 pears, peeled, halved lengthwise, and cored

about ½ cup (2½ oz/75 g) all-purpose (plain) flour seasoned with salt and freshly ground pepper

1 rabbit, about 2½ lb (1.25 kg), quartered

¼ cup (2 fl oz/60 ml) brandy

1 cup (8 fl oz/250 ml) dry white wine

bouquet garni of 1 fresh thyme sprig, 1 fresh parsley sprig, 1 bay leaf, and 6 peppercorns

salt and freshly ground pepper to taste

❧ In a saucepan, combine the leeks, onion, carrot, tomato, and garlic with enough stock just to cover. Bring to a boil over high heat and boil until the vegetables are tender, about 15 minutes. Let cool slightly, then pass the vegetables and liquid through a food mill or purée in a blender. Set aside.

❧ At the same time, in a saucepan, combine the turnips with salted water to cover. Bring to a boil and boil until tender-crisp, 10–15 minutes. Drain well

and pat dry. Spread a little flour on a plate and dip the turnips in it, tapping off the excess. In a frying pan, pour olive oil to a depth of ¼ inch (6 mm) and warm over medium-high heat. Add the turnips and fry, turning as needed, until golden, 2–3 minutes. Remove from the heat and set aside.

❧ While the vegetables are cooking, place the pears in a saucepan with water or stock to cover, bring to a simmer, and cook until barely tender, about 15 minutes. Using a slotted spoon, transfer to a dish and set aside.

❧ Spread the seasoned flour on a plate and dip the rabbit pieces in it, coating evenly. In a large, heavy frying pan, pour oil to a depth of ¼ inch (6 mm) and warm over medium-high heat. Add the rabbit pieces and brown well on all sides, 5–10 minutes. Using tongs or a slotted spoon, transfer the rabbit pieces to a *cazuela* or heavy pot. Pour the brandy over the rabbit and ignite it with a long match. Pour on the wine, bring to a boil over high heat, and cook rapidly to burn off the alcohol, 2–3 minutes.

❧ Meanwhile, place the ingredients for the bouquet garni on a square of cheesecloth (muslin), bring the corners together, and tie securely with kitchen string. Add the bouquet garni and 1½ cups (12 fl oz/375 ml) of the stock to the rabbit, bring to a boil, reduce the heat to low, and simmer until the rabbit is tender, 35–45 minutes, adding the puréed vegetables about halfway through cooking and the turnips and pears for the last 10 minutes of cooking.

❧ When the rabbit is cooked through, remove the bouquet garni and discard. Season the rabbit with salt and pepper. Transfer to a warmed serving dish and serve immediately.

serves 4

The leaves clipped from turnips are never discarded by the frugal Spanish cook, who instead stirs them into braises and soups.

Estremadura

Gambas com Caril

shrimp with curry

In the fifteenth century, Vasco da Gama rounded the Cape of Good Hope and later returned with cinnamon, cloves, nutmeg, pepper, and curry powder. This recipe is based on one from Goa, a Portuguese colony until it was seized by India in 1961. Serve with rice and piri-piri sauce (page 64).

1 lb (500 g) medium or large shrimp (prawns), peeled and deveined

salt to taste

1 tablespoon curry powder

½ teaspoon ground ginger (optional)

1 tablespoon fresh lemon juice

3 tablespoons unsalted butter

1 yellow onion, chopped

2 cloves garlic, minced

1 red bell pepper (capsicum), seeded and chopped

1 tablespoon all-purpose (plain) flour

½ cup (4 fl oz / 125 ml) shrimp or fish stock

½ cup (4 fl oz / 125 ml) light (single) cream

freshly ground pepper to taste

¼ cup (⅓ oz / 10 g) chopped fresh flat-leaf (Italian) parsley or fresh cilantro (fresh coriander)

☙ Sprinkle the shrimp with salt. In a small bowl, dissolve the curry powder and the ginger, if using, in the lemon juice. (Use the ginger if the curry powder lacks ginger or includes only a small amount.)

☙ In a large frying pan over medium heat, melt the butter. Add the onion, garlic, and bell pepper and sauté until tender, about 10 minutes. Add the dissolved spices and the flour and stir well. Add the stock and cream and cook, stirring constantly, until thickened, about 8 minutes. Season with salt and pepper. Add the shrimp and cook until they turn pink, 2–4 minutes.

☙ Transfer to a warmed serving dish and sprinkle with parsley or cilantro. Serve immediately.

serves 4

Catalonia

Calamares con Guisantes

squid with peas

Fish and shellfish are favorites of the Catalan table, and the local fishermen haul in a varied catch, from squid to baby octopuses, small lobsters to slithery eels, slim sole to silvery sardines. Most proprietors of waterfront restaurants put together attractive displays of their offerings, making it easy for potential diners to survey the bountiful harvest before selecting a place to eat. One of the most popular treatments for fish or shellfish on these seaside menus is to combine it with peas in a salsa verde, a sauce made from fresh mint or parsley and olive oil.

This squid recipe is especially appealing because of the addition of tomatoes and a picada of bread and garlic. I love it because of the generous amount of garlic, but you can choose to use less. You can also prepare this dish with clams.

2 lb (1 kg) squid, cleaned (see glossary, page 250)

4 lb (2 kg) English peas in the pod, shelled

½ cup (4 fl oz/125 ml) olive oil

2 heads garlic, cloves separated and peeled

2 slices coarse country bread, crusts removed

1 tablespoon all-purpose (plain) flour

3 tomatoes, peeled, seeded, and chopped

½ cup (4 fl oz/125 ml) dry white wine, or as needed

¼ cup (⅓ oz/10 g) chopped fresh mint

¼ cup (⅓ oz/10 g) chopped fresh flat-leaf (Italian) parsley

☙ Cut the squid bodies crosswise into 1-inch (2.5-cm) rings; set aside with the whole tentacles.

☙ Bring a saucepan three-fourths full of salted water to a boil. Add the peas and cook until tender, 3–5 minutes. Drain and immerse in cold water to stop the cooking. Drain and set aside.

☙ In a large frying pan over medium heat, warm the olive oil. Add the garlic and sauté until golden, about 5 minutes. Using a slotted spoon, transfer to paper towels to drain. Add the bread to the same oil over medium-high heat and fry, turning once, until crisp and golden, 5–7 minutes. Transfer to paper towels to drain. Break up the bread and place in a mortar, blender, or food processor along with the garlic. Pound or process until finely ground.

☙ Add the flour to the same oil over medium heat and, when it starts to color, add the tomatoes and wine, stirring well. Add the bread-garlic mixture along with half each of the mint and parsley and simmer for 15 minutes. If the sauce is too thick, add a little more wine or water. It needs to be spoonable and have a nice liquid consistency. Remove from the heat, let cool slightly, and pour into a blender or food processor. Process until smooth. If the purée is too thick, thin with a little water.

☙ Return the sauce to the pan and bring to a boil over high heat. Add the squid and stir well. Cook for a minute or two. Stir in the peas and heat for a minute longer until the peas are heated through and the squid is just tender.

☙ Transfer to a warmed platter and garnish with the remaining mint and parsley. Serve at once.

serves 6

VEGETABLES AND GRAINS

Vast market gardens and rice fields yield riches for the Iberian table.

THE MOORS INTRODUCED rice to Iberia in the eighth century, planting it extensively in the area around the city of Valencia, where the soil and climate were well suited to its cultivation. Emerald-green paddies still surround Lake Albufera—"little sea" in Arabic—a great freshwater lagoon just south of the city and separated from the sea by a slim sandbar lined with pine trees. The lagoon is filled with eels, just as it was in the days of the Moors, and, not surprisingly, many of the region's earliest rice dishes combined the newly planted grain with the slippery water creatures. Eventually, rice cultivation spread to Aragon's Ebro River delta and later to the marshlands around the Guadalquivir River in southern Andalusia and to the Calasparra region near the ninth-century town of Murcia, whose medieval quarter still projects a Moorish ambience.

The earliest recorded Iberian recipes for rice were sweet dishes, cooked in milk, and a fourteenth-century book refers to sweet rice scented with cinnamon and almonds in the Arab tradition. Medieval texts mention *manjar blanco,* a dish of ground rice, chicken, almonds, and sugar, and famed author Ruperto de Nola, in an early sixteenth-century cookbook, refers to rice cooked in meat broth. By the eighteenth and nineteenth centuries, rice had become a staple of the Spanish recipe repertoire, and many rice dishes were part of the Lenten menu. While long-grain rice is grown in limited amounts for export and for certain soups and side dishes, different varieties of medium-grain rice are cultivated and harvested for locally made paellas and puddings.

Although Spanish cuisine boasts a number of different rice preparations, paella, of course, is the most famous of them. It is believed to have originated with shepherds on the shores of Lake Albufera, who assembled it from what was on hand, usually snails, eels, green beans, olive oil, and rice. It was prepared over an open fire at midday (being too heavy to consume at night) and eaten communally from the great pan in which it was cooked, and mouthfuls of the rice were alternated with mouthfuls of green (spring) onion. The classic paella of Valencia calls for rabbit or chicken,

Preceding spread: The sun lights up the windows and balconies on a village street in Spain's Basque country. **Left:** Succulent snails and a myriad of other ocean-dwelling delicacies are plucked from the waters off the west coast of Portugal. **Below top:** Noodles such as these star in various Spanish regional dishes, including *fideos a la malagueña* and Valencian *fideuá.* **Below bottom:** A pile of long, flat green beans tempts shoppers at a market in Lisbon.

snails, and beans, and purists disdain the notion of combining fish and shellfish with meats, or even certain types of fish with certain varieties of shellfish. But as with all good ideas, paella has evolved, and contemporary cooks in Barcelona, for example, prepare paellas that mix chicken, sausage, and shellfish.

The Portuguese rice repertoire is no match for that of its neighbor, but rice is cultivated in well-watered areas along the country's west coast, especially in the flatlands along the Mondego and Vouga Rivers in Beira Litoral, and is used in various dishes. In Minho, for example, it is cooked with eels and wine *(arroz de lampreia),* octopus *(polvo com arroz),* and duck *(arroz de pato),* while cooks in Minho, Douro, and elsewhere in the north and north-west prepare rice with ham and chicken stock in the hearty dish known as *arroz de sustância.*

The Moors also introduced noodles to Iberia, which arrived with a Greek label, *itria.* With the passage of time, the named evolved into *alatria.* But eventually that ancient term died, too, and was replaced by yet another, *fideos,* derived from the Arabic *fada,* meaning "abundant" or "overflowing." In Spain, unlike

Below top: A young gourmand-in-training takes in the bright colors and animated atmosphere of a busy Spanish marketplace. **Below bottom:** Andalusia's *pueblos blancos,* which spill over hilltops or nestle in valleys, are white-washed in the Moorish style to deflect the region's intense seasonal heat. **Right:** A vendor unloads his daily delivery of potatoes to a market in Toledo.

Below top: Antonio Gaudí's architectural treasures can be found all over his native Barcelona. This elegantly sculptured turret stands on the rooftop of his Casa Mila. **Below bottom:** Many of Madrid's tapas bars are decorated with murals rendered in painted tiles. Here, a colorful portrayal of bulls rises above rows of regional wines. **Right:** A busy market vendor in San Sebastián expertly bags her produce for a waiting customer.

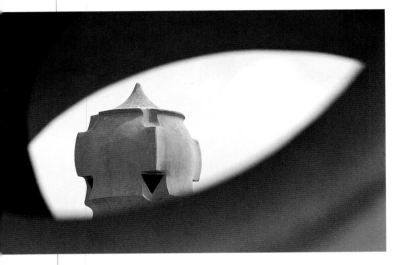

Italy, noodles are not served al dente. Instead, they are cooked until quite soft, often in the pan with the stock or sauce ingredients. The Spaniards have not been resistant to the charms of Italian pasta altogether, however. Cannelloni *(canalones)* are on many menus in Barcelona, the result of a wave of popularity for Italian food that swept through Spain in the 1800s. Smaller shapes are used in soups: *estrellas* (stars), *piñones* (pine nuts), and *fideos finos,* very thin angel-hair-type pasta. Other examples, such as *macarrones, tiburones* (shells), and *tallarines* (strips), are served with meat, fish, or tomato sauces.

Both Spain and Portugal are known for their fine market gardens, fertile plots that, like rice, owe their establishment to the Moors. They planted spinach, eggplants (aubergines), oranges, and lemons in the sunny south, where such crops thrived in the felicitous climate. Some seven centuries later, with the discovery of the New World, these Iberian market gardens, called *huertas* in Spain and *terras saloias* in Portugal, expanded to include corn, tomatoes, squashes, potatoes, peppers (capsicums), beans, and other vegetables.

The tables of Portugal and Spain would be far different today without the seeds from these two disparate parts of the world. Cornmeal is used to make *broa,* the signature bread of northern Portugal, and to thicken Portuguese soups. Winter squashes go into sweet pastries in Spain and soups and stews in Portugal. Tomatoes, of course, are used in all manner of dishes in both countries, from Portuguese white beans with tomato sauce to a Spanish stew of fava (broad) beans, artichokes, and chopped tomatoes. The Spanish and Portuguese are serious potato eaters, too, and each kitchen boasts a long list of favorites, including Spain's spicy *patatas bravas* and classic *patatas panaderas* (oven-roasted) to Portugal's addictive *batatas fritas* (chips) and *batatas com louro* (with bay leaves). And New World

Above top: Small kitchen gardens allow families to grow a profusion of vegetables and herbs for the table. **Above bottom:** The outdoor market in Ordizia, a small Basque village, is as much a spot to meet old friends as it is a place to buy freshly baked bread. **Right:** In Barcelona's Gothic quarter, the brick façade of the city's huge cathedral, the structure a sea of octagonal towers and soaring spires, glows in the golden hour before sunset.

peppers also have been enthusiastically embraced by the cooks in both countries, who regularly add them to salads, stews, and sautés and use them extravagantly as garnishes.

The Moors introduced styles of vegetable preparation as well, in particular stuffed vegetables, a culinary tradition that most scholars credit early Persian cooks with originating. Today, Spanish cooks fill mushrooms with spicy chorizo, eggplants with a cinnamon-and-nutmeg-scented meat mixture, and peppers with salt cod or crabmeat. They also stuff onions, artichokes, zucchini (courgettes), and cabbage leaves, all in the spirit of the Middle Eastern dolma.

Vegetables are seasonal glories, and the Iberians respect that. In particular, they anxiously await the arrival of spring, which brings some of the year's most treasured culinary treats. City dwellers and country people in Aragon, Andalusia, and elsewhere go in search of reed-slim, pleasantly bitter wild asparagus, or *espárrago triguero,* which they bake with eggs, grill, or boil and dress with olive oil and vinegar. The year's first green onions, called *calçots,* are so special that they have their own festival, the *calçotada,* held in the small town of Valls, in Tarragona Province. At this convivial eating marathon, grilled onions are served on a terra-cotta roof tile, anointed with a chile-laced almond, pepper, and tomato sauce, and eaten with great gusto.

Wild mushrooms are popular, too, in both spring and fall, prepared with garlic, olive oil, and parsley as a tapa, tucked into omelets, simply broiled, or added to soups. The prized fungi are especially sought after in Catalonia and the Basque provinces, where experienced foragers, armed with baskets or buckets and knives, carefully comb the forest's rim, always keeping the best hunting locations a secret.

The mushroom hunt has a long history in Spain and Portugal, dating back to a time when seasonal foraging defined the character of the cuisine. The shepherds, who centuries ago put their lakeside paellas together from what they found nearby, were cooks in this same tradition, and even today, the best Iberian pantries are stocked with locally cultivated grains and seasonal vegetables.

Andalusia

Fideos a la Malagueña

vermicelli with seafood, málaga style

The Costa del Sol is celebrated for its beautiful white sand beaches, sheer cliffs rising from a deep-blue sea, and cloudless days. Sadly, much of this visually stunning coastline has been marred by the construction of ugly high-rise hotels and sprawling beach resorts, and Málaga, the region's chief port and a city with a long and interesting history, has ceded much of its beauty to this runaway real estate. The well-kept waterfront and the wide, shaded esplanade that runs along it offer a welcome respite from the towering urban skyline, however. This dish, which calls for thin noodles rather than the more common rice, is a popular menu item in Málaga's many seaside restaurants.

1 lemon

3 artichokes

1 lb (500 g) fava (broad) beans (about ¼ lb/ 125 g shelled)

3 lb (1.5 kg) small clams, preferably Manila, well scrubbed

½ cup (4 fl oz/125 ml) water

¼ cup (2 fl oz/60 ml) extra-virgin olive oil

1 large yellow onion, chopped

4 cloves garlic, minced

4 tablespoons (⅓ oz/10 g) chopped fresh flat-leaf (Italian) parsley

1 cup (6 oz/185 g) peeled, seeded, and chopped tomato (fresh or canned)

1 teaspoon saffron threads, crushed and steeped in 2 tablespoons dry white wine

1 teaspoon sweet paprika

2 green bell peppers (capsicums), seeded and diced

1 bay leaf, crumbled

10 oz (315 g) dried vermicelli or spaghetti, broken into 2-inch (5-cm) lengths

1 cup (8 fl oz/250 ml) dry white wine

1 lb (500 g) large shrimp (prawns), peeled and deveined

salt and freshly ground pepper to taste

Fill a large bowl with cold water. Cut the lemon in half and squeeze the juice into the water. Working with 1 artichoke, remove all the leaves until you reach the pale green heart. Pare away the dark green area from the base. Cut the artichoke into quarters lengthwise and scoop out and discard the choke from each piece. Drop into the lemon water to prevent discoloration. Repeat with the remaining artichokes. Set aside.

Shell the fava beans. Bring a saucepan three-fourths full of water to a boil, add the favas, and boil for 30 seconds. Drain, rinse under cold water, and slip the beans from their tough skins. Set aside.

Place the clams in a large, deep frying pan, discarding any that are broken or open. Add the water, cover, and place over high heat. Cook, shaking the pan occasionally, until the clams open, 3–5 minutes. Uncover and, using a slotted spoon, transfer the clams to a bowl or deep platter, discarding any that failed to open. Cover and set aside. Pour the cooking liquid through a fine-mesh sieve lined with cheese-cloth (muslin) placed over a bowl. (You may want to simmer the shrimp shells in this liquid for several minutes to intensify its seafood flavor.) Reserve the cooking liquid.

In a paella pan or large frying pan over medium heat, warm the olive oil. Add the onion and sauté until tender, about 8 minutes. Add the garlic and 2 tablespoons of the parsley and sauté for 2 minutes to release the fragrance of the garlic. Add the tomato, saffron and wine, paprika, bell peppers, and bay leaf and stir well. Drain the artichokes and add to the pan along with the favas, pasta, wine, and reserved clam liquid. Simmer, uncovered, for 10 minutes.

Add the shrimp and clams. When the pasta and vegetables are tender and the shrimp are cooked, after about 5 minutes, season with salt and pepper.

Transfer to a warmed platter and sprinkle with the remaining 2 tablespoons parsley. Serve at once.

serves 6

Heat-loving vegetables – peppers, tomatoes, eggplants – flourish under the Andalusian sun.

Alentejo

Favas com Coentro à Portuguesa

fava beans with cilantro

This ragout of favas with garlic and cilantro is an ideal accompaniment to poultry or pork. Served with rice, it can also be a main dish. The presence of cilantro reveals the southern (Arabic) origin of this dish. A similar Catalan dish, habas a la catalana, *calls for mint rather than cilantro and sausage instead of bacon.*

4 lb (2 kg) fava (broad) beans, shelled, or 1 lb (500 g) frozen baby lima beans

2 tablespoons olive oil

2 oz (60 g) bacon, finely diced

1 yellow onion, chopped

2 cloves garlic, finely minced

¾–1 cup (6–8 fl oz / 180–250 ml) water

1 small bay leaf

salt and freshly ground pepper to taste

½ cup (¾ oz / 20 g) chopped fresh cilantro (fresh coriander)

☙ If using fava beans, bring a saucepan three-fourths full of water to a boil, add the favas, and boil for 30 seconds. Drain, rinse under cold water, and slip the beans from their tough skins. Set aside. If using lima beans, reserve.

☙ In a saucepan over medium heat, warm the oil. Add the bacon and cook until crisp, about 3 minutes. Transfer to paper towels to drain. Add the onion to the fat remaining in the pan and sauté until tender, about 8 minutes. Add the garlic and sauté for a minute to release its fragrance, then add the beans, enough water just to cover, and the bay leaf. Cover and simmer until the beans are tender, 10–15 minutes for the favas or 8–10 minutes for the limas. Add water as needed to maintain the original level.

☙ Return the bacon to the pan and season with salt and pepper. Add the cilantro, toss gently, and transfer to a warmed bowl. Serve at once.

serves 4–6

Andalusia

Berenjenas con Queso

fried eggplant with cheese

The presence of sugar and sweet spices in this Andalusian dish are clues to its Arabic heritage. Early Spanish and Maghrebi manuscripts record the use of eggplants in the Iberian kitchen as far back as the thirteenth century. Look for the smallest globe eggplants you can find. If only large ones are available, each half will serve two guests.

4 small globe eggplants (aubergines), about ½ lb (250 g) each, peeled and cut in half lengthwise

⅓ cup (3 fl oz/80 ml) olive oil, plus olive oil for deep-frying

1 yellow onion, finely chopped

1 tablespoon dried mint or 2 tablespoons chopped fresh mint

¼ teaspoon ground cinnamon, plus a pinch

¼ teaspoon ground cloves

¼ teaspoon freshly grated nutmeg

¼ teaspoon freshly ground pepper

4 eggs

½ cup (2 oz/60 g) fine dried bread crumbs

2 oz (60 g) fresh goat cheese, finely crumbled

salt to taste

¼ cup (2 oz/60 g) sugar

½ cup (2½ oz/75 g) all-purpose (plain) flour

☸ In a large pot over high heat, combine the eggplants with lightly salted water to cover. Bring to a boil and boil for 10 minutes. Drain well. Finely chop 4 of the eggplant halves and set aside.

☸ Scoop out the soft pulp from each remaining eggplant half, leaving a shell ½ inch (12 mm) thick. Chop the pulp and set aside.

☸ In a frying pan over medium heat, warm the ⅓ cup (3 fl oz/80 ml) oil. Add the onion and sauté until it starts to take on color, about 10 minutes. Add all of the chopped eggplant and the mint and sauté for 2 minutes. Add the ¼ teaspoon cinnamon, the cloves, the nutmeg, and the pepper and reduce the heat to low. Lightly beat 2 of the eggs and add to the pan. Stir for a few minutes, then add the bread crumbs and goat cheese. Season with salt and add a few teaspoons of the sugar. Stir well and remove from the heat. Let cool slightly, then fill the hollowed-out eggplant halves with the sautéed mixture.

☸ In a large, deep, wide frying pan, pour in olive oil to a depth of 2 inches (5 cm) and heat to 375°F (190°C) on a deep-frying thermometer. Meanwhile, in a shallow bowl, beat the remaining 2 eggs. Spread the flour on a plate.

☸ Dip a stuffed eggplant half into the beaten eggs, turning to coat evenly, and then into the flour. Slip, filled side down, into the hot oil. Repeat with a second eggplant half. Fry, turning once, until crisp and golden on both sides, 5–6 minutes. Using a slotted spoon, transfer to paper towels to drain, then arrange on a warmed serving dish. Cover to keep warm. Repeat with the remaining eggplant halves.

☸ In a small bowl, stir together the remaining sugar and the pinch of cinnamon. Sprinkle over the eggplant halves and serve hot.

serves 4

New Castile

Pisto Manchego

summer vegetable stew

Pisto evolved from an ancient stew called alboronia, *Moorish for "eggplant." The original* alboronia *is thought to have included Arabic seasonings such as cumin, saffron, and cilantro (fresh coriander). Over time, vegetables from the New World were introduced into the mix, as this recipe illustrates.*

2 large eggplants (aubergines), about 1½ lb (750 g) total weight

salt and freshly ground pepper to taste

¾ cup (6 fl oz / 180 ml) olive oil

2 large yellow onions, chopped

1 lb (500 g) bell peppers (capsicums), a mixture of red and green, seeded and chopped

½ cup (2½ oz / 75 g) all-purpose (plain) flour

2 lb (1 kg) tomatoes, peeled, seeded, and diced

1 teaspoon dried oregano

2 tablespoons pine nuts, toasted

❦ Peel the eggplants and cut into 1½-inch (4-cm) pieces. Place in a colander, sprinkling salt between the layers, and let drain for 1 hour.

❦ In a large frying pan over medium heat, warm ¼ cup (2 fl oz / 60 ml) of the olive oil. Add the onions and sauté until tender, 8–10 minutes. Add the peppers and sauté until softened, about 5 minutes longer.

❦ Meanwhile, rinse the eggplant pieces and pat dry. Place the flour in a shallow bowl. In another large frying pan over high heat, warm the remaining ½ cup (4 fl oz / 120 ml) oil. Dip the eggplant in the flour, tapping off the excess. In batches, add to the hot oil and fry, turning as needed, until golden, 5–8 minutes. Using a slotted spoon, transfer to a plate.

❦ When all of the eggplant pieces have been fried, add them to the onion-pepper mixture along with the tomatoes, oregano, salt, and pepper. Reduce the heat to low and simmer until the flavors are well blended and the tomatoes have broken down into a saucelike consistency, about 20 minutes.

❦ Spoon into a bowl and garnish with the pine nuts. Serve warm or at room temperature.

serves 6

Peppers

Today, it is difficult to imagine Spanish and Portuguese food without its sweet peppers (capsicums). But these contemporary staples of the Iberian table did not arrive until the fifteenth and sixteenth centuries, when the great Portuguese explorers and Spanish conquistadores carried them to the Old World from the New. The chile made the same voyage, but the Portuguese took to its fiery taste with far more enthusiasm than the Spanish, introducing it with great success at home and in their overseas colonies.

Red and green bell peppers are known as *pimentos* in Portugal and *pimientos* in Spain. *Chilindrón,* a popular sauce in Aragon and Navarre, is but one of the many Spanish recipes in which peppers play a central role. In Portugal, cooks assemble platters of roasted peppers in oil and vinegar or make *massa pimentão* (see glossary, page 248), a dry rub for roasting meats.

Spain's most prized peppers are the slightly spicy *piquillo* and the mildly hot *romesco*. The best *piquillos* come from Navarre, where they are cultivated in the valley that lines the Ebro River. Much of the crop is roasted over wood fires, peeled, and packed into jars, for stuffing with squid, salt cod, eggs and mushrooms, or other fillings. The *romesco* pepper, smaller and usually dried, is the basis of the famed Catalan *salsa romesco* (page 184).

Minho

Arroz de Pato à Moda de Braga

rice with duck and sausage

There are two ways to prepare this dish. One calls for putting the duck, sausage, and ham in a pot, covering them with water, and then simmering them until the duck is tender. The meats are removed, the stock is skimmed of fat, and the rice is cooked in the stock. This usually produces rather mushy rice and a somewhat oily dish, however. I prefer the second method, which calls for roasting the duck and sausage, then placing the meats on top of cooked rice and baking them together in the oven until piping hot. If you use a dry sausage, you will not need to bake it first—simply cut it into pieces and proceed with the recipe.

Although versions of this dish are served all over Portugal, cooks in the lovely old town of Braga, with its countless fine churches and famous Holy Week celebration, are known for their superb renditions.

1 duck, 5 lb (2.5 kg), with the wing tips, feet, and excess fat removed

salt and freshly ground pepper to taste

1 lemon, halved

½ lb (250 g) chouriço (see note)

2 cups (14 oz / 440 g) long-grain white rice

2 tablespoons olive oil

2 cups (8 oz / 250 g) chopped yellow onion

1 large carrot, peeled and grated

⅓ lb (5 oz / 155 g) presunto or prosciutto, sliced ⅛ inch (3 mm) thick and coarsely chopped

½ cup (4 fl oz / 125 ml) chicken stock, or as needed

2 tablespoons grated lemon zest

2–3 tablespoons unsalted butter, melted

¼ cup (⅓ oz / 10 g) chopped fresh flat-leaf (Italian) parsley

orange slices

❦ Preheat an oven to 450°F (230°C).

❦ Prick the duck all over with a fork to allow the fat to drain. Sprinkle with salt and pepper and rub inside and outside with the lemon halves. Place it on a rack, breast side up, and roast until tender, about 1 hour. Remove from the oven and let cool. Leave the oven set at 450°F (230°C). Remove the meat from the bones, discard the skin, and tear the meat into bite-sized pieces or dice it. Set aside.

❦ If using a fresh *chouriço*, prick the sausage with a fork in a few spots, place in a baking dish, and bake until cooked through, about 15 minutes. Remove from the oven and transfer to a cutting board. Reserve some of the drippings. Let the sausage cool and then cut into 1-inch (2.5-cm) chunks. Set aside. Reduce the oven temperature to 350°F (180°C).

❦ Meanwhile, bring a saucepan three-fourths full of salted water to a boil. Add the rice and boil until just tender, about 10 minutes. Drain, rinse under cool water, drain again, and set aside.

❦ In a large frying pan over medium heat, warm the olive oil along with the reserved drippings. Add the onion and carrot and sauté until the onion is tender, about 10 minutes. Add the ham, sausage, rice, stock, and lemon zest and cook until some of the liquid is absorbed, 5–8 minutes. Transfer the rice mixture to a *cazuela* or baking dish. Top with the duck meat and drizzle with the melted butter.

❦ Bake in the oven until piping hot, 15–20 minutes. Remove from the heat and season with salt and pepper. Sprinkle with the parsley and garnish with the orange slices. Serve at once.

serves 6

Estremadura

Peixinhos da Horta

batter-fried green beans

In Lisbon's Bairro Alto, locals and visitors alike flock to the many tascas, *small eateries celebrated for their homestyle food and reasonable prices. This dish, a specialty of the capital, is commonly on the menus. The name literally means "garden fish," a charming nickname for these crisp beans showered with coarse salt.*

1 lb (500 g) green beans, trimmed

all-purpose (plain) flour for dusting, plus
¾ cup (4 oz/125 g)

olive oil for deep-frying

1 teaspoon baking powder

½ teaspoon table salt

1 egg

½ cup (4 fl oz/125 ml) dry white wine,
or as needed

coarse sea salt

☙ Bring a saucepan three-fourths full of salted water to a boil. Add the beans and boil until tender-crisp, 3–4 minutes. Drain immediately and rinse under cold water to stop the cooking. Drain again and pat dry with paper towels. Sprinkle the beans lightly with flour, tapping off any excess.

☙ In a wide, deep frying pan, pour in olive oil to a depth of 2 inches (5 cm) and heat to 375°F (190°C) on a deep-frying thermometer.

☙ While the oil is heating, make the batter: Into a bowl, sift together the ¾ cup (4 oz/125 g) flour, the baking powder, and the table salt. Make a well in the center and add the egg. Using a fork, gradually mix the flour mixture and egg until well combined. Then add as much wine as needed to form a thick batter.

☙ In batches, dip the beans into the batter and slip them into the oil. Deep-fry until golden, about 2 minutes. Using tongs or a wire skimmer, transfer to paper towels to drain.

☙ Arrange the beans on a warmed platter, sprinkle with coarse sea salt, and serve immediately.

serves 4

Levante

Paella a la Valenciana

paella with chicken and snails

Paella takes its name from the two-handled shallow pan, called a paellera, *in which it is customarily cooked. The dish originated in Valencia, where it is typically made with a medium-grain rice, rabbit or chicken, tomatoes, beans, and often snails. In Spain, rosemary and snails rarely appear in the same recipes, as local snails used in cooking feed on wild rosemary. Elsewhere, however, where canned snails are the only choice, rosemary must be added to the dish, which accounts for its presence in this recipe. Less custom-bound versions of paella call for shellfish and occasionally sausage, ham, or meatballs.*

Spanish cooks traditionally prepare paella outdoors over an open fire, or on specially designed gas ring burners built in graduated sizes to accommodate various sizes of paelleras. *But it can be cooked on a conventional stove top with great success, although you'll probably need two burners for a large paella pan. The golden crust that forms on the bottom, called the* socarrat or quemada, *is greatly desired.*

1 rounded cup (8 oz/250 g) dried large
white beans

1 chicken or rabbit, 2½ lb (1.25 kg), cut into
small serving pieces

salt and freshly ground pepper to taste

½ cup (4 fl oz/125 ml) olive oil

1 large yellow onion, chopped

2 cloves garlic, minced

4 tomatoes, peeled, seeded, and chopped

4–5 cups (32–40 fl oz/1–1.25 l) chicken stock
or part stock and part water, heated

24 canned snails, drained

½ lb (250 g) green beans, trimmed, blanched for
3–5 minutes, and drained

½ teaspoon saffron threads, crushed and steeped
in 2 tablespoons of the heated stock

2 fresh rosemary sprigs, chopped

2½ cups (17 oz/530 g) Spanish medium-grain
rice such as Bomba or Calasparra

lemon wedges

❦ Pick over the beans, discarding any stones or misshapen beans. Rinse well and place in a bowl with water to cover generously. Let soak overnight in the refrigerator.

❦ The next day, drain the beans and place in a saucepan with water to cover by about 3 inches (7.5 cm). Bring to a boil over high heat, reduce the heat to low, cover, and simmer gently until tender, about 1 hour. Remove from the heat, drain, and set aside.

❦ Rinse the chicken or rabbit pieces, pat dry, and season with salt and pepper. In a paella pan or very large frying pan, warm the olive oil. Add the chicken or rabbit and brown well on all sides, 5–8 minutes. Using a slotted spoon, transfer the pieces to a plate and set aside.

❦ Add the onion, garlic, and tomatoes to the oil remaining in the pan over medium heat and cook, stirring occasionally, until the vegetables have softened, about 10 minutes.

❦ Return the chicken or rabbit to the pan, add the stock or stock and water, and simmer, uncovered, for 10 minutes. Add the snails, white beans, green beans, saffron and stock, rosemary, and rice. Stir well and cook, uncovered, over medium heat without stirring until the rice is nearly tender and the liquids are nearly absorbed, about 20 minutes. (You can also slip the pan, uncovered, in a 325°F/165°C oven for the last 20 minutes of cooking.) Check occasionally to make sure the mixture is not burning or cooking too quickly. Halt the cooking when the rice still seems a bit underdone. It will finish cooking off the heat, where it will absorb the last of the juices. Cover and let stand for 5–10 minutes.

❦ Serve the paella hot directly from the pan. Garnish with lemon wedges.

serves 6–8

Patriotic Valencians insist that the local water makes the difference between a good paella and a great one.

Romesco Sauce

Most visitors to the southern Catalan city of Tarragona, with its breathtaking vista of the Mediterranean, come to see the architectural treasures and to sample the fine local still wines and *cavas*. But the gastronome who makes a pilgrimage to this ancient city of Roman Spain is surely in search of *salsa romesco* in its place of origin.

Romesco is a nut-thickened sauce made from the dried sweet-piquant *romesco* pepper, olive oil, and garlic. The nuts can be almonds or hazelnuts (filberts), both of which grow in orchards surrounding the city, or pine nuts, or a combination. The sauce, usually an appealing terra-cotta color, can vary from mild to surprisingly hot. Some scholars believe that Roman cooks introduced an early version of the sauce, minus the New World pepper, to the Tarragonese kitchen, thus its name.

It is a versatile sauce, enhancing every food it accompanies, whether slathered on grilled onions (at right), seafood, or rabbit fresh off the *parrillada* or served as a dip for fried potatoes at a tapas bar. Thinned with oil and vinegar, it becomes a dressing for a salad of potatoes and salt cod (page 62). The sauce also shares its name with yet another famous Tarragonese dish, *romesco de peix,* a mixed seafood stew flavored with the same ingredients that go into the sauce.

Calçots y Espárragos con Romesco

grilled wild onions and asparagus with romesco sauce

In spring, when calçots *(wild green onions) appear at Barcelona's famed La Boquería market, local cooks rush to fire up their grills. As cooks outside of Spain cannot easily find* calçots, *large green onions or, better yet, baby leeks are good substitutes. For variety, I have grilled some asparagus spears along with the onions. The romesco pepper traditionally used for the sauce is also difficult to find away from Iberia, but the more widely available dried ancho chile is a good substitute.*

ROMESCO SAUCE

2 ancho chiles

2 small red bell peppers (capsicums)

1 tablespoon olive oil (optional)

1 slice coarse country bread (optional)

4 cloves garlic, chopped

½ cup (2½ oz/75 g) hazelnuts (filberts), toasted and peeled (see glossary, page 248)

½ cup (3 oz/90 g) blanched almonds, toasted

2 tablespoons tomato paste

¼ cup (2 fl oz/60 ml) red wine vinegar, or to taste

4 teaspoons sweet paprika

½ teaspoon cayenne pepper, or more to taste

¾ cup (6 fl oz/180 ml) olive oil

salt to taste

16 very fat green (spring) onions or baby leeks, each about ¾ inch (2 cm) in diameter

16 large asparagus spears, tough ends removed

¼ cup (2 fl oz/60 ml) extra-virgin olive oil

salt and freshly ground black pepper to taste

To make the sauce, in a small saucepan, combine the ancho chiles with water to cover. Bring to a boil, remove from the heat, and let stand for 20 minutes.

Meanwhile, preheat a broiler (griller). Cut the bell peppers in half lengthwise and remove the stems, seeds, and ribs. Place, cut sides down, on a baking sheet. Broil (grill) until the skins blacken and blister. Remove from the broiler, drape the peppers loosely

with aluminum foil, and let cool for 10 minutes. Peel away the skins and cut the peppers into medium-sized pieces. Set aside.

♛ If using the bread, in a small frying pan over medium heat, warm the olive oil. Add the bread and fry, turning once, until crisp and golden on both sides, 3–5 minutes total. Remove from the pan, break into pieces, and add to a blender or food processor.

♛ Drain the ancho chiles and remove the stems and seeds. Tear or cut into pieces.

♛ Add the garlic, hazelnuts, and almonds to the blender or food processor and pulse until finely ground. Add the bell peppers, chiles, tomato paste, ¼ cup (2 fl oz/60 ml) vinegar, paprika, and ½ teaspoon cayenne pepper and process to combine. With the motor running, slowly pour in the olive oil until the mixture emulsifies. Season with salt. Taste and adjust with more vinegar and cayenne, if needed. You should have about 2½ cups (20 fl oz/625 ml) sauce. Pour into a bowl, cover, and refrigerate until needed. Bring to room temperature before serving.

♛ Prepare a fire in a charcoal grill.

♛ Trim off the roots from the green onions or leeks but keep the bulbs intact. Trim off all but 4 inches (10 cm) of the green tops. Bring a saucepan three-fourths full of salted water to a boil. Add the onions or leeks and boil until the bulbs are tender and crack slightly when pinched with tongs, 8–15 minutes; the timing depends upon the size. Drain and rinse under cold water. Drain again. Slip 4 onions or leeks onto each of 4 skewers for easier handling.

♛ Bring a saucepan three-fourths full of salted water to a boil. Add the asparagus and cook until barely tender, about 5 minutes. Drain and rinse under cold water. Drain again. Slip 4 asparagus spears onto each of 4 skewers.

♛ Brush the green onions or leeks and the asparagus with the olive oil and sprinkle with salt and black pepper. Place on the grill rack and grill, turning as needed, until well browned and a little charred. Remove the vegetables from the skewers and arrange on a warmed serving platter. Serve hot with bowls of *romesco* sauce on the side.

serves 4

Catalonia

Berenjenas Rellenas
a la Catalana

stuffed eggplants

This eggplant main course is somewhat reminiscent of Greek moussaka in flavor. Beef was used in the earliest versions of this recipe, according to Muslim tradition. Today, pork is the more likely ingredient.

4 small globe eggplants (aubergines), about ½ lb (250 g) each

olive oil for brushing, plus 4 tablespoons (2 fl oz / 60 ml) olive oil

½ lb (250 g) ground (minced) beef or pork

1 yellow onion, finely chopped

2 cloves garlic, minced

¼ cup (2 fl oz / 60 ml) dry white wine

½ teaspoon ground cinnamon

1 tablespoon all-purpose (plain) flour

⅓ cup (3 fl oz / 80 ml) milk

freshly grated nutmeg to taste

salt and freshly ground pepper to taste

2 eggs

½ cup (2 oz / 60 g) fine dried bread crumbs

❀ Preheat an oven to 350°F (180°C).

❀ Cut the eggplants in half lengthwise and scoop out the soft pulp from each half, leaving a shell ½ inch (12 mm) thick. Reserve the pulp. Put the eggplant shells in a baking pan and brush them with olive oil. Bake until soft, about 20 minutes.

❀ Meanwhile, chop the eggplant pulp coarsely. In a frying pan over high heat, warm 3 tablespoons of the olive oil. Add the meat and sauté until browned, 8–10 minutes. Add the onion, garlic, and eggplant and sauté until softened, 5–8 minutes. Stir in the wine and cinnamon and cook until all the liquid has been absorbed, 3–5 minutes. Remove from the heat.

❀ Make a tiny batch of béchamel sauce: In a small saucepan over low heat, warm the remaining 1 tablespoon oil. Add the flour and stir for a few minutes until well combined; do not allow to brown. Add the milk and stir until the sauce thickens, about 5 minutes. Season with nutmeg, salt, and pepper. Remove from the heat and fold into the meat mixture.

❀ Lightly beat 1 of the eggs, add to the meat mixture, and mix well. Taste and adjust the seasonings. Oil a baking dish in which the eggplant shells will fit comfortably in a single layer. Spoon the meat mixture into the shells, dividing it evenly. Beat the remaining egg and spoon it over the tops of the filled eggplants, then sprinkle with the bread crumbs.

❀ Bake until golden brown on top, about 20 minutes. Serve immediately.

serves 8

Alentejo

Batatas com Coentro

potatoes with cilantro

Although peeling the potatoes is traditional for this dish, you may leave them unpeeled. If you prefer the texture of roasted new potatoes, rub the potatoes with olive oil and roast them in a 400°F (200°C) oven until tender, about 30 minutes. Let them cool a bit, cut them in half, and fry them in the same manner.

12–18 small new potatoes, peeled if desired

3 tablespoons unsalted butter

¼ cup (2 fl oz / 60 ml) olive oil

⅓ cup (½ oz / 15 g) chopped fresh cilantro (fresh coriander)

salt and freshly ground pepper to taste

❀ In a saucepan over medium heat, combine the potatoes with salted water to cover. Bring to a gentle boil, cover, and cook until tender, about 35 minutes. Drain and let cool slightly.

❀ In a large frying pan over high heat, melt the butter with the oil. Add the potatoes and fry, turning often, until they take on color, about 3 minutes. Sprinkle with the cilantro, season with salt and pepper, and turn in the oil for a minute or two longer.

❀ Transfer the potatoes to a warmed serving bowl and serve.

serves 4–6

Catalonia

Espinacas con Pasas y Piñones

spinach with raisins and pine nuts

The Moorish origin of this popular Catalan dish is revealed in the combination of raisins and nuts, the raisins imparting a sweetness to the spinach that eighth-century Moors no doubt appreciated as much as contemporary Catalans. The sweet addition of fruits and nuts to a savory dish can be seen in other local fare, such as rabbit with pears (page 160) or duck with prunes and pine nuts.

Some recipes suggest boiling the spinach, but this is not necessary. Just sauté it in the water clinging to the leaves after rinsing. A handful of chopped onion and ham is occasionally added to the dish for a saltier, sharper flavor. Acelgas a la malagueña is Swiss chard prepared the same way but, in true Moorish fashion, without the serrano ham.

¼ cup (1½ oz/45 g) raisins

3 tablespoons olive oil

1 small yellow onion, chopped (optional)

3 oz (90 g) serrano *ham,* chopped (optional)

2 lb (1 kg) spinach, stems removed

¼ cup (1½ oz/45 g) pine nuts, toasted

salt and freshly ground pepper to taste

❧ In a bowl, combine the raisins with hot water to cover. Let stand until plumped, about 30 minutes. Drain well and set aside.

❧ In a large frying pan over medium heat, warm the olive oil. Add the onion and the ham, if using, and sauté until the onion is tender, 8–10 minutes. Add the spinach and stir constantly until the spinach is wilted, just a few minutes.

❧ Stir in the drained raisins and the pine nuts and season with salt and pepper. Transfer to a warmed serving dish and serve at once.

serves 4

Catalonia

Cebollas Rellenas

stuffed onions

As with the stuffed eggplants (aubergines) on page 187, beef was traditionally used for the filling in this one-time Moorish dish, with pork introduced by Christian Spain as a test of faith for converted Jews and Muslims. Another test would be to soak the bread in milk instead of water, or to mix in grated cheese, both violations of kosher law. Some versions of this recipe omit the frying of the stuffed onions and simply bake them in a cazuela. Still others use chicken stock and wine instead of the beef stock.

8 yellow or red (Spanish) onions, ½–¾ lb (250–375 g) each

6 oz (185 g) ground (minced) beef or pork

1 cup (2 oz/60 g) fresh coarse bread crumbs soaked in milk or water to cover and then squeezed dry

2 tablespoons chopped fresh flat-leaf (Italian) parsley

2 cloves garlic, minced

2 eggs, beaten

salt to taste

1 cup (5 oz/155 g) all-purpose (plain) flour

olive oil for deep-frying

½ cup (4 fl oz/125 ml) beef stock, heated

❦ Preheat an oven to 350°F (180°C). Oil a baking dish in which the onions will fit in a single layer.

❦ Peel the onions, then cut a slice 1 inch (2.5 cm) thick off the top of each one. Cut a very thin slice off the bottom as well, so the onions stand upright.

❦ Bring a large saucepan three-fourths full of salted water to a boil. Add the onions and boil until just beginning to soften, 10–15 minutes. The onions should still be firm but not hard. Using a slotted spoon, transfer the onions to a plate and set aside. Reserve the cooking water.

❦ In a bowl, combine the meat, bread crumbs, parsley, garlic, all but a few teaspoons of the beaten eggs, and the salt. Mix well.

❦ Using a spoon and working from the top, scoop out the center of each onion, leaving a shell about ½ inch (12 mm) thick. Fill the onion shells with the meat mixture, dividing it evenly. Brush the top of the filling with the reserved egg. Spread the flour on a plate, and lightly coat each onion with the flour.

❦ In a large, deep, wide frying pan, pour in olive oil to a depth of 2–3 inches (5–7.5 cm) and heat to 350°F (180°C) on a deep-frying thermometer. Add the onions in batches and fry, turning as needed, until pale gold on all sides, 5–7 minutes. Using the slotted spoon, transfer the onions, filling side up, to the prepared baking dish. When all of the onions have been fried, pour the beef stock into the baking dish and add enough of the reserved cooking water to reach about halfway up the sides of the onions.

❦ Bake the onions uncovered, basting with the cooking liquid every 10 minutes or so, until they are golden and tender when pierced with a knife, about 30 minutes.

❦ Remove from the oven. Serve hot or warm, directly from the baking dish.

serves 8

Levante

Coliflor con Ajos y Pimentón

cauliflower with garlic and paprika

The province of Murcia, with its charming capital city of the same name, is known for its fine vegetable gardens, or huertas, *and the cauliflowers and cabbages grown there are especially flavorful.*

2 lb (1 kg) small cauliflowers, cut into florets

2 teaspoons fresh lemon juice

⅓ cup (3 fl oz/80 ml) olive oil

2 or 3 thick slices coarse country bread, crusts removed (about 3 oz/90 g)

1 tablespoon sweet paprika

2 cups (16 fl oz/500 ml) water

salt to taste

3 cloves garlic, coarsely chopped

2 tablespoons pine nuts, toasted

3 tablespoons chopped fresh flat-leaf (Italian) parsley

freshly ground pepper to taste

❦ Fill a bowl with water and add the cauliflower florets and lemon juice. Set aside until needed.

❦ In a large frying pan over medium heat, warm the olive oil. Add the bread slices and fry, turning once, until crisp and golden on both sides, 3–5 minutes total. Remove from the pan, break into pieces, and place in a blender or food processor.

❦ Add the paprika to the oil remaining in the pan over low heat and cook for a minute or two to release its fragrance. Add the water and bring to a boil. Drain the cauliflower and add to the pan. Season with a little salt and cook, uncovered, until the cauliflower is tender, 10–15 minutes.

❦ Meanwhile, add the garlic, pine nuts, and parsley to the blender or food processor and pulse until well crushed. When the cauliflower is tender, add about ¼ cup (2 fl oz/60 ml) of the cauliflower cooking water, pulse once, and then transfer the mixture to the frying pan. Stir to mix and cook for 5 minutes over low heat to blend the flavors.

❦ Season with salt and pepper, transfer to a warmed serving bowl, and serve.

serves 6

Paprika

Spanish cooking relies on a handful of spices to give it its unique character. Arguably the most widely used item in this indispensable pantry is *pimentón,* or paprika, which adds color and flavor to stews, soups, sausages, and sauces.

Spanish paprika, which is made by drying and then grinding ripe, red peppers (capsicums), is similar to its more famous relative of the same name, Hungarian paprika. But the Spanish product is a rich orange-red, rather than the deep, dark red of its central European kin. The best version is *pimentón de La Vera* from northern Extremadura, which is infused with a distinctive smoky flavor, a product of smoke-drying over oak. Three types, their differences depending upon the variety of pepper used, are available: sweet, medium-hot, and hot.

In Portugal, two types, sweet and hot, are used. Like their Spanish counterparts, they add a distinctive orange-red hue and lively flavor to sausages such as *linguiça* and *chouriço,* as well as to various pork dishes.

Andalusia

Cazuela de Espárragos Trigueros

baked asparagus with eggs

Because of its high cost, asparagus has always been associated with upper-class dining in Spain. Wild asparagus season is an eagerly awaited spring event, and enterprising vendors who have hunted down the prized spears in rural glades can be seen selling them from makeshift stands or big baskets on the roadsides or in open-air markets. The deep green, pencil-thin stalks have a slight bitterness, unlike their sweeter cultivated counterparts. They are used in omelets (page 33) or baked with eggs in ramekins, as in this recipe. Try to find pencil-thin asparagus at your market, to replicate the spirit of this Andalusian favorite.

1 lb (500 g) pencil-thin asparagus spears

¼ cup (2 fl oz/60 ml) olive oil

4 cloves garlic, peeled but left whole

2 slices coarse country bread, crusts removed

1 teaspoon sweet paprika

¼ teaspoon saffron threads

8 peppercorns

½ teaspoon salt, plus a pinch

2 tablespoons white wine vinegar

3 eggs

5 tablespoons (2½ fl oz/75 ml) water

✤ Preheat an oven to 350°F (180°C).

✤ Trim off any tough ends from the asparagus, cutting at the point at which they turn white, then cut the spears into 2-inch (5-cm) lengths. Bring a saucepan three-fourths full of salted water to a boil. Add the asparagus and boil until tender but firm to the bite, 2–3 minutes. Drain, reserving 2 cups (16 fl oz/500 ml) of the cooking water. Set the asparagus and water aside separately.

✤ In a frying pan over medium heat, warm the oil. Add the garlic and fry until golden, about 8 minutes. Using a slotted spoon, transfer the garlic to a blender or food processor. Add the bread slices to the oil remaining in the pan over medium-high heat and fry, turning once, until crisp and golden on both sides, 3–5 minutes total. Remove with the slotted spoon, break into pieces, and add to the blender or food processor. Reserve the oil in the frying pan.

✤ Add the paprika, saffron, peppercorns, and the ½ teaspoon salt to the blender or food processor and pulse until finely ground. Add 1 cup (8 fl oz/250 ml) of the reserved cooking liquid and process briefly to mix.

✤ Return the frying pan to low heat. Add the asparagus and sauté until warmed through, about 2 minutes. Add the bread mixture and vinegar and stir over low heat until blended, 3–4 minutes. If the mixture seems a little dry, add some of the reserved cooking liquid to moisten.

✤ In a bowl, whisk together the eggs, water, and the pinch of salt. Divide the asparagus mixture among 4 gratin dishes or ramekins. Top with the egg mixture, dividing evenly.

✤ Bake until the eggs are set, 15–20 minutes. Remove from the oven and serve immediately.

serves 4

Trás-os-Montes

Arroz de Sustância

nourishing rice

This simple rice dish is served in Trás-os-Montes and in neighboring Douro, where hearty preparations such as this one are especially welcome during the cold winter months. Strips of roasted green pepper are sometimes added for decoration.

2 tablespoons olive oil

½ lb (250 g) lean pork, cut into 1-inch (2.5-cm) cubes

½ lb (250 g) lean beef, cut into 1-inch (2.5-cm) cubes

¼ lb (125 g) thinly sliced ham, cut into 1-inch (2.5-cm) pieces

1 yellow onion, chopped

1 cup (7 oz/220 g) long-grain white rice

2½ cups (20 fl oz/625 ml) chicken stock

2 tablespoons fresh lemon juice

¼ lb (125 g) linguiça or chouriço, *thinly sliced*

salt to taste

roasted green or red bell pepper (capsicum) strips

lemon wedges

In a large saucepan over medium heat, warm the olive oil. Add the pork and beef and sauté until lightly browned, 7–8 minutes. Add the ham and onion and sauté until the onion is tender, about 10 minutes. Add the rice, stir well to coat with the oil, then add the stock, lemon juice, and sausage. Raise the heat to high and bring to a boil. Reduce the heat to low, cover, and cook until the rice is tender, about 25 minutes. Season with salt.

Transfer to a warmed serving dish. Garnish with roasted pepper strips and accompany with lemon wedges. Serve warm.

serves 4

Levante

Arroz a Banda

seafood-flavored rice

Valencia is the home of Spanish rice cultivation and rice-based cuisine. Arroz a banda is an unusual rice dish in that it is served in two parts. The seafood is cooked in a broth, sometimes with potatoes, and set aside for a second course. The broth is strained and reduced, and the rice is browned in oil, then cooked in the flavorful fish broth. The rice is served as a first course by itself—a banda, or apart—accompanied with a very garlicky alioli. A similar dish, fideos a banda, is made with dried thin pasta that is browned and cooked slowly in fish stock.

ALIOLI

8 cloves garlic

2 teaspoons coarse salt

2 egg yolks

3–4 tablespoons fresh lemon juice

1½ cups (12 fl oz / 375 ml) olive oil

4 cups (32 fl oz / 1 l) fish stock (see glossary, page 250)

1 or 2 dried red chiles

1½ lb (750 g) white fish fillets such as halibut, monkfish, or cod

1 lb (500 g) shrimp (prawns), peeled and deveined (optional)

lemon wedges

RICE

6 tablespoons (3 fl oz / 90 ml) olive oil

4 cloves garlic, minced

2 tomatoes, peeled, seeded, and chopped, or 2 tablespoons tomato paste

2 teaspoons sweet paprika

2 cups (14 oz / 440 g) Spanish medium-grain rice such as Bomba or Calasparra

¼ teaspoon saffron threads, crushed

salt and freshly ground pepper to taste

To make the *alioli*, finely mash the garlic cloves with the coarse salt. Place the egg yolks in a blender or mini food processor, add 3 tablespoons of the lemon juice, and pulse to blend. With the motor running, gradually drizzle in the olive oil and process until an emulsion forms. Add the garlic and pulse to blend. Taste and adjust with salt and lemon juice as needed. If the *alioli* is too thick, thin with a bit of cold water. Cover and refrigerate until serving.

Make the fish stock as directed, adding the chiles along with the herbs. Pour the stock into a wide, shallow saucepan, place over low heat, and bring to a gentle simmer.

Add the fish fillets and cook gently until opaque throughout, 5–10 minutes, depending on the thickness of the fillets. Using a slotted spatula, transfer the fillets to a deep platter. Add the shrimp, if using, and simmer until they turn pink and begin to curl, 2–3 minutes. Using a slotted spoon, transfer them to the platter holding the fillets. Spoon a little stock over the fish and shrimp to keep them moist, then cover to keep warm. Reserve the fish stock.

To make the rice, in a paella pan or wide frying pan over medium heat, warm the olive oil. Add the garlic, sauté until it starts to turn pale gold, and then add the tomatoes or tomato paste. Cook for about 5 minutes to blend the flavors, then add the paprika. Cook for 2 minutes, then add the rice and sauté, stirring often, until opaque, about 3 minutes. Add the saffron, salt, and pepper and stir well. Add the reserved fish stock, raise the heat to high, bring to a boil, and cook for 5 minutes. Reduce the heat to low and cook, uncovered, until the rice has absorbed the stock, about 15 minutes. (Alternatively, place in a preheated 350°F/180°C oven for 15 minutes.) Cover and let stand off the heat for 10 minutes.

Taste and adjust the seasonings. Transfer the rice to a warmed bowl or platter. Serve with the *alioli*, then serve the fish and the shrimp (if used) as a second course, garnished with lemon wedges.

serves 6

In spring, emerald shoots appear in the flooded rice fields that lay within shouting distance of bustling Valencia.

Saffron

In the fall, lavender fields of crocuses blanket the provinces of Ciudad Real, Albacete, Cuenca, and Toledo in New Castile, sharing the hot, dry climate with grapes, olives, and wheat. It is from these fields, and from smaller crops in Teruel, Andalusia, Murcia, Valencia, and the Balearic Islands, that Spain harvests its world-famous saffron.

The harvest runs from September to November, depending upon the region. At dawn, the fields are filled with men and women who quickly and carefully pluck the flowers one by one, before they open to the morning sun. The blossoms are spread out in the shade and, on the same day, a trio of stigmas, long, slender filaments, is plucked from the center of each flower by hand. This is the saffron, which is roasted over a gentle charcoal or gas fire to dry and then stored in a dark place free of humidity.

Because it takes some five thousand flowers, all gathered and processed by hand, to yield a single ounce of the salable filaments, saffron is the world's costliest spice. Ancient Greeks and Romans reportedly bathed in saffron-tinged water, and in later centuries the spice was believed to remedy coughs, cure infertility, and soothe the pain of a teething baby. Nowadays, however, these delicate filaments, with their deep red tips, small white-yellow bases, and high price tags, are primarily reserved for use in the kitchen. Fortunately, only a few so-called threads are usually needed to impart a sunny color and intoxicating taste to any dish.

Each year, saffron is honored in a colorful harvest festival held in the small town of Consuegra, in the province of Ciudad Real. On the last Sunday in October, the towns-people gather for La Rosa del Azafrán, a celebration during which the woman who succeeds in plucking the most saffron filaments from the blossoms is crowned queen.

Andalusia

Habas a la Granadina

favas with artichokes, granada style

Lovely Granada, wedged between the Sierra Nevada mountain range and the most productive agricultural land in Andalusia, was the last stronghold of the Moors. Perched on one of its tallest hills is the grand pink-gold Alhambra palace, the glorious summer home of the caliphs. From its courtyard, the visitor can look across to the Albaicín, the old Moorish quarter, a spirited neighborhood of whitewashed houses, stately cypresses, and cobblestone streets.

Although no one would dispute Granada's beautiful setting and rich history, most guidebooks describe the local fare as disappointing. This springtime Granadan vegetable stew, its ingredients drawn from nearby fields and its seasonings of cumin and saffron holdovers from the long-ago Arab rulers, dampens such criticism.

1 lemon

4 artichokes

4 lb (2 kg) fava (broad) beans

2 tablespoons extra-virgin olive oil

1 small yellow onion, chopped

2 or 3 cloves garlic, minced

1 teaspoon ground cumin

1 teaspoon sweet paprika

1 tomato, peeled, seeded, and chopped

½ teaspoon saffron threads, steeped in 2 tablespoons boiling water

1 bay leaf

1 fresh mint sprig, plus 2 tablespoons chopped

2 fresh flat-leaf (Italian) parsley sprigs, plus 2 tablespoons chopped

salt and freshly ground pepper to taste

❀ Fill a large bowl with cold water. Cut the lemon in half and squeeze the juice into the water. Working with 1 artichoke, remove all the leaves until you reach the pale green heart. Pare away the dark green area from the base. Cut the artichoke into quarters lengthwise and cut away and discard the choke from each piece. Drop the quarters into the lemon water to prevent discoloration. Repeat with the remaining artichokes. Set aside.

❀ Shell the fava beans. Bring a saucepan three-fourths full of water to a boil, add the favas, and boil for 30 seconds. Drain, rinse under cold water, and slip the beans from their tough skins. Set aside.

❀ In large frying pan over medium heat, warm the olive oil. Add the onion and sauté until tender, about 8 minutes. Add the garlic, cumin, and paprika and cook for 2 minutes longer to release their fragrance. Add the tomato and cook for 1 minute.

❀ Drain the artichokes and add to the pan along with the favas, the saffron and boiling water, and enough additional water just to cover the vegetables. Add the bay leaf and the mint and parsley sprigs and simmer, uncovered, until the vegetables are tender, about 15 minutes. If there seems to be too much liquid, raise the heat to high to reduce it. Discard the bay leaf and any large herb sprigs.

❀ Stir in the chopped mint and parsley and season with salt and pepper. Transfer to a dish and serve.

serves 4

Levante

Arroz con Costra

baked rice from alicante

*Here is a baroque version of arroz al horno, or
"baked rice." Meatballs, chicken, pork, and chickpeas
are buried in the rice in this specialty of Elche, a small
town in Alicante Province surrounded by date-palm
groves. This is an ideal dish for home entertaining, as
it can be assembled up to four hours in advance and
then finished in the oven just before serving.*

MEATBALLS

*½ lb (250 g) ground (minced) lean pork or veal,
or a mixture*

*½ cup (1 oz/30 g) fresh bread crumbs, soaked
in milk or water to cover and then squeezed dry*

¼ cup (1½ oz/45 g) almonds, ground

*3 tablespoons chopped fresh flat-leaf (Italian)
parsley*

1 egg

grated zest of 1 lemon

salt and freshly ground pepper to taste

1 red bell pepper (capsicum)

6 tablespoons (3 fl oz/90 ml) olive oil

3 cloves garlic, peeled but left whole

4 cups (32 fl oz/1 l) chicken stock

*1 whole chicken breast, boned with skin intact
and cut into 1-inch (2.5-cm) pieces (about
½ lb/250 g meat)*

*½ lb (250 g) pork, cut into 1-inch (2.5-cm)
cubes*

salt and freshly ground pepper to taste

*¼ lb (125 g) thick-cut bacon, cut into ¼-inch
(6-mm) dice, or sweet pork sausage, sliced*

*2 cups Spanish medium-grain rice such as
Bomba or Calasparra*

*1 cup (7 oz/220 g) drained, cooked or canned
chickpeas (garbanzo beans)*

7 eggs

¼ cup (2 fl oz/60 ml) milk

❦ To make the meatballs, in a bowl, combine the
ground pork and/or veal, bread crumbs, almonds,
parsley, egg, lemon zest, salt, and pepper. Mix well
and form into tiny meatballs each about 1 inch (2.5
cm) in diameter. Set aside.

❦ Preheat a broiler (griller). Cut the bell pepper in
half lengthwise and remove the stem, seeds, and ribs.
Place, cut sides down, on a baking sheet. Broil (grill)
until the skin blackens and blisters. Remove from the
broiler, drape the pepper loosely with aluminum foil,
and let cool for 10 minutes, then peel away the skin.
Place in a blender or food processor and set aside.

❦ Preheat an oven to 350°F (180°C).

❦ In a large ovenproof frying pan over low heat,
warm the olive oil. Add the garlic cloves and sauté
until tender, 2–3 minutes. Using a slotted spoon,
transfer the garlic to the blender or food processor
with the roasted red pepper. Add ½ cup (4 fl oz/
125 ml) of the chicken stock and process to form
a smooth purée. Set aside.

❦ Sprinkle the chicken and pork pieces with salt
and pepper. Heat the oil remaining in the frying pan
over high heat. Add the chicken and brown well on
all sides, 5–8 minutes. Using the slotted spoon, transfer to a plate. One at a time, brown the pork pieces,
meatballs, and the bacon or sausage over high heat in
the same oil. Set aside with the chicken.

❦ Meanwhile, in a saucepan over high heat, bring
the remaining 3½ cups (28 fl oz/875 ml) stock to a
boil, then reduce the heat to low to maintain a bare
simmer. When you have finished browning the
meats, add the rice to the oil remaining in the frying
pan over medium heat. Stir well, then add the
reserved pepper purée and cook for a few minutes
until well blended. Add the simmering stock, the
chickpeas, and the meats. Bring to a boil, reduce the
heat to low, and cook uncovered, stirring often, until
the flavors are blended and some of the liquid is
absorbed, about 7 minutes. Transfer to the oven and
bake, uncovered, until most of the liquid is absorbed,
about 10 minutes. (If making ahead, stop at this
point. Cover and refrigerate until ready to serve.
Reheat in a 325°F/165°C oven until warmed
through, then continue as directed.)

❦ In a bowl, whisk together the eggs and milk until
blended. Pour the egg mixture evenly over the rice.
Raise the oven temperature to 500°F (260°C) and
continue to bake until the top is browned, 5–8 minutes. (If the top fails to brown after 8 minutes and the
pan is flameproof, slip it under the broiler for a few
minutes until browned.)

❦ Remove from the oven and let stand for 10 minutes before serving, then serve directly from the pan.

serves 6

Levante

Arroz Negro

black rice

The Mediterranean coast that runs from Catalonia to Andalusia, a serpentine stretch on which Mother Nature lavished considerable attention, invites travelers to dream of seafood feasts. Sadly, the package-holiday industry has saddled much of this landscape with a tidal wave of concrete towers and beach playgrounds. But interesting restaurants can still be found in the cities and towns—Peñíscola, Castellón de la Plana, Gandía, Cullera—that dot the coast.

This dish is often found on the local menus. Its dramatic black color is achieved with the addition of squid or cuttlefish ink. As it can be difficult to extract sufficient ink from the squid purchased for making the recipe, I recommend buying packets of the ink, which can be found at specialty-food stores or fish markets.

Garnish with a dollop of alioli (page 194).

1 lb (500 g) squid

1 lb (500 g) mussels, well scrubbed and debearded

½ cup (4 fl oz / 125 ml) water

1¼ cups (10 fl oz / 310 ml) olive oil

2 yellow onions, chopped

2 green bell peppers (capsicums), seeded and finely chopped

3 or 4 cloves garlic, minced

1 cup (6 oz / 185 g) peeled, seeded, and chopped tomato (fresh or canned)

5 cups (40 fl oz / 1.25 l) water or fish stock, or as needed

2 cups (14 oz / 440 g) Spanish medium-grain rice such as Bomba or Calasparra

1–2 tablespoons squid ink (see note)

16 jumbo shrimp (prawns) or a mixture of crayfish and shrimp

salt and freshly ground pepper to taste

✴ To clean each squid, pull the head and clinging innards free from the body. Discard the innards, reserving the ink sac. Cut the tentacles from the head and squeeze out the small, hard beak from the mouth at the base of the tentacles. Pull out and discard the transparent quill-like cartilage from the body pouch. Rinse out the body and rub off the mottled violet skin covering it, then rinse the tentacles. Leave the tentacles whole. Cut the bodies into rings ½ inch (12 mm) wide. Set aside.

✴ Place the mussels in a deep frying pan, discarding any that fail to close to the touch. Add the water, cover, and place over high heat. Cook, shaking the pan occasionally, until the mussels open, about 5 minutes. Uncover and, using a slotted spoon, transfer the mussels to a bowl, discarding any that failed to open. Pour the cooking liquid through a fine-mesh sieve lined with cheesecloth (muslin) placed over the bowl of mussels. Set aside.

✴ In a paella pan or large, deep frying pan over medium heat, warm half of the olive oil. Add the onions, bell peppers, and garlic and sauté until tender, about 10 minutes. Add the tomato and sauté for a few minutes until it releases its liquid. Add about 1 cup (8 fl oz/250 ml) of the water or fish stock and simmer for 20 minutes to blend the flavors. Add the rice, the remaining 4 cups (32 fl oz/1 l) water or stock or as needed to cover, and 1 tablespoon squid ink. Simmer over medium heat until the rice has absorbed about half of the liquid, about 10 minutes.

✴ While the rice is cooking, heat the remaining olive oil in a frying pan over high heat. Add the shrimp or the crayfish and shrimp and sauté until they turn pink and begin to curl, 2–3 minutes. Remove from the heat. When the rice is ready, season with salt and pepper. Add the shrimp or crayfish and shrimp, cooked mussels and their juices, and the squid to the rice. If the rice is not as dark as you would like, add the remaining tablespoon of squid ink. Reduce the heat to low and simmer until the flavors are blended and the rice is cooked through, 10–15 minutes longer.

✴ Transfer to a warmed platter and serve at once.

serves 4–6

Alioli

Spanish recipes for the thick, pungent, opalescent *alioli* (in Catalan, *allioli*) date as far back as the tenth century, but the sauce itself is much older. Its name comes from the Latin *allium,* for garlic, and *oleum,* for oil, and most scholars agree that the ancient Romans introduced it to the Spanish kitchen. Today, this classic sauce is equally beloved and claimed by cooks in Catalonia and the Levante, where it is used for dipping, spreading, and enjoying with everything from fish, shellfish, and meats to rice dishes and vegetables.

In the past, this simple sauce was always prepared and served in a mortar. It was nothing more than raw garlic crushed to a paste with salt and olive oil and occasionally thickened with bread crumbs. It was a very fragile emulsion, however, and Catalan cooks began adding egg yolks to stabilize the mix, producing the garlic mayonnaise that most people associate with the name today.

In some parts of Catalonia, a batch of *alioli* is enchanced by the addition of honey, almonds, walnuts, herbs, or puréed quince, apples, or pears. And for those who shy away from raw garlic, there is even a mild version, *mousseline d'all,* made with cloves of buttery roasted garlic.

New Castile

Patatas a la Importancia

potatoes "of importance"

Potatoes are a staple of the Spanish diet and are grown throughout the country. This tasty Castilian dish is "important" enough to be a meal in itself.

olive oil for deep-frying

3 eggs

about 1½ cups (7½ oz / 235 g) all-purpose (plain) flour

4 large russet potatoes (about 2 lb / 1 kg), peeled and sliced ½ inch (12 mm) thick

1 large yellow onion, finely chopped

5 cloves garlic, minced

2 cups (12 oz / 375 g) peeled, seeded, and chopped tomato (fresh or canned)

pinch of sugar (optional)

2 cups (16 fl oz / 500 ml) beef stock

salt and freshly ground pepper to taste

☙ In a wide, deep frying pan, pour in olive oil to a depth of 2 inches (5 cm) and heat to 350°F (180°C) on a deep-frying thermometer. While the oil is heating, break the eggs into a shallow bowl and whisk until blended. Spread the flour on a plate.

☙ When the oil is ready, working in batches, dip the potato slices into the beaten eggs and then into the flour and slip them into the hot oil. Fry until golden, 3–5 minutes. Using a slotted spoon, transfer to a flameproof *cazuela* or large frying pan and set aside.

☙ Drain off all but about 2 tablespoons of the oil from the frying pan and place over medium heat. Add the onion and garlic and sauté until tender, about 10 minutes. Add the tomato and simmer until slightly thickened, about 5 minutes. If the tomato tastes tart, add the sugar. Stir in 1 tablespoon flour, then pour the mixture over the potatoes.

☙ Pour the stock over the potatoes and season with salt and pepper. Place over low heat and cook, uncovered, until tender, about 35 minutes. Serve hot directly from the *cazuela* or pan.

serves 4–6

Navarre

Menestra de Primavera

spring vegetable stew

The measurements don't have to be precise in this vegetable dish from Navarre, but the ingredients must be fresh and full of flavor. The abundant vegetable plots of the region's Ebro Valley contribute to the rich mix.

1 red bell or fresh pimiento pepper (capsicum)

3 lb (1.5 kg) fava (broad) beans (about ¾ lb/ 375 g shelled)

2 lb (1 kg) English peas, shelled (about 10 oz/ 315 g shelled peas)

1 lemon

6 small or medium artichokes

¼ cup (2 fl oz/60 ml) olive oil

4 green (spring) onions, including tender green tops, chopped

2 or 3 cloves garlic, minced

½ lb (250 g) ham, diced

1 tablespoon all-purpose (plain) flour

salt and freshly ground pepper to taste

1 teaspoon sweet paprika

3 tablespoons tomato sauce

6 tablespoons (3 fl oz/90 ml) water or vegetable or chicken stock

chopped fresh flat-leaf (Italian) parsley or mint

❀ Preheat a broiler (griller). Cut the bell pepper or pimiento in half lengthwise and remove the stem, seeds, and ribs. Place, cut sides down, on a baking sheet. Broil (grill) until the skin blackens and blisters. Remove from the broiler, drape the pepper loosely with aluminum foil, and let cool for 10 minutes, then peel away the skin and chop the pepper. Set aside.

❀ Shell the fava beans. Bring a saucepan three-fourths full of water to a boil, add the favas, and boil for 30 seconds. Drain, rinse under cold water, and slip the beans from their tough skins. Refill the saucepan with salted water and bring to a boil. Add the fava beans and boil until tender but still firm, 5–10 minutes, depending upon their size. Drain and set aside.

❀ Refill the same saucepan with salted water and bring to a boil. Add the peas and boil until tender but still firm, 3–7 minutes; again, the timing will depend upon their size. Drain and set aside.

❀ Fill a large bowl with cold water. Cut the lemon in half and squeeze the juice into the water. Working with 1 artichoke, remove all the leaves until you reach the pale green heart. Pare away the dark green area from the base. Cut the artichoke into quarters lengthwise and scoop out and discard the choke from each piece. Drop into the lemon water to prevent discoloration. When all the artichokes are trimmed, drain and place in a saucepan with salted water to cover. Bring to a boil and cook until tender, 15–20 minutes; the timing will depend upon the size of the artichokes.

❀ In a large frying pan over medium heat, warm the olive oil. Add the green onions and garlic and sauté very briefly. Add the chopped pepper and the ham and sauté for a minute or two longer. Add the cooked peas, favas, and artichokes, and swirl them in the oil for a minute or two. Then sprinkle with the flour, salt, pepper, and paprika and stir in the tomato sauce and water or stock. Bring to a simmer and cook over medium-low heat for about 10 minutes to thicken the pan juices.

❀ Taste and adjust the seasonings. Transfer to a platter, garnish with parsley or mint, and serve.

serves 4–6

SWEETS

Spanish and
Portuguese cooks
shine brightest in
the world of baking
and confectionery.

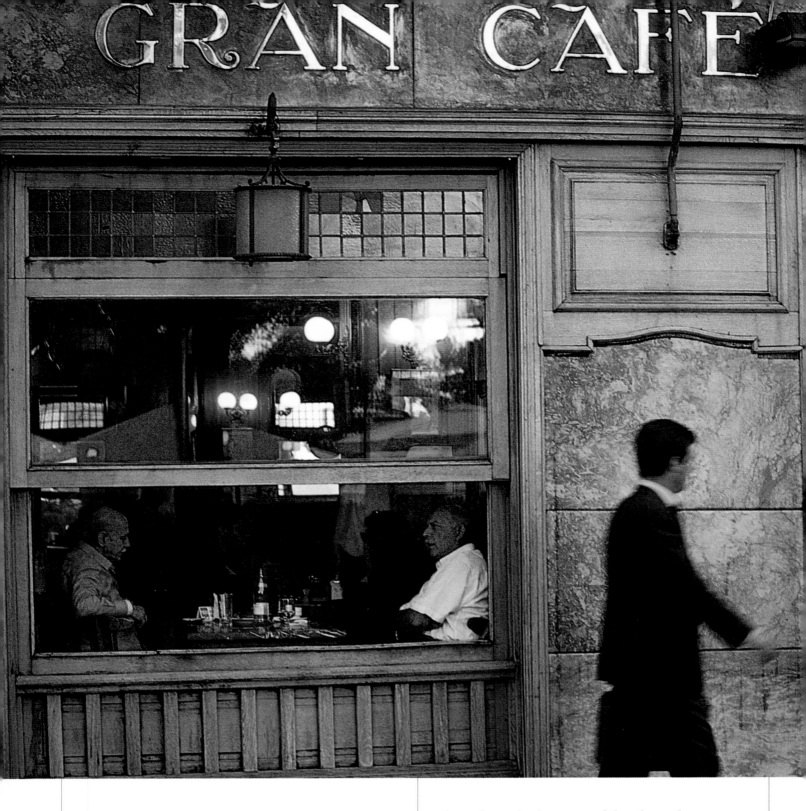

THE EGG SWEETS of Portugal and Spain are anomalies in these calorie- and cholesterol-conscious days. They are traditional delicacies that seem almost too rich for contemporary tastes. Of course, far simpler fare—apple fritters, honey-drizzled cheese, mixed-fruit compotes, rice pudding, peaches in red wine, pineapple in port, baked figs—is served in these two nations of sweet lovers as well. But it is in the realm of baking and confectionery that Iberian cooks distinguish themselves, showing off a wealthy heritage.

The Moors introduced these sweet, rich egg confections to Spain and Portugal, fashioning them from the harvests of the almond groves and sugarcane they planted in the area. The reconquest of the peninsula by the Spanish in the mid–thirteenth century prompted the flourishing of Christianity and with it a convent building boom. The nuns who took up residence in the new structures began making the centuries-old egg sweets, which they gave as gifts to the many patrons who funded the religious orders with generous donations. But by the nineteenth century, faced with a downturn in receipts, the sisters were forced to sell their confections. Today, many convent kitchens, along with an abundance of pastry

and candy shops, continue to sell these traditional sweetmeats to locals and visitors who appreciate their history and exquisite taste.

But it was something far simpler than carefully rendered Moorish recipes that helped to define the dessert legacy of Spain and Portugal: it was a surplus of egg yolks. Spanish and Portuguese wine makers used egg whites for fining, or clarifying, their sherry and port, to remove any particles that might cloud them. Large numbers of leftover yolks were the result. Although today egg whites are used for clarifying only the finest wines, egg-yolk sweets are well established.

Preceding spread: A Barcelona sweet shop displays a riotously colored assortment of treats guaranteed to tempt young and old alike. **Left:** Madrid's Gran Café de Gijón has been a haven for artists and intellectuals for more than a century. **Below top:** A glistening conserved orange is just one of many ways to satisfy a discriminating sweet tooth. **Below bottom:** From the market to the table: egg-based desserts abound on both Spanish and Portuguese menus, from silky custards to sunny yellow cakes.

Among the most famous of the Portuguese egg sweets are *aletria,* fine noodles covered with egg-yolk custard; *barrigas-de-freira,* or "nun's tummies," egg-yolk mounds flavored with cinnamon; *papos de anjo,* or "angel's cheeks," small egg-yolk disks doused with sugar syrup; and *ovos moles,* a stunningly rich mixture of sugar and egg yolks that is the most fundamental of all the Portuguese egg sweets and a specialty of the convents around Aveiro, in Beira Litoral. *Ovos moles,* often sold packed in small wooden casks in local pastry shops, are commonly used as a filling for thin pastry layers or for sandwiching between a pair of airy meringues.

Less exotic egg-yolk-rich desserts such as *pudim flan; queijadas,* small custard-cheese tarts; and *sopa dourada,* a bread pudding built from sponge cake and flooded with custard, are made as well. Egg whites are not forgotten, however. *Suspiros,* which translate as "sighs," are light meringues that often conceal a fresh strawberry filling in spring when the season's first berries appear in the markets.

Toucinho-de-céu is the famous "bacon from heaven," an egg-yolk custard made with ground almonds and squash. More than one locale insists that it originated there, among them the Convento de Odivelas, near Lisbon; the small town of Murça, near Vila Real in Trás-os-Montes; Guimarães, near Oporto; and even Jérez in Spain, where it is called *tocino de cielo* and has been given an apocryphal nun's story to prove its claim.

As *tocino de cielo* illustrates, Spain has its own versions of these rich sweets, from confections to custards to cakes. *Yemas,* for example, are simply Spanish *ovos moles,* and *crema catalana* is Spanish *pudim flan.* Then comes the double-rich combination of *brazo de gitano,* similar to *sopa dourada,* where the theme of sponge cake (*pão de ló* in Portuguese, *bizcocho* in Spain) and custard prevails. Milk-based sweets such as *arroz con leche, leche frita,* and the various custard recipes are most frequently found in northern Spain, home to the country's most productive dairy farms.

The legacy of the Arab sweet tooth is also evident in the abundance of dried-fruit confections. Among the most popular are those

Above: On Madrid's chaotic Puerta del Sol, this billboard for Tio Pepe sherry advertises the flavors of "bottled Andalusian sunshine." **Right top:** Almonds newly shaken from the tree may be ground into marzipan, ribboned through cookies, or chopped and mixed with honey and egg whites for *turrón*, rich nougat traditionally eaten at Christmastime. **Right middle:** Wheels of Manchego are distinguished by the crosshatched pattern on their sides. The markings, once the result of the woven baskets used to press the curds, are now imprints left from plastic molds. **Right bottom:** Crisp pastry layers topped with paper-thin apple slices on display in a Spanish *pastelería*.

made with figs and nuts and sometimes chocolate. These fruits, accompanied with a glass of port or Madeira, are a wonderful sweet ending to a meal. A paste or preserve made by cooking down quince with sugar until it is thick and the color of amber is popular in Spain and Portugal, with the *marmelada* made at the convent at Odivelas near Lisbon among the most famous versions. It is eaten as a jam or sweetmeat, often with a soft, fresh white cheese such as majorero, a goat cheese from the Canary Islands, or with the sharper Manchego. Another unusual sweet, *doce de chila,* is thin strands of candied squash flavored with cinnamon or lemon. Its close Spanish relative is *cabello de ángel,* or angel's hair, so named because of its resemblance to the golden strands that cover the heads of angels in countless paintings.

Nowhere in the world will you find such an assortment of nut-based sweets as on the Iberian Peninsula. Marzipan, the paste of ground almonds and sugar that is known as *maçapão* or *massapão* in Portuguese and *mazapán* in Spanish, is one of the most commonly encountered, although its origins are widely debated. Some believe its name comes from the Arabic *mautaban*, from *uataba*, meaning "white," and that it was brought by the Moors. Others place its beginnings in ancient Rome, where it was prepared as part of the rituals that accompanied the arrival of spring. Still others claim it was first made in Toledo in the early thirteenth century by nuns in the Convent of San Clemente as a substitute for the flour shipments that could not reach the city due to the fierce battles being fought by the Moors and the royal forces of Castile. In this scenario,

the name comes from *maza* (mallet) and *pan* (bread). Today, antique marzipan molds can still be seen in the convent, and a number of shops on Plaza de Zocodover, in the heart of Toledo's Old Quarter, specialize in the sweet almond paste, which they sell shaped into whimsical forms. The groves of almond trees of the Algarve guarantee that Portuguese confectioneries carry a beautiful assortment of marzipan sweets as well.

Equally sweet and almondy is Spanish *turrón*. Every Christmas, Spanish friends send me a box of this nougat, a traditional holiday confection made from toasted almonds, egg whites, and honey. Like so many other sweets enjoyed by contemporary Spaniards, *turrón* arrived with the Moors, and a similar candy is still made today in the Near East, where it is called halvah. After the Moors were expelled, *turrón* continued to be produced, and in the sixteenth century it was considered such a luxury in the region that local officials presented it as a gift to visiting dignitaries. The most famous *turrón* comes from the hilltown of Jijona, in Alicante Province in Levante, and it is sold in two styles, so-called soft Jijona and crackly or hard Alicante. A number of small factories are located in the town, and at Christmastime the locally produced nougat is sold in countless shops and stalls all along the Levantine coast.

Every holiday on the Spanish calendar has its distinctive sweet, however. For example, just after Christmas, pastry shops in Catalonia fill their shelves with the ring-shaped cake of the king, *tortell de reis* in Catalan, in celebration of Epiphany, on January 6. A dried bean or trinket is traditionally hidden inside each cake, and it is believed to bring good luck to whoever finds it. (The Portuguese make a similar holiday cake, called *bolo-rei,* which is baked from late November through Epiphany. Alas, coming upon the bean is unlucky in this case, for it means the finder must buy the cake the next year.) A few months later, on Good Friday, Catalan cooks prepare doughnuts dusted with fine sugar, and then bake a *mona de Pasqua,* a ring cake adorned with hard-boiled eggs, for Easter Monday.

The Iberian love of sweet flavors extends to beverages as well. A small nutlike tuber, called chufa in both English and Spanish, and also known as tigernut, ground almond, earth almond, or rush nut, is used in the making of *horchata,* a milky-looking, nutty-tasting, sugar-sweetened drink flavored with cinnamon or lemon. It is consumed primarily in the area around Valencia, where chufas are cultivated, and it is particularly popular in the summertime, when Valencians sip it as a refreshing pick-me-up anytime from midday to late evening. It can be purchased in bottles, but the locals know it is best drunk in the bars, called *horchaterías,* where it is freshly made and served as is or *granizado,* with shaved ice.

Many Valencians, not surprisingly, claim *horchata* as their own, declaring the small, sandy region of Alboraya, just north of the city, its birthplace. But as is the case with many of the sweet indulgences enjoyed by Iberians, from sugary egg-yolk confections to thick preserves, the Moors brought the tradition, carrying both the tuber and the cool, creamy refreshment to the peninsula.

Left: Spanish markets, with their plump figs, tart kumquats, and clusters of juicy grapes, are a fruit lover's paradise. **Above:** The perfect end to any Spanish meal is a *café solo,* with sugar or without.

Douro

Delícia de Laranja

orange cake

Portugal's orange groves are mainly in the Algarve and around Setúbal. Algarve oranges are large, seedless navels, the consummate eating orange, while those from Setúbal are smaller and primarily used for preserves. While a cut orange is the dessert of choice for most Portuguese, this cake makes a more festive ending.

1¼ cups (6½ oz / 200 g) all-purpose (plain) flour

½ teaspoon baking powder

3 eggs, separated

½ cup (4 oz / 125 g) plus 2 tablespoons unsalted butter

⅔ cup (5 oz / 155 g) granulated sugar

grated zest of 1 orange

½ cup (4 fl oz / 120 ml) fresh orange juice

¼ cup (1 oz / 30 g) confectioners' (icing) sugar

orange sections (optional)

☙ Preheat an oven to 350°F (180°C). Butter and flour an 8-inch (20-cm) round cake pan.

☙ In a small bowl, sift together the flour and baking powder. In a medium bowl, using an electric mixer, beat the egg whites until soft peaks form.

☙ In a large bowl, using the electric mixer set on high speed, beat together the butter and the granulated sugar until light and fluffy. Beat in the egg yolks, one at a time. Reduce the speed to low and slowly beat in the flour mixture, the orange zest, and ¼ cup (2 fl oz / 60 ml) of the orange juice. Fold the beaten egg whites into the yolk mixture just until combined. Spoon the batter into the prepared pan.

☙ Bake until a skewer inserted into the center emerges clean, 30–40 minutes. Remove from the oven and let cool in the pan on a rack for 10 minutes. Then turn out onto the rack and let cool to lukewarm. Transfer the cake to a platter.

☙ In a small bowl, stir together the remaining ¼ cup (2 fl oz / 60 ml) orange juice and the confectioners' sugar until the sugar dissolves and pour evenly over the cake. Garnish with orange sections, if desired.

serves 6–8

Madeira

In 1419, Portuguese explorers discovered a small, heavily forested volcanic island about five hundred miles (800 km) off the mainland and named it Madeira. By the beginning of the sixteenth century, vineyards had been planted, and wine was being made, but only enough to sell to the island's residents and to arriving sailors who believed the rustic product was a protection against scurvy. It would be another two hundred years before Madeira would become the drink of kings and czars and of the colonists of America.

Today, much of the cultivatable land of this sun-drenched, mountainous island is blanketed with tall pergolas covered with grapevines. Come September, farmers pick the fat, sugar-laden grapes, beginning with the vineyards at the sea and slowly working their way up the towering peaks where cooler weather dictates a later harvest.

The ripe grapes are crushed, fermented, and then put in *estufas,* or "hothouses," a system unique to Madeira production in which the wine is "cooked" for several months. It is then fortified with brandy and aged, resulting in four distinct types: dry, straw gold Sercial, and semidry, golden Verdelho, both fine aperitif wines, and semisweet Bual and sweet Malmsey, rich red dessert wines.

Galicia

Torta de Santiago

almond sponge cake

This cake is a specialty of Galicia, where granite walls outline each farmer's plot and granite crosses stand at many rural crossroads. The top of the cake is traditionally decorated with a cross in confectioners' sugar, in honor of Saint James, Spain's patron saint.

1 lb (500 g) blanched almonds (about 3 cups)

2¼ cups (18 oz / 560 g) granulated sugar

¾ cup (6 oz / 180 g) unsalted butter, at room temperature

7 eggs

⅓ cup (2 oz / 60 g) all-purpose (plain) flour

grated zest and juice of 1 large lemon

confectioners' (icing) sugar

❀ Preheat an oven to 350°F (180°C). Butter a 9-inch (23-cm) springform pan.

❀ Spread the almonds on a baking sheet and toast briefly just until their aroma is released, 8–10 minutes. Transfer to a plate, let cool, and then place in a blender or food processor with a few tablespoons of the granulated sugar. Process until finely ground.

❀ In a bowl, using an electric mixer, beat together the butter and the remaining granulated sugar until fluffy. Beat in the eggs, one at a time, beating well after each addition. Stir in the flour, ground almonds, and lemon zest. Pour into the prepared pan.

❀ Bake until a skewer inserted into the center emerges clean, about 1 hour. Remove from the oven and prick the top of the cake with a fork. Sprinkle with the lemon juice. Release the pan sides and slide the cake from the pan bottom onto a rack to cool.

❀ Transfer the cake to a serving plate and dust the top with confectioners' sugar before serving.

serves 8–10

New Castile

Leche Frita

fried custard

Although fried custard is popular all over Spain, this particular recipe comes from La Mancha. Some versions of leche frita *omit the butter and flour base and use only cornstarch (cornflour). A few combine cornstarch with flour. The goal is to have the custard firm enough to hold its shape when cut, be creamy in texture, and not floury tasting. For an aromatic finish, flambé the* leche frita *with anise liqueur.*

3 cups (24 fl oz/750 ml) milk

1 lemon zest strip, 2 inches (5 cm) long

1 vanilla bean, slit in half lengthwise

¾ cup (6 oz/185 g) unsalted butter

½ cup (2½ oz/75 g) all-purpose (plain) flour

pinch of salt

¾ cup (6 oz/185 g) granulated sugar

6 egg yolks, plus 1 or 2 whole eggs

4–5 cups (1–1¼ lb/500–625 g) fine dried bread crumbs

clarified unsalted butter or vegetable oil for frying

confectioners' (icing) sugar

ground cinnamon (optional)

☙ Oil an 8-by-10-inch (20-by-25-cm) baking pan and place it in the freezer to chill well.

☙ Pour the milk into a saucepan and add the lemon zest strip and vanilla bean. Place over medium-high heat, bring to a boil, and reduce the heat to low. Simmer for 10 minutes, then remove from the heat and let steep for 1 hour. Strain the milk, discarding the lemon zest and vanilla bean, and reheat the milk just until small bubbles appear along the pan edges. Remove from the heat.

☙ In a separate saucepan over low heat, melt the butter. Add the flour and salt and cook, stirring constantly, for 5 minutes to blend well. Gradually whisk in the granulated sugar and the hot milk and slowly bring to a boil, stirring often and cooking until thickened, about 5 minutes.

☙ Gradually whisk in the egg yolks and continue to stir until the mixture is very thick, 5–7 minutes. Remove from the heat and pour the mixture into

the chilled baking pan. Using a rubber spatula, spread to an even thickness of about 1 inch (2.5 cm). Cover and refrigerate until fully set, at least 2 hours or as long as overnight.

☙ To serve, cut the custard into 8 squares or diamonds. In a shallow bowl, beat 1 whole egg until foamy. (Start with 1 egg and use the second only if needed.) Spread the bread crumbs on a plate.

☙ In a large frying pan, add clarified butter or vegetable oil to a depth of ½ inch (12 mm) and place over medium heat. When the butter or oil is hot, working in batches, dip the custard pieces into the egg, coating evenly, and then in the bread crumbs, again coating evenly. Add to the frying pan and fry, turning once, until golden on both sides, 6–8 minutes total. Using a slotted spatula, transfer to a baking sheet lined with paper towels to drain briefly. Keep warm until all the pieces are fried.

☙ Arrange the fried custard pieces on a platter. Dust them with confectioners' sugar or, if desired, with confectioners' sugar mixed with a little cinnamon, and serve at once.

serves 8

Alentejo

Arroz Doce

rice pudding

Rice pudding in Portugal is a celebratory dessert, served throughout the country at major events. This version, which calls for three egg yolks, is the classic. The fanciest puddings are topped with an ornate design stenciled in ground cinnamon.

4 cups (32 fl oz/1 l) milk

⅔ cup (5 oz/155 g) sugar

1 tablespoon unsalted butter

1 lemon zest strip, 3 inches (7.5 cm) long

1 cinnamon stick

6 cups (48 fl oz/1.5 l) water

pinch of salt

⅔ cup (4½ oz/140 g) short-grain white rice

3 egg yolks

ground cinnamon

chopped toasted almonds

☙ Pour the milk into a saucepan and add the sugar, butter, lemon zest strip, and cinnamon stick. Place over medium-high heat and heat until small bubbles appear along the edges of the pan. Remove from the heat and let steep for 30 minutes.

☙ Meanwhile, pour the water into a saucepan and bring to a boil over high heat. Add the salt and the rice, reduce the heat to low, and cook, stirring occasionally, until tender, 15–20 minutes. Drain the rice.

☙ Add the rice to the milk mixture and return to low heat. Cook, stirring often, until thickened, 20–30 minutes. Remove from the heat and scoop out and discard the lemon zest and cinnamon stick.

☙ In a bowl, whisk the egg yolks until frothy. Whisk ½ cup (4 fl oz/125 ml) of the hot milk mixture into the egg yolks. Return the mixture to the saucepan and cook over very low heat, stirring constantly, for about 5 minutes.

☙ Spoon the pudding into custard cups. Sprinkle with cinnamon and almonds. Serve at room temperature or slightly chilled.

serves 6–8

Catalonia

Panellets

sweet potato cookies

These nut-coated cookies are a traditional Catalan treat on All Saints' Day. Sometimes cocoa or cooked chestnuts are added to the sweet potato dough, making the panellets *even richer.*

½ lb (250 g) sweet potatoes, peeled and cut into chunks

1 lb (500 g) almonds (about 3 cups), chopped

2 cups (1 lb/500 g) sugar

½ cup (2½ oz/75 g) all-purpose (plain) flour

2 eggs, separated

1 tablespoon grated lemon zest

1 teaspoon vanilla extract (essence)

1 cup (5 oz/155 g) pine nuts

1 cup (5 oz/155 g) hazelnuts (filberts), coarsely chopped

☙ In a saucepan over medium-high heat, combine the sweet potatoes with water to cover. Bring to a boil and boil until very tender, about 15 minutes. Drain well and place in a large bowl. Mash well with a fork or potato masher. Let cool.

☙ Add the almonds, sugar, flour, egg yolks, lemon zest, and vanilla to the sweet potatoes and mix with a wooden spoon or an electric mixer until well blended. Using your hands, knead the mixture for few minutes until the dough holds together. Cover with a kitchen towel and let rest for 30 minutes.

☙ Preheat an oven to 350°F (180°C). Oil 4 baking sheets, or line them with parchment (baking) paper.

☙ In a shallow bowl, lightly beat the egg whites. In another shallow bowl, stir together the pine nuts and hazelnuts. To form each cookie, pinch off a piece of the dough the size of a walnut and roll it into a ball between your palms. Flatten the ball a bit, brush it with the egg whites, and roll it in the nuts, coating evenly. Place on a prepared baking sheet, spacing the cookies about 1 inch (2.5 cm) apart.

☙ Working in batches, bake until golden, about 15 minutes. Remove from the oven and transfer the cookies to wire racks to cool. The cookies will keep in an airtight container for up to 1 week.

makes about 6 dozen cookies

Catalonia

Buñuelos de Manzana

apple fritters

Although most of Spain's apples are grown in Asturias and Levante, Catalans are recognized as the masters of the apple fritter. The batter must be assembled ahead of time, but for the best results, beat the egg whites just before you are ready to fry the apples.

1 lb (500 g) apples such as Golden Delicious, Gala, Fuji, or McIntosh, peeled, halved, cored, and sliced lengthwise ½ inch (12 mm) thick

2 tablespoons granulated sugar

1 tablespoon anise liqueur such as anís del mono or brandy

2 eggs, separated

½ cup (4 fl oz/125 ml) milk

1 tablespoon olive oil, plus olive oil or vegetable oil for deep-frying

pinch of salt

1 cup (5 oz/155 g) plus 1 tablespoon all-purpose (plain) flour

confectioners' (icing) sugar

♨ Place the sliced apples in a shallow bowl, add the granulated sugar and liqueur or brandy, and toss to coat. Let stand for a few hours at room temperature.

♨ In a separate bowl, whisk together the egg yolks, milk, the 1 tablespoon olive oil, the salt, and the flour. Cover and refrigerate for 1–2 hours.

♨ In a bowl, beat the egg whites until they form stiff peaks, and fold into the batter just until combined.

♨ In a deep frying pan, pour in oil to a depth of 2 inches (5 cm) and heat to 350°F (180°C) on a deep-frying thermometer. In batches, dip the apple slices in the batter and then slip them into the hot oil. Fry, turning once, until golden, 3–4 minutes total. Using a slotted spoon, transfer to paper towels to drain.

♨ Arrange the fritters on a warmed platter and sift confectioners' sugar over the top. Serve piping hot.

serves 4

Coffeehouses

In Spain and Portugal, the coffeehouse is a beloved institution, with much of its prominence due to historical circumstance. Both countries included important coffee-growing colonies in their one-time empires—Brazil, East Timor, Mozambique, and Angola in the case of Portugal and most notably Colombia in the case of Spain—which gave the populace a taste for fine coffees. Indeed, in Lisbon and other Portuguese cities, shops selling coffee beans often offer some three dozen different blends and individual coffees.

In Spain, the coffee drinker generally selects from a quintet of choices: *solo,* or black coffee; *cortado,* similar to an Italian espresso with a streak of milk; *café con leche,* coffee with milk; *leche manchada,* milk "stained" with coffee; and *café del tiempo,* coffee with ice and a lemon slice—a hangover cure. The Portuguese boast an equally refined coffee menu: The *bica,* a demitasse of superstrong coffee, is the equivalent of an Italian espresso and a coffeehouse standard. The *café* is a rather powerful brew served in restaurants and homes. People who prefer a lighter beverage choose *carioca,* basically half water and half coffee. A *galão* is hot milk and strong coffee mixed together and served in a glass, similar to an Italian caffè latte. And a child in this coffee-loving society drinks a *garoto,* or "urchin," a tiny cup of hot milk flavored with coffee.

But Iberian coffeehouses are more than just a place to drink a superb coffee. They are busy outposts for everything from family gossip to political debates to storytelling. People head to their regular coffeehouse to read the newspaper, visit with an old friend, talk over a business deal, or hook up a romantic rendezvous.

Membrillo

quince preserves

Although you can buy quince preserves in markets that specialize in Iberian or Latin American foods, you should try making your own, as the texture will be a little softer and more appealing. Membrillo is served with a fresh soft cream cheese, a youngish Manchego, or a mild goat cheese and crackers or toasted bread.

> 2 lb (1 kg) quinces
> 4 cups (32 fl oz / 1 l) water
> 3½–4 cups (1¾–2 lb / 875 g–1 kg) sugar
> 1 teaspoon ground cinnamon

❧ Wipe the fuzz off the quinces and rinse well. Peel each quince, cut in half, and remove the core and seeds. Reserve the peels, cores, and seeds and place in a square of cheesecloth (muslin). Bring the corners together and tie securely with kitchen string.

❧ Slice the quinces and place in a heavy pot, preferably one of enamel-lined cast iron. Add water to cover and the cheesecloth pouch. Bring to a boil over high heat, reduce the heat to low, and cook slowly, uncovered, until very tender, 20–40 minutes; the timing will vary from batch to batch. You may want to stop the cooking a few times, for about an hour or two, to let the quinces rest and redden. Add more water if the mixture begins to dry out. (This process can even be done over 1 or 2 days, without refrigerating between simmerings.)

❧ When the quinces are red and very tender, remove the cheesecloth bag and discard. Using a potato masher, mash the quinces, or purée them in a food processor. Combine the pulp and cooking water, 3½ cups (1¾ lb/875 g) of the sugar, and the cinnamon and cook very slowly, stirring often, until thick, about 20 minutes. Taste and add more sugar if the preserves seem too tart.

❧ Ladle into hot, sterilized canning jars to within ¼ inch (6 mm) of the top. Wipe each rim clean with a hot, damp kitchen towel, cover with a sterilized canning lid, and seal tightly with a screw band. Process the jars in a hot-water bath for 10 minutes, check the seals, label, and store in a cool pantry for up to 1 year. Jars that do not form a good seal can be refrigerated for up to 1 month.

makes about 2 pt (1 l)

Trás-os-Montes

Papos de Anjo

egg cakes in syrup

What the name of this convent sweet means is debatable. Indeed, nearly everyone gives a different answer when asked to translate papos. Some say it means angel's breasts, others angel's cheeks or double chins. The cakes are round, tender, and bathed in a vanilla-scented syrup.

8 egg yolks

2 egg whites

pinch of salt

2 cups (1 lb/500 g) sugar

1 cup (8 fl oz/250 ml) water

1 teaspoon vanilla extract (essence)

⚜ Preheat an oven to 350°F (180°C). Grease 12 standard muffin cups or ½-cup (4–fl oz/125-ml) custard cups with butter. Place in a baking pan.

⚜ In a bowl, using an electric mixer set on high speed, beat the egg yolks until they are thick and pale and fall in a wide, slowly dissolving ribbon when the beaters are lifted. In a separate bowl, beat the egg whites with the salt until they form stiff peaks. Fold the whites into the yolks just until combined. Divide the mixture evenly among the prepared muffin cups or custard cups. Pour hot water into the baking pan to reach halfway up the sides of the molds.

⚜ Bake until a knife inserted into the center of a cake comes out clean, 15–20 minutes. Remove the baking pan from the oven and let the cakes cool in the pan for 5 minutes. Remove the molds from the water bath and invert them onto a large platter. Prick each cake in a few places with a wooden skewer.

⚜ In a heavy saucepan over high heat, combine the sugar and water. Bring to a boil, stirring until the sugar dissolves, and then boil until the mixture reaches the thread stage, about 230°F (110°C) on a candy thermometer, or until it is very thick. Remove from the heat and stir in the vanilla.

⚜ Using a large spoon, dip each cake into the syrup, moving it gently to coat it well, and then return it to the platter. Pour the remaining syrup over the cakes. Cover and chill well before serving.

makes 12 small cakes

Beira Litoral

Ovos Moles

soft eggs

A specialty of Aveiro, where they are sold in little wooden barrels and savored by the spoonful, ovos moles are golden yellow egg creams. Although these rich sweets are quite decadent just as they are, some Portuguese cooks enrich them even further with the addition of ground toasted nuts.

In Spain, a similar mixture of thickened egg yolks and syrup is made, poured out onto a marble slab coated with confectioners' (icing) sugar, and then rolled into rounds and wrapped in paper. These little candies are called yemas, *or "yolks."*

1¼ cups (10 oz/315 g) sugar

⅓ cup (3 fl oz/80 ml) water

8 egg yolks

⚜ In a heavy saucepan over high heat, combine the sugar and water. Bring to a boil, stirring until the sugar dissolves, and then boil until the mixture reaches the soft-ball stage, 234°–238°F (112°–114°C) on a candy thermometer. Remove from the heat and let cool a bit.

⚜ In a bowl, using an electric mixer set on high speed, beat the egg yolks until thick and pale. Very slowly add the hot syrup in a thin stream, beating constantly. Pour the mixture into a clean saucepan, place over low heat, and cook, stirring constantly, until the mixture coats a spoon, 5–8 minutes. Do not allow it to boil. Remove from the heat and let cool completely. The mixture will thicken as it cools.

⚜ Spoon into small cups or goblets or a single large serving bowl. Serve at room temperature.

serves 4–6

Sleepy Aveiro, once a maritime power, today is known for its eel dishes and toothsome sweets.

Estremadura

Toucinho-do-Céu

"heavenly bacon"

The birthplace of this centuries-old dessert, which today is prepared all over Portugal, is hotly debated among food scholars, with the Convento de Odivelas, located near Lisbon and known for its exquisite sweets, the leading contender. But the Spanish claim the dessert (tocino de cielo), too, citing this story: One day in Jerez an absentminded nun set out to make an egg-and-milk custard. But she forgot to add the milk, producing a rather firm, dark brown dessert that looked remarkably like a slab of bacon, thus the name.

3 tablespoons unsalted butter, softened

2 tablespoons plus 1¼ cups (10 oz / 315 g) sugar

7 tablespoons (3½ fl oz / 105 ml) water

12 egg yolks

1½ cups (6 oz / 185 g) finely ground almonds, plus chopped almonds for garnish (optional)

¾ teaspoon ground cinnamon

🌱 Preheat an oven to 400°F (200°C). Using the butter, grease an 8-inch (20-cm) springform pan, preferably nonstick. Sprinkle with 1 tablespoon sugar.

🌱 In a heavy saucepan over high heat, combine the 1¼ cups (10 oz / 315 g) sugar and water. Bring to a boil, stirring until the sugar dissolves, and then boil until the mixture reaches the thread stage, about 230°F (110°C) on a candy thermometer, or until very thick. Remove from the heat and let cool.

🌱 In a bowl, using an electric mixer set on high speed, beat the egg yolks until light and fluffy. Very slowly add the hot syrup in a thin stream, beating constantly. Beat in the ground almonds and cinnamon. Pour into a clean saucepan over low heat, and cook, stirring, until slightly thickened, about 5 minutes. Do not allow it to boil. Pour into the pan.

🌱 Bake until a skewer inserted into the center of the custard emerges clean, about 10 minutes. Let cool for 15 minutes, then run a knife blade around the inside edge of the pan and unmold onto a platter. Sprinkle with the remaining 1 tablespoon sugar and top with the chopped almonds, if using. Cut into wedges to serve.

serves 8

Algarve

Figos Recheados

chocolate-and-almond stuffed figs

Figs, both green and purple-black varieties, have been grown in the Algarve for centuries. The Portuguese eat the plump, sweet fruits fresh in the warm summer months and dry the surplus for use in innumerable sweets during the rest of the year. Indeed, dried figs from the Algarve were so highly regarded in the 1600s that they were exported to the Levant and Flanders. Almonds, introduced by the Moors, are cultivated in the Algarve as well. Here, they are combined with chocolate, introduced from Mexico, and the mixture is stuffed into moist dried figs for an ideal after-dinner sweet. Pour a glass of port or Madeira for each guest.

¼ *cup (1½ oz/45 g) blanched whole almonds, plus 12 extra*

2 tablespoons sugar

1 oz (30 g) semisweet (plain) chocolate, finely chopped

12 large dried figs

❧ Preheat an oven to 350°F (180°C).

❧ Spread all the almonds on a baking sheet and toast them until they take on color and are fragrant, 8–10 minutes. Remove from the oven and let cool. Set aside the 12 almonds. Combine the remaining almonds, the sugar, and the chocolate in a food processor. Pulse until well combined.

❧ Cut the stems off the figs, then cut a slit in the top of each fig and stuff with 1–2 teaspoons of the chocolate–nut mixture. Pinch the openings closed. Place the figs, stem ends up, on a baking sheet.

❧ Bake for 5 minutes. Turn the figs over and bake for 5 minutes longer to heat through.

❧ Remove from the oven and press 1 almond into each slit. Serve warm or at room temperature.

serves 6

Andalusia

Brazo de Gitano

gypsy's arm

Andalusia is home to Spain's Gypsies and flamenco, and this custard-filled cake symbolizes the arm of a Gypsy raised in the dramatic gesture of the dance. In the recipe, a classic génoise is rolled around a sweet filling of chocolate custard. A sherry-flavored version calls for folding in ¼ cup (4 fl oz / 125 ml) sweet sherry in place of the chocolate. This is a dessert for a special occasion, but it is not difficult to make, as the custard can be prepared the day before, covered, and stored in the refrigerator, and the finished cake can be assembled up to six hours in advance and refrigerated. Bring to room temperature before serving.

FILLING

2½ cups (20 fl oz / 625 ml) milk

1 lemon or orange zest strip

1 cinnamon stick

4 oz (125 g) semisweet (plain) chocolate, chopped

8 egg yolks

¾ cup (6 oz / 185 g) granulated sugar

½ cup (2½ oz / 75 g) all-purpose (plain) flour

1 tablespoon unsalted butter

SPONGE CAKE

5 eggs

½ cup (4 oz / 125 g) granulated sugar

1 teaspoon grated lemon zest

1 cup (4 oz / 125 g) sifted all-purpose (plain) flour

¼ cup (2 oz / 60 g) clarified unsalted butter, melted and cooled

confectioners' (icing) sugar

ground cinnamon

♛ To make the filling, pour the milk into a saucepan and add the citrus zest strip and cinnamon stick. Place over medium-high heat, bring almost to a boil, and reduce the heat to low. Simmer for 15 minutes, then remove from the heat and strain, discarding the zest and cinnamon stick.

♛ Meanwhile, place the chocolate in a heatproof bowl over (but not touching) simmering water in a saucepan. Heat, stirring occasionally, until melted. Remove from the heat.

♛ In a bowl, using an electric mixer set on high speed, beat the egg yolks until thick and pale. Add the granulated sugar and continue to beat until the mixture is very thick and falls in a wide, slowly dissolving ribbon when the beaters are lifted. Stir in the flour, mixing well, and gradually add the hot milk while stirring constantly. Transfer to a large saucepan and cook over medium heat, stirring constantly, until the mixture thickens to the consistency of pudding, about 5 minutes. Remove from the heat, stir in the butter, and then fold in the melted chocolate. Nest the bowl in a larger bowl filled with ice and let cool completely, stirring from time to time.

♛ While the custard is cooling, make the sponge cake: Preheat an oven to 375°F (190°C). Butter an 11-by-15-inch (28-by-38-cm) jelly-roll pan. Line the bottom with parchment (baking) paper and butter the parchment.

♛ In a heatproof bowl, whisk together the eggs and granulated sugar. Place over (but not touching) simmering water in a saucepan and continue to whisk until the mixture is warm and the sugar is dissolved. Remove from over the water and, using an electric mixer set on high speed, beat until very thick and pale, 8–10 minutes. Beat in the lemon zest, and then fold in the flour. Using a rubber spatula, fold in the butter. Pour the batter into the prepared pan and smooth the top with the spatula.

♛ Bake until golden and springy to the touch, about 10 minutes. Meanwhile, sprinkle a kitchen towel slightly larger than the dimensions of the cake with confectioners' sugar. Remove the cake from the oven, invert the pan onto the towel, and lift off the pan. Peel off the parchment paper. Working carefully, roll up the cake and towel together into a cylinder. Keep covered with a kitchen towel until ready to fill.

♛ To fill the cake, unroll it on a work surface and remove the towel. Spread the cake with the room-temperature custard and roll it up once again. Carefully transfer to a serving plate. If not serving immediately, cover with plastic wrap and refrigerate.

♛ To serve, dust heavily with confectioners' sugar flavored with a little cinnamon and cut into slices.

serves 8

Sangria

In Andalusia, a land of citrus groves and Moorish echoes, locals and visitors alike seek a cool, refreshing antidote to the long, blistering hot summers. A tall, iced glass of sangria, a drink that originated here but is now drunk all over the country and in neighboring Portugal, is often the choice. To make it, a fruity red wine is mixed with sparkling water and then a few orange and lemon slices are added. Sometimes a glass of brandy is splashed into the pitcher to fortify the wine. The result is a wonderfully thirst-quenching drink that bears little resemblance to the tutti-frutti mixture of the same name so often served in bars and restaurants beyond the Iberian Peninsula—mixtures that inexplicably include everything from bananas and peaches to apples and nectarines.

To make an authentic Spanish sangria for four people, pour a bottle of fruity, dry red wine over a half dozen ice cubes in a pitcher. Add ¼ cup (2 fl oz/60 ml) brandy; 2 tablespoons sugar; 1 or 2 lemons, sliced paper-thin; 2 oranges, sliced paper-thin and slices quartered, and 3 cups (24 fl oz/750 ml) chilled sparkling water. Stir well, pour into chilled glasses, and sip slowly to beat the heat of an Andalusian afternoon.

Aragon

Melocotón al Vino

peaches in wine

Most travelers pass up landlocked Aragon, skipping its handsome mudéjar *towers at Tereul and medieval villages tucked away in isolated northern valleys. They never see the* jota *performed, a centuries-old regional dance in which the participants leap high repeatedly at a furious pace, or the bullfighting festivals in early fall that draw locals rather than the tourists who flock to Pamplona, in neighboring Navarre. But anyone who pursues good food knows that Aragon is famous for its peaches, and savvy travelers stop at the height of the summer to eat the juicy fruit right off the trees and to take some home for steeping in sugar and Aragon's rough dry red wine. Throughout the rest of the year they enjoy jars of the peaches in syrup sold at shops throughout the region.*

4 large freestone peaches
2½ cups (20 fl oz/625 ml) dry red wine
½ cup (4 oz/125 g) sugar
zest of 1 lemon, cut into strips
1 cinnamon stick
⅓ cup (3 fl oz/80 ml) brandy (optional)

❧ Bring a saucepan three-fourths full of water to a boil. One at a time, add the peaches and blanch for about 20 seconds to loosen the skin. Using a slotted spoon, transfer the peaches to a bowl of cold water. Slip off the skins, cut the peaches in half through the stem end, and remove the pit. Set the peaches aside in a heatproof bowl.

❧ In a saucepan over medium heat, combine the wine, sugar, lemon zest, and cinnamon stick and bring to a boil, stirring to dissolve the sugar. Add the brandy, if using, then remove from the heat and pour over the peaches. Let cool, cover, and let steep in the wine for 2 days in the refrigerator.

❧ To serve, spoon the peaches, along with some of the liquid, into glass bowls or goblets. Serve cold.

serves 4

New Castile

Torrijas

bread fritters

In the region of New Castile, especially in Madrid, desserts tend to be simple and rustic. Torrijas are typical in that everyday ingredients—bread, egg, milk, and honey—are turned into a satisfying sweet. These fritters are also called pan de Santa Teresa, *after the nun, a respected teacher and writer, who reformed the Carmelite order in the sixteenth century.*

6–8 thick slices day-old white bread, crusts removed

2 cups (16 fl oz/500 ml) milk, or as needed

orange or lemon zest strips

1 cinnamon stick

sweet sherry to cover (optional)

3 eggs

olive oil for frying

warmed honey or cinnamon-sugar

❦ Cut each bread slice into 2 triangles. Place in a single layer in a shallow baking pan or baking dish.

❦ Pour the 2 cups (16 fl oz/500 ml) milk into a saucepan over medium heat, add the citrus zest and cinnamon stick, and heat until small bubbles appear along the edges of the pan. Remove from the heat and let steep for about 30 minutes. Remove the cinnamon stick and citrus zest from the milk and pour the milk over the bread. If it does not cover the bread, add more milk or add sherry as needed to cover. Let stand for 10 minutes to absorb the milk.

❦ In a shallow bowl, whisk the eggs until blended. In a large frying pan, pour in olive oil to a depth of ¼ inch (6 mm) and warm over medium-high heat.

❦ In batches, dip the bread into the beaten eggs and slip into the hot oil. Fry, turning once, until golden on both sides, 6–8 minutes total. Transfer to individual plates and drizzle with warm honey or sprinkle with cinnamon-sugar. Repeat with the remaining bread slices, using more oil as needed. Serve at once.

serves 6

Balearic Islands

Flaon

minted cheese tart from ibiza

Ibiza is the southernmost island of the Balearic chain and the one closest to the mainland. Pine, almond, and olive trees flourish in its dry climate, as do herbs such as mint, fennel, marjoram, and thyme. Mint is featured in this lovely cheese tart, an ancient recipe that calls for a yeast-leavened pastry dough. Spanish cooks use cheese in many of their desserts, such as the Asturian quesada paseiga, *a kind of cheesecake made from a soft curd cheese produced in Cantabria. The Portuguese bake delicious cheese tarts, too, with perhaps* queijada de Sintra *the best known of them. It uses the local soft, fresh sheep's milk cheese called* requeijão, *which is made from whey and is much like Italian ricotta. For a special occasion, sprinkle the tart with cinnamon and garnish with fresh mint sprigs.*

PASTRY SHELL

1 teaspoon active dry yeast

½ cup (4 fl oz / 125 ml) milk, barely warmed

2 cups (10 oz / 315 g) all-purpose (plain) flour

1 tablespoon sugar

¼ cup (2 oz / 60 g) chilled lard or unsalted butter, or 2 tablespoons of each, cut into bits

1 egg

FILLING

1 lb (500 g) whole-milk ricotta or cream cheese

1 cup (8 oz / 250 g) sugar

4 eggs

¼ cup (2 fl oz / 60 ml) anise liqueur such as anís del mono *or* Pernod

12 fresh mint leaves

pinch of ground cinnamon (optional)

☙ To make the pastry shell, in a large bowl, sprinkle the yeast over the warm milk and let sit until frothy, 5–8 minutes.

☙ Meanwhile, place the flour and sugar in a food processor and pulse briefly to combine. Add the lard or butter and pulse until the mixture resembles coarse crumbs. Add the milk mixture and the egg and pulse just until the dough comes together. Turn out onto a lightly floured work surface and knead until smooth, about 5 minutes. Cover with a kitchen towel and let rest for 20 minutes.

☙ Preheat an oven to 350°F (180°C). Butter a 10-inch (25-cm) tart pan with a removable bottom.

☙ Lightly flour the work surface and roll out the dough into an 11-inch (28-cm) round. Transfer the round to the prepared tart pan, pressing it smoothly against the bottom and sides. Trim the edges even with the pan rim. Set aside.

☙ To make the filling, in a bowl, using an electric mixer, beat together the cheese, sugar, and eggs until creamy. Add the liqueur and mix well. If desired, chop 2 of the mint leaves and mix them in as well. Beat in the cinnamon, if using.

☙ Pour the cheese mixture into the pastry-lined pan. Arrange the mint leaves on top, gently pushing them into the surface.

☙ Bake until the top of the tart is pale gold, 25–30 minutes. Transfer to a rack and let cool completely. Remove the pan rim and slide the tart onto a plate. Serve at room temperature.

serves 8

Filloas

crepes filled with sautéed apples

If you like, garnish these leaf-thin crepes with whipped cream flavored with apple brandy.

CREPES

3 eggs

1 cup (8 fl oz/250 ml) milk

¾ cup (6 fl oz/180 ml) water

1½ cups (7½ oz/235 g) all-purpose (plain) flour

pinch of salt

2 tablespoons unsalted butter, melted, plus extra melted butter for frying

FILLING

3 tablespoons unsalted butter

1 lb (500 g) Golden Delicious apples, peeled, halved, cored, and sliced lengthwise ½ inch (12 mm) thick

3 tablespoons sugar

½ teaspoon ground cinnamon (optional)

❦ To make the crepes, in a bowl, whisk together the eggs, milk, water, flour, salt, and the 2 tablespoons melted butter. Let the batter rest for 30 minutes.

❦ Meanwhile, make the filling: In a frying pan over medium heat, melt the butter. Add the apples and sauté until softened, 10–12 minutes. Sprinkle with the sugar, raise the heat to medium-high, and sauté until the apples begin to caramelize, 10–15 minutes more. Sprinkle with cinnamon, if using. Keep warm.

❦ Lightly brush a 7–7½-inch (18–19-cm) crepe pan with melted butter and place over medium heat. When the pan is hot, ladle in about 3 tablespoons of the batter and swirl to coat the bottom. Cook over medium heat until just set, 2–3 minutes. Using your fingers, turn the crepe and cook on the second side until set, about 1 minute longer. Do not allow it to color. Slide the crepe onto a clean kitchen towel, then wrap tightly in aluminum foil to keep warm. Brush the pan again with butter and repeat until all of the batter is used. You should have 12 crepes.

❦ Place several spoonfuls of the warm apples in the middle of each crepe and fold into quarters. Divide among individual plates and serve.

serves 4–6

Douro

Pudim Flan

port-scented custard

Flan is the most popular dessert in almost every taberna and tasca in Spain and Portugal. The addition of port here places this silken dessert on the dinner tables of Oporto, a city celebrated for its role in putting the distinctive wine on the world's enological map. This recipe doubles easily.

1 cup (8 fl oz/250 ml) milk

1 cup (8 fl oz/250 ml) heavy (double) cream

1 cinnamon stick

zest of 1 orange, in long strips

1 cup (8 oz/250 g) sugar

2 tablespoons water

3 whole eggs plus 2 egg yolks

2 tablespoons tawny port

½ teaspoon vanilla extract (essence)

❦ Pour the milk and cream into a saucepan and add the cinnamon stick and orange zest strips. Place over medium-high heat and heat until small bubbles appear along the edges of the pan. Remove from the heat and let steep for 1 hour.

❦ Have ready six ½-cup (4–fl oz/125-ml) ramekins or custard cups. In a small, heavy saucepan over high heat, combine ½ cup (4 oz/125 g) of the sugar and the water and heat, stirring until the sugar dissolves and the mixture comes to a boil. Continue to boil, without stirring, until the mixture is golden brown, 6–8 minutes. Be careful not to let it get too dark, or the custard will taste bitter. Remove from the heat and carefully pour the hot syrup into the ramekins or custard cups, dividing it evenly and quickly swirling the cups to coat with the caramel. Place the molds in a large baking pan. Set aside.

❦ Preheat an oven to 325°F (165°C).

❦ Strain the milk-cream mixture through a fine-mesh sieve, discarding the orange zest and cinnamon stick. Return the liquid to the pan and place over medium-high heat. Heat until small bubbles appear along the edges of the pan. Remove from the heat.

❦ In a bowl, using an electric mixer set on high speed, beat together the whole eggs and egg yolks until frothy. Gradually add the remaining ½ cup (4 oz/125 g) sugar, beating until the mixture is pale yellow and thick, about 10 minutes. Add the hot milk-cream mixture, a little at a time, beating constantly. Stir in the port and vanilla. Pour the mixture through a fine-mesh sieve placed over a pitcher. Then pour the strained mixture into the caramel-lined molds, dividing evenly. Pour hot water into the baking pan to reach halfway up the sides of the molds. Cover the pan with aluminum foil.

❦ Bake until a knife inserted into the center of a custard emerges clean, about 30 minutes. Remove the custards from the water bath, let cool, and refrigerate until chilled.

❦ At serving time, run a knife around the inside edge of each mold and unmold into shallow dessert bowls, allowing any caramel in the molds to drizzle over the custards. Serve immediately.

serves 6

Port

The Douro River twists and turns for some 140 miles (215 km) through the narrow—and beautiful—valley of the same name and then crosses into Spain. On either side of the waterway rise steep hills covered with terraced vineyards. Only the upper portion of the Douro, near the city of Oporto, is port wine country, however, a land of hot summers, wet winters, and picturesque manor houses.

Port is one of world's best fortified wines. Although it is unquestionably a Portuguese product, it owes its existence to the British, who, during a disagreement with the French in the early eighteenth century, decided to look elsewhere for their refreshment. The British ambassador executed an agreement that put Portuguese wines on London tables for a fraction of the cost of their French rivals.

But the wines that reached Britain were unpleasantly sharp, as their sugars had nearly vanished. Enterprising English merchants, who had settled in Oporto in the sixteenth century, hit upon the idea of fortifying them with brandy before fermentation was finished, thereby wiping out the bitter yeasts and maintaining some of the sugars. With that move, modern-day port was born.

Basically two kinds of port exist, vintage port and wood port. Vintage port is made exclusively of wine pressed from the best vineyards in the same year. These are products of great character, created when the weather and soil cooperate perfectly.

Tawny and ruby ports are the so-called wood ports. The former are blended wines from different years that spend a long time in wood before bottling. They take their name from their pale, or tawny, color, a result of redness lost during prolonged cask storage. The payoff is a memorable, soft finish. Ruby ports, somewhat younger blended wines, are named for their distinctive color as well.

Minho

Sopa Dourada

golden soup

The name of this dessert comes from its colorful components: golden Portuguese sponge cake, or pão-de-ló, covered either with ovos moles *(page 224) or with an egg-yolk-loaded custard. In Minho,* sopa dourada *is served during the Christmas holidays, and some cooks give it a more festive air by decorating it with colorful candied fruits or slivered nuts. One variation,* barrigas-de-freira, *or nun's tummies, adds a spoonful of cocoa to the soft egg custard and crumbles the sponge cake.*

CUSTARD

4 cups (32 fl oz/1 l) half-and-half (half cream)

2 cups (16 fl oz/500 ml) heavy (double) cream

1 cinnamon stick

1 tablespoon grated lemon zest

7 whole eggs plus 6 egg yolks

1 cup (8 oz/250 g) sugar

¼ teaspoon freshly grated nutmeg

1 teaspoon vanilla extract (essence)

SPONGE CAKE

6 eggs

1 cup (8 fl oz/250 g) sugar

pinch of salt

½ cup (2 oz/60 g) plus 2 tablespoons sifted all-purpose (plain) flour

6 tablespoons (2 oz/60 g) blanched almonds, toasted and finely ground

¼ teaspoon almond extract (essence)

2 teaspoons grated lemon zest

☙ To make the custard, pour the half-and-half and cream into a saucepan and place over medium heat until small bubbles appear along the pan edges. Remove from the heat and add the cinnamon stick and lemon zest. Let steep for 2 hours.

☙ In a bowl, whisk together the whole eggs and egg yolks, sugar, nutmeg, and vanilla. Pour the steeped milk though a fine-mesh sieve held over the bowl holding the egg mixture. Stir to mix.

☙ To make the cake, preheat an oven to 325°F (165°C). Butter a 10½-by-15-inch (26½-by-38-cm) jelly-roll pan. Line the bottom with parchment (baking) paper and butter the parchment.

☙ In a heatproof bowl, whisk together the eggs, sugar, and salt. Place over (but not touching) simmering water in a saucepan and continue to whisk until the mixture is warm and the sugar is dissolved. Remove from over the water and, using an electric mixer set on high speed, beat until the mixture is very thick and falls in a wide, slowly dissolving ribbon when the beaters are lifted.

☙ Sift together the flour and ground almonds over the eggs. Using a rubber spatula, gently fold them in along with the almond extract and lemon zest. Pour the batter into the prepared pan and smooth the top.

☙ Bake until a skewer inserted into the center of the cake emerges clean and the top is springy to the touch, 10–15 minutes. Remove from the oven and let cool in the pan on a rack for about 5 minutes. Run a knife around the inside edge of the pan to loosen the cake and turn the cake out onto the rack. Peel off the parchment. Let cool completely.

☙ Preheat the oven to 350°F (180°C). Butter a 2-qt (2-l) baking dish with 3-inch (7.5-cm) sides.

☙ To assemble the pudding, cut the cake into 1-inch (2.5-cm) cubes or thin slices, then distribute evenly in the prepared dish, covering the bottom completely. Pour the custard over the cake, filling the dish. The cake will float to the top. Place the dish in a baking pan. Pour hot water into the pan to reach three-fourths of the way up the sides of the dish.

☙ Bake until a knife inserted into the center emerges almost clean, about 40 minutes. The pudding will still jiggle slightly when the dish is shaken. Let cool for 45 minutes before serving.

serves 8

At harvest, almonds are shaken from the trees, their hard green coverings peeled away, and the nuts left to dry in the sun.

Bolo Podre

"rotten" cake

A favorite in Alentejo, this delicious honey cake is made with olive oil rather than butter. Despite its unappealing name, its dark, rustic appearance is really quite handsome.

2½ cups (10 oz/315 g) sifted all-purpose (plain) flour or whole wheat (wholemeal) flour

1 tablespoon ground cinnamon

1½ teaspoons baking powder

½ teaspoon ground cloves

6 eggs, separated

½ cup (4 oz/125 g) granulated sugar or ½ cup (3½ oz/105 g) firmly packed brown sugar

grated zest of 1 orange

1 cup (8 fl oz/250 ml) olive oil or vegetable oil

1 cup (12 oz/375 g) dark honey

¼ cup (2 fl oz/60 ml) brandy

♛ Preheat an oven to 350°F (180°C). Butter a 10-inch (25-cm) springform pan.

♛ In a bowl, sift together the flour, cinnamon, baking powder, and cloves. In another bowl, using an electric mixer set on high speed, beat the egg yolks and sugar until pale and thick. Beat in the orange zest, then drizzle in the oil, beating constantly. Slowly add the honey and brandy, beating until smooth. Reduce the speed to low and add the flour mixture in 3 batches. Beat well after each addition.

♛ In a clean bowl, using clean beaters, beat the egg whites until soft peaks form. Fold into the cake batter. Pour into the prepared pan.

♛ Bake until a skewer inserted into the center of the cake emerges clean and the edges of the cake begin to shrink from the sides of the pan, 45–50 minutes. Let cool in the pan on a rack for 15 minutes, then run a small knife around the inside edge of the pan to loosen the cake. Release and remove the pan sides and let cool.

♛ Transfer the cake to a plate. Cut into very thin slices to serve, as the cake is quite rich.

serves 8–10

Catalonia

Crema Quemada

"burnt" cream

Sometimes called crema de San José, as it is traditionally served on Saint Joseph's Day, this classic caramelized custard is on the menu of nearly every Barcelona restaurant. Unlike pudim flan (page 236), which is poured into a caramelized mold, this custard is chilled and then caramelized, or "burnt," on top just before serving, like a French crème brûlée.

2 tablespoons cornstarch (cornflour)

1 cup (8 fl oz/250 ml) milk

1 cup (8 fl oz/250 ml) half-and-half (half cream) or heavy (double) cream

3 lemon zest strips, each 2 inches (5 cm) long

1 cinnamon stick

6 egg yolks

½ cup (4 oz/125 g) granulated sugar

6 tablespoons (3 oz/90 g) firmly packed brown sugar or granulated sugar

✠ In a small bowl, dissolve the cornstarch in a few tablespoons of the milk. Set aside. Pour the remaining milk and the cream into a saucepan and add the lemon zest strips and cinnamon stick. Place over medium-high heat and heat until small bubbles appear along the edges of the pan. Remove from the heat and discard the lemon zest and cinnamon stick.

✠ In a bowl, using an electric mixer set on high speed, beat together the egg yolks and the ½ cup (4 oz/125 g) granulated sugar until thick and pale. Gradually whisk in about ½ cup (4 fl oz/125 ml) of the hot milk-cream mixture. Return the mixture to the pan, whisk in the cornstarch-milk mixture, and place over low heat. Simmer, stirring, until the custard thickens enough to coat a spoon, about 10 minutes. Pour through a fine-mesh sieve placed over a pitcher. Then pour it into six ½-cup (4-fl oz/ 125-ml) flameproof custard cups or ramekins, dividing evenly. Let cool, cover, and chill well.

✠ Preheat a broiler (griller). Place the molds on a baking sheet. Sprinkle 1 tablespoon brown or granulated sugar over the top of each chilled custard and slip under the broiler. Broil (grill) until the sugar is melted and bubbling. Serve at once.

serves 6

Andalusia

Pan de Higos

fig loaf

The warm climate of southern Spain produces a bumper crop of figs. Locals consider them among the delights of summer eating, enjoying them fresh or poached in light sugar syrup. When the population is sated, the balance of the figs is dried and used in cakes or other sweets. This rich, sweet confection, an echo of the Moorish table that once fed the region, is traditionally served during the Christmas holidays.

1½ lb (750 g) dried Mission figs, stems removed and finely chopped

½ cup (3 oz/90 g) almonds, toasted and finely chopped

½ cup (2½ oz/75 g) hazelnuts (filberts), toasted and finely chopped

¼ cup (1 oz/30 g) confectioners' (icing) sugar, plus more for sprinkling foil

1 teaspoon ground cinnamon

½ teaspoon ground cloves

1 tablespoon grated lemon zest

2 tablespoons anise liqueur such as anís del mono *or brandy

2 oz (60 g) semisweet (plain) chocolate, melted

In a food processor, combine the figs, almonds, hazelnuts, the ¼ cup (1 oz/30 g) confectioners' sugar, cinnamon, cloves, and lemon zest. Pulse until well combined. Stir in the liqueur or brandy and chocolate to moisten the mixture, which will be very stiff.

Sprinkle a large square of heavy-duty aluminum foil with confectioners' sugar. Shape the fig mixture into a large loaf and wrap it in the foil. (Alternatively, use 2 foil squares and make 2 small loaves.) Refrigerate for at least 2 days or for as long as 3 months.

To serve, dip a very sharp knife in hot water and cut the loaf into slices.

serves 8–12

Chocolate

On his fourth voyage to the New World, in 1502, Columbus sent back the first cacao beans to Spain. The recipients, alas, were mystified as to what to do with the bitter seeds, and Columbus provided no insights. Nearly two decades later, however, Hernán Cortés, who had drunk cups of chocolate at Aztec dinner tables, returned to Spain not only with the beans, but also with the knowledge of how to use them.

The Spanish did not at first realize the cacao bean's dessert possibilities, but they did manage to fashion the beans into tablets, which they sweetened with sugar and later with cinnamon and vanilla. They jealously guarded the secrets of chocolate production. The tablets were used to make hot chocolate, a sweet, molten liquid that, despite early objections from the Catholic Church, who viewed it as potentially sinful, soon took the country by storm.

Today, chocolate is used in sweets, of course, but it also flavors savory dishes in Aragon and Navarre, such as small white onions in a chocolate-flavored sauce. And many Spaniards still enjoy a big cup of thick, hot chocolate for breakfast as well, often accompanied by a *churro,* a wonderful loop or finger of deep-fried dough—a cruller of sorts—dusted with sugar.

Basque Country

Panchineta

almond custard tart

Steeping the almonds in the milk intensifies the almond flavor of this simple Basque tart. It is an ideal dessert for entertaining, as the crust can be baked ahead of time and the custard fully prepared and chilled. Then, just before serving, assemble the tart and heat it in a moderate oven. Most versions of this recipe call for a prebaked puff pastry shell, but you can use a rich tart pastry in its place.

1 sheet frozen puff pastry, about 12 by 14 inches (30 by 35 cm) and ¼ inch (6 mm) thick, thawed in the refrigerator

1¾ cups (14 fl oz / 430 ml) milk

⅓ cup (3 oz / 90 g) sugar

1 cup (5½ oz / 170 g) almonds, toasted

2 whole eggs plus 3 egg yolks

¼ cup (1½ oz / 45 g) all-purpose (plain) flour

¼ teaspoon salt

⅔ cup (2½ oz / 75 g) sliced (flaked) almonds, lightly toasted

2 tablespoons unsalted butter, at room temperature

1 teaspoon vanilla extract (essence)

1 teaspoon almond extract (essence)

❀ To prepare the puff pastry shell, unfold the sheet of puff pastry and, using a sharp knife, cut into a 9-inch (23-cm) round. Using a fork, prick all over the center of the round, leaving a 1-inch (2.5-cm) border. (This will allow the edges to puff up when baked.) Wrap in plastic wrap and freeze for 1 hour or as long as 12 hours before baking.

❀ Preheat an oven to 400°F (200°C). Lightly butter a baking sheet.

❀ Transfer the round to the prepared baking sheet. Bake for 10–12 minutes, remove from the oven, and prick again with a fork. Reduce the oven temperature to 350°F (180°C), return to the oven, and bake until crisp and pale golden brown, about 10 minutes longer. Remove from the oven and let cool.

❀ To make the custard, combine the milk and sugar in a saucepan and place over medium heat. Heat, stirring to dissolve the sugar, until small bubbles appear along the edges of the pan. Remove from the heat, add the 1 cup (5½ oz / 170 g) toasted almonds, and let steep for 1 hour. Strain and discard the almonds.

❀ Pour the almond milk into a clean saucepan and bring to a boil over medium heat. In a bowl, whisk together the whole eggs, egg yolks, flour, and salt until blended. Gradually add about ½ cup (4 fl oz / 125 ml) of the hot milk to the egg mixture, whisking until well blended. Then return the mixture to the saucepan. Place over medium heat and cook, whisking constantly, until the mixture comes to a boil. Continue to whisk for 2–3 minutes to remove the raw flour taste. Remove from the heat and pour the custard into a bowl nested in a bowlful of ice. Stir in the butter and the vanilla and almond extracts until the butter melts. Cover with plastic wrap, pressing it directly onto the surface, and refrigerate until cold.

❀ Preheat an oven to 325°F (165°C). Pour the custard evenly into the prebaked puff pastry shell. Strew the toasted sliced almonds over the top. Bake until lightly browned and warmed through, 5–10 minutes. Remove from the heat and serve warm.

serves 8

Estremadura

Farófias

snow pancakes

This light, not-too-sweet dessert is traditionally served for Carnival and New Year's.

3 eggs, separated, plus 2 egg yolks

pinch of salt

1 cup (8 oz/250 g) sugar

4 cups (32 fl oz/1 l) milk

1 vanilla bean, split in half lengthwise

cinnamon-sugar

In a bowl, using an electric mixer, beat the egg whites with the salt until foamy. Gradually beat in ½ cup (4 oz/125 g) of the sugar until the mixture forms stiff peaks.

Pour the milk into a wide saucepan and add the vanilla bean. Place over low heat and bring to a gentle simmer. Using a large spoon and working in batches, drop in the egg whites by spoonfuls, forming ovals. Simmer for 2–3 minutes. Turn the ovals over and cook gently until set, 2–3 minutes longer. Using a slotted spoon, transfer the ovals to paper towels to drain. You want to make at least 12 snow pancakes, allowing 2 per person. If you make them smaller, they may poach a bit more quickly. Remove the pan from the heat and pour the milk through a fine-mesh sieve placed over a measuring pitcher.

To make the custard sauce, beat the egg yolks lightly in a heatproof bowl placed over (not touching) barely simmering water in a saucepan. Stir in the remaining ½ cup (4 oz/125 g) sugar, then stir in 3 cups (24 fl oz/750 ml) of the strained milk. Continue to cook, stirring constantly, until the mixture thickens and coats a spoon, 5–8 minutes. Pour the custard through the sieve into a serving bowl, cover the bowl with plastic wrap, pressing it directly onto the surface of the custard, and refrigerate until cold.

To serve, gently spoon the custard into individual bowls and place the egg-white ovals on top. Sprinkle with cinnamon-sugar.

serves 6

GLOSSARY

The following entries cover key Spanish and Portuguese ingredients and basic recipes called for in this book. For information on items not found below, please refer to the index.

ANCHOVIES

Thriving in Mediterranean waters along the coast of Catalonia, where they are known as *boquerones* or *anchoas* (or in Portuguese, *anchovas*), these shimmering blue-green fish measure no more than 6 inches (15 cm) long. When freshly caught, they may be fried and eaten whole, or they are sometimes pickled with vinegar. The bulk of the catch is preserved by layering the fish with salt. Whole salted anchovies are packed in cans, to be filleted at home before use. They can be found in some delicatessens. Salted anchovy fillets immersed in olive oil in small, flat tins or in glass jars are more commonly available. Jars of anchovy fillets are generally preferable because they offer the buyer a chance to assess their quality at a glance.

BEANS, DRIED

Dried beans are popular, economical staples in Spain and Portugal alike. Some of the most popular varieties, used in this book, include the chickpea (garbanzo bean), a large, pea-shaped tan bean that was introduced to southern Spain by Phoenician traders; large, creamy-textured white beans or butter beans such as those the Spanish call *alubias* and the Portuguese call *feijão manteiga;* and small white beans known by the Spanish *judías blancas* or the Portuguese *feijão branco,* for which Great Northern or navy beans are an acceptable substitute.

TO PREPARE DRIED BEANS, first pick them over to remove any foreign matter or misshapen or discolored specimens. Then, rinse the beans and soak them to rehydrate them, ensuring quicker and more even cooking. Soaking may be done overnight by placing the beans in a large bowl and adding fresh cold water to cover by at least 2–3 inches (5–7.5 cm) or more quickly by putting them in a pot, adding cold water to cover generously, bringing the water to a simmer, and then leaving the beans to soak in the pot, covered but off the heat, for 1–1½ hours. To cook the soaked beans, drain their water completely, cover them with fresh water in a large pot, bring to a full rolling boil, and continue boiling for 10 minutes. Then reduce the heat to a simmer and continue cooking until the beans are tender to the bite, at least 1 hour. Cooked beans will keep in the refrigerator in a sealed container for several days or in an airtight container in the freezer for up to 1 year.

BREAD, COARSE COUNTRY

In big cities and small villages throughout Iberia, local bakers produce robust, chewy loaves of bread from simple doughs of hard-wheat flour, yeast, salt, and water. Seek out similar loaves at small boutique bakeries, which usually label them coarse country bread or peasant bread.

TO MAKE BREAD CRUMBS, trim off and discard the crusts from a loaf and process the bread in a food processor until the crumbs are as coarsely or as finely textured as desired. To dry the crumbs, spread them on a baking sheet and bake in a preheated 325°F (165°C) oven for

CHEESES

In the Spanish and Portuguese countryside, farmers raise many cows, sheep, and goats for their milk, which is turned into a wealth of local cheeses. Many of these products never find their way beyond the region, much less to other countries. Several types of cheese, however, have won considerable fame and are produced on a larger scale, sometimes in quantities sufficient to be sold abroad. Some of these are featured in this book.

CABRALES ~ Spain's signature blue-veined cheese, this specialty of Cantabria is made from a mixture of sheep's, goat's, and cow's milk, formed into short cylinders, and aged in limestone caves for 3–6 months. It is comparable in flavor to French Roquefort, which may be substituted, although Cabrales has a somewhat sharper flavor.

GOAT CHEESE ~ Many forms of goat's milk cheese are enjoyed in both Spain and Portugal. Some of the best-known types include Cádiz, a strong-tasting aged cheese from the Spanish region of the same name; Catalan mató, a soft, fresh white cheese that is often enjoyed with honey as a dessert; and Portugal's cabreiro, a lightly salted goat cheese that is eaten in both its soft, fresh form and as a somewhat firmer, tangier, briefly aged cheese.

QUESO FRESCO ~ Fresh, uncured cow's milk cheese, known by the generic term *queso fresco,* is a popular ingredient, for which Italian whole-milk ricotta may be substituted.

MANCHEGO ~ Spain's most famous cheese, this specialty of La Mancha, from which it gets its name, is traditionally made from sheep's milk, although cow's milk is now used as well. In its earliest days, it was made and eaten by the shepherds who tended large flocks in the area. Today it is available in Spain in fresh *(fresco)* and lightly aged *(semicurado)* forms, but the most common and widely exported type is labeled *curado,* which has been aged for at least 6 months. It has a rich, tangy flavor and a firm, somewhat brittle texture. Thinly sliced, it is served as a tapa or sometimes as a dessert with fruit or quince preserves.

about 15 minutes. For toasted crumbs, continue baking the coarse or fine dried crumbs, stirring once or twice, until lightly golden, about 15 minutes longer.

CHOCOLATE

Although Columbus reputedly encountered chocolate in Nicaragua on his fourth voyage in 1502, it was Spanish explorer Hernán Cortés who first brought cacao beans back to Spain from Mexico's Aztec court in 1528. Soon, chocolate caught on as a popular breakfast drink, where it is still enjoyed to this day, whisked into boiling milk. (The Portuguese do not favor chocolate as greatly.) For cooking or eating, seek out semisweet chocolate, a lightly sweetened form made with at least 40 percent—but preferably 50 percent—cocoa butter. Unsweetened chocolate, also known as bitter or cooking chocolate and sold in small blocks, is composed of half cocoa butter and half cocoa solids. It is unpalatable on its own but adds rich chocolate taste to recipes that also contain a sweetener. In Catalonia, cooks favor *xocolata a la pedra,* "chocolate on the stone," a cooking chocolate flavored with cinnamon and sugar (similar to Mexican Ybarra brand chocolate). It may be used to make breakfast hot chocolate, in desserts, or in savory dishes such as *estofado de buey a la catalana* (page 107).

CILANTRO

Also known as fresh coriander or Chinese parsley, the fresh, green leaves of the plant that also yields the spicy seeds known as coriander first came to Spain and Portugal with the Moors. It remains popular in the cuisines of both countries as a seasoning for all manner of savory recipes, adding its sharp, somewhat astringent flavor to soups, stews, and vegetable dishes.

CURRY POWDER

Portuguese explorer Vasco da Gama first encountered and brought home this Indian spice blend while searching for a trade route to the East in the early 16th century. Known as *caril* in Portuguese, it is sold as commercial mixtures that usually include coriander, cumin, chile, fenugreek, and turmeric, as well as such possible additions as cardamom, cinnamon, clove, allspice, fennel, and ginger. Portuguese cooks use it frequently but sparingly to add just a hint of intriguing spice to soups or stews.

FAVA BEANS

From springtime into summer, gardens all over the Iberian Peninsula yield profuse crops of fava (broad) beans, known as *habas* in Spain and *favas* in Portugal. Larger, older fava beans develop a thick, tough skin around each bean, which requires peeling to appreciate fully the tender, pale green bean inside.

TO SHELL AND PEEL FAVA BEANS, simply use your thumbs to split each pod open along its seam, then sweep a thumb along the inside of the pod to pop out the beans. If the skins covering the beans are thick, immerse the beans in boiling water for about 30 seconds, drain, and peel each one by splitting the skin with a thumbnail or slitting it with the tip of a small, sharp knife and slipping it off. For the best taste and texture, always shell and peel fava beans as close to their cooking time as possible.

FIGS, DRIED

Figs are popular throughout Portugal and Spain, whether served alongside *presunto* or *serrano* ham to start a meal or for dessert, perhaps accompanied by a glass of port. The summer fig crop is so abundant that many of the fruits are dried, often for use in confections. For the finest dried fig flavor, seek out dried Mission figs, which have a particularly intense, rich taste.

GARLIC

A definitive pungent flavoring in the kitchens of both Spain and Portugal, and a natural partner to olive oil, garlic was originally introduced to the region during the Roman Empire. While it is most often used in the form of familiar cloves separated from whole heads of garlic, a favorite specialty is slender green shoots of fresh garlic, known by the Spanish *ajos tiernos.* These are occasionally found canned in specialty-food stores. Garlic chives, frequently stocked in Asian and farmers' markets, may be substituted.

GRAPE LEAVES

Grapevine leaves are popular edible wrappers in the countries bordering the Mediterranean, a purpose for which they are used in Spain and Portugal as well. If you can find fresh leaves, rinse them well before use, then blanch briefly to soften. Bottled leaves packed in brine, found in ethnic and specialty-food stores, should also be gently rinsed, to reduce their saltiness, before using.

HAM

Both Portugal and Spain boast superb country-style hams that may be served thinly sliced as a first course or used as a distinctive source of flavor in sauces, soups, stews, braises, and other dishes. In Portugal, this air-cured ham is known as *presunto.* It has a sweet, smoky flavor and a deep chestnut color. Spain's finely marbled *serrano,* or "mountain," ham has an intense, almost sweet flavor. (See page 28 for information on where and how the hams are produced.) A suitable substitute for *presunto* or *serrano* ham is prosciutto, the famed air-cured ham of Parma, Italy. Other similar hams, including French Bayonne, German Westphalian, or American Smithfield, may also be used.

LARD

While olive oil is the favored cooking fat throughout Iberia, kitchens in those areas in which pigs are raised will naturally stock lard (rendered pork fat) as well, prizing it for the rich flavor it contributes. Packaged lard may be found in the refrigerated case of food stores.

NUTS

Nut trees grow throughout Spain and Portugal, providing cooks with their rich-tasting, crisp meats to use whole, sliced, chopped, or pulverized in savory and sweet dishes alike. Most popular of all are almonds, *almendras* in Spanish and *amêndoas* in Portuguese, the cultivation of which was introduced to the region by the Moors. Their use ranges from whole nuts fried in olive oil and served as appetizers to ground almonds used to lend body to *romesco* sauce and *picadas* and to cakes and confections. Chestnuts, which thrive in the Pyrenees, are a particular autumn specialty, traditionally sold roasted in streetside carts. Richly flavored, spherical hazelnuts (filberts) are favorite ingredients in sauces and nougat candies. Pine nuts, the small, slender nuts of the stone pine tree, add a rich, resinous flavor to everything from salads to stuffings, batters to candies. Walnuts are also popular, particularly in sauces and sweets.

TO TOAST NUTS, bake them in a single layer in a 325°F (165°C) oven until they just begin to darken, 5–10 minutes, depending upon their size. Remove from the oven and let cool to room temperature. Toasting also loosens the skins of hazelnuts and walnuts, which may then be removed by rubbing the still-warm nuts inside a towel.

OLIVE OIL

Spain is the world's largest producer of olive oil, much of which comes from huge olive plantations in Andalusia. Harvested from autumn into early winter, the olives are first pressed mechanically, without use of heat, chemicals, or other extractants, to yield olive oil that is classified extra-virgin or virgin, depending upon its degree of acidity. Spanish extra-virgin oil is generally characterized by a fruity, aromatic quality. Olive oil without the virgin or extra-virgin designations is a product blended from virgin and refined (filtered) oils, which gives it a far milder taste. In contrast, Portuguese olive oil generally has an even more intense aroma and flavor, resulting from the olives being picked late in the harvest and then being left on the ground to age for up to 10 days before pressing.

OLIVES

Unripened green and ripe black olives, cured either by soaking them in an alkaline brine or by layering them with salt, are eaten in Spain and Portugal alike. Among the most popular olives in Spain are the small, green Manzanilla, the small, black Jonquillo, and the large, greenish brown Obregón varieties. In Portugal, where green olives are widely preferred, the finest are considered to be those of the Alentejo region. Any good-quality black or green olives may be substituted.

TO PIT OLIVES, use a cherry pitter or an olive pitter, both tools specially designed to grip the small fruit while pushing out its hard pit with a squeeze of the hand. Alternatively, hit the olive with a meat pounder and pull out the pit.

ONIONS

These pungent, aromatic bulbs are staple savory ingredients of Spanish and Portuguese kitchens. Among the popular varieties are green (spring) onions, the immature form of an onion especially grown to be enjoyed in its entirety, both the small white bulb and long green leaves. The *calçot*, a wild green onion from the Valls region of Catalonia, is much sought-after in spring (see page 184). Red onions are mild, purple-red onions often referred to outside of Spain as a Spanish onion. Within Spain, however, certain red varieties are paradoxically called *cebollas francesas,* French onions.

PAPRIKA

A source of vibrant color and flavor in both Spanish and Portuguese cooking, this finely ground brick-red spice derives from a type of dried red pepper. It is used primarily in two forms: hot (*picante,* or "spicy," in Spanish, and *colorau,* or "red," in Portuguese) and sweet (*dulce* in Spanish and *colorau-doce* in Portuguese). The Spanish also make a medium-hot paprika, labeled *agridulce. Pimentón de La Vera,* made from smoke-dried peppers and named for a valley in Extremadura, is especially prized. Sweet or hot Hungarian paprika may be substituted for Spanish or Portuguese products.

PEPPERS

Carried home from the New World to the Iberian Peninsula, a wide variety of mild peppers (capsicums) and chiles are used today in the cooking of Spain and Portugal. Two of Spain's most important peppers are the small, triangular, red *pimiento del piquillo,* generally fire-roasted and sold packed in jars, and the smaller, more piquant *romesco.* The most common role for the *romesco* is in the Catalan *salsa romesco* (see page 184), a versatile nut-rich sauce that marries perfectly with seafood. Dried ancho chiles are an acceptable substitute. Red and green bell peppers are also widely used. One of the many Spanish recipes in which they are a central ingredient is *chilindrón,* a popular sauce for lamb or poultry in Aragon and Navarre, made with bell peppers, tomatoes, onions, paprika, and sometimes *serrano* ham. In Portugal, cooks regularly prepare *massa de pimentão,* a paste of roasted red bell peppers, garlic, and olive oil, for rubbing on meat before roasting it.

QUINCE

This autumn-harvested tree fruit, known as *membrillo* in Spain and *marmelo* in Portugal, looks like a large, lumpy green cross between an apple and a pear. When raw, its flesh tastes unpleasantly bitter. Cooked with sugar, however, quince develops a wonderfully sweet, aromatic flavor. Throughout the two countries, it is most often cooked down to the consistency of a thick, solid, pink jam, also known as *membrillo* in Spain and called *marmelada* in Portugal. This may be used in desserts or served as a complement to cold cuts such as *serrano* ham or *presunto.*

RICE

Rice grows abundantly in the marshlands of Spain's Valencia Province, as well as those along Portugal's Atlantic coastline. Spanish cooks prefer medium-grain rices, such as the Bomba and Calasparra varieties, which have a firm texture and give off a good amount of starch, producing the desirable consistency for paellas. In the absence of Spanish rice, Italian Arborio, Carnaroli, or Vialone rice or one of the medium-grain California varieties can be substituted. Medium-grained varieties are also favored in Portugal for use in popular rice puddings, although long-grained rices are used in soups and stews.

SAFFRON

Taking its name from the Arabic for "yellow," and known as *azafrán* in Spain and *açafrão* in Portugal, this rare and costly spice is the dried stigmas of a purple crocus flower, *Crocus sativa*. Native to Asia Minor and introduced to Iberia by the Moors, it has become a signature seasoning of Spanish cooking, particularly in paella. Portuguese cooks use it more sparingly. The best form to buy is saffron threads, the actual whole dried stigmas. The flavor of powdered saffron tends to dissipate more rapidly, and it is also more easily subject to adulteration with less costly ingredients like turmeric. Before the threads are added to a dish, they are generally treated in one of two ways to release their maximum flavor and aroma: slowly toasted in a dry pan over low heat, or lightly crushed and then steeped for a few minutes in a warm liquid such as wine, stock, milk, or water.

SALT

Coarse forms of salt add intense flavor and at times even a touch of texture to savory dishes. Granules or "corns" of kosher salt, produced for the koshering of meats in homes that follow strict Jewish dietary guidelines, are made without additives and taste about half as salty as ordinary table salt. Kosher salt can be found in the seasonings or kosher food sections of well-stocked food stores. Sea salt, most commonly available in coarse crystals, is made by evaporating seawater and tends to have a fresh, yet complex flavor. Look for it in well-stocked markets and in specialty and health-food stores.

SALT COD, BONELESS

Not long after Columbus first discovered the New World, Portuguese fishermen were plying the waters off Newfoundland for codfish, which they preserved first by gutting, filleting, and salting while still at sea and then by sun-drying once back home. The Spanish, meanwhile, were introduced to the uses of salt cod at the same time by cooks in the south of France. Today, in both countries, the strong, briny-tasting, tender fish, *bacalao* in Spanish and *bacalhau* in Portuguese, remains a popular basis for appetizers and main courses. Before use, salt cod must be soaked in cold water to reduce its saltiness. Look for filleted salt cod for the recipes in this book.

TO REHYDRATE SALT COD, immerse the fish in a bowl of cold water. Cover and refrigerate, changing the water 4–6 times, for 24–36 hours. The soaking time will depend upon how heavily salted and how thick the cod is. When ready, the fish will be puffy and lighter in color. Drain and proceed as directed in individual recipes.

SARDINES

These small, slender, silvery-blue fish, an immature form of the pilchard, are popular throughout Iberia. In Portugal in particular, people resist eating them during cold months, waiting until late spring when the fish are especially plump and sweet tasting, ideal for grilling.

SAUSAGES

One by-product of widespread pig farming in Spain and Portugal is the existence of a great variety of fresh and cured pork sausages, of which several types are included in this book.

BLOOD SAUSAGE ~ This sausage, *morcilla* in Spanish and *morcela* in Portuguese, gains rich flavor and texture, as well as a deep brownish red color, from the inclusion of pig's blood. Many regions of Spain and Portugal produce blood sausages, which may also include such ingredients as ground pork, bacon, rice or potatoes, and almonds or pine nuts, and such seasonings as garlic, cinnamon, and paprika. Typical examples include Spain's *butifarra negra* and paprika-laced *morcilla asturiana*.

BUTIFARRA ~ Also called *butifarra blanca*, this popular fresh white pork sausage of Catalonia is typically flavored with cinnamon, nutmeg, and cloves. Sweet Italian sausage is an acceptable substitute.

CHORIZO/CHOURIÇO ~ There are countless variations on this popular Iberian sausage, but lean and fat pork, garlic, herbs, and generous amounts of paprika (the source of its deep red color) are always part of the mix. Depending upon the region and the sausage maker, these sausages are sold fresh, dried to various stages, and sometimes even slightly smoked.

LINGUIÇA ~ A dry, cured sausage enjoyed in Portugal, *linguiça* is made from coarsely ground (minced) pork shoulder laced with garlic and paprika. The name derives from its resemblance to a long tongue.

SHERRY

Produced exclusively in the Jerez and Manzanilla regions of southwestern Spain, these fortified wines gain their distinctive quality from the area's chalky soil, from the white grape variety known as Palomino Fino, and from the unique process by which they are produced (see page 51). The two main types of sherry are known as fino and oloroso. Finos, among which are the crisp, dry manzanilla and the dry, nutty amontillado, are pale, fragrant, young aperitif wines that are staples of southern Spain's tapas bars. Olorosos, which are darker and stouter, include sweet cream sherry and full-bodied brown sherry, both of which are sipped at the end of a meal.

SQUID AND SQUID INK

Many fishmongers sell squid already cleaned. To clean squid yourself, pull the head and clinging innards free from the body. Discard the innards. If the ink is not called for in the recipe, discard the ink sac as well. Cut the tentacles from the head and squeeze out the small, hard beak from the mouth. Pull out and discard the transparent quill-like cartilage from the body pouch. Rinse the body and rub off the mottled violet skin covering it, then rinse the tentacles. Cut the body and tentacles, or leave whole, as needed.

The black ink adds striking color and subtle flavor to a variety of Spanish and Portuguese seafood dishes. In general, smaller squid have proportionately more ink for their size than larger squid. Since squid release ink as a defense mechanism when being caught, it's wise to buy extra ink for dishes calling for it. Most seafood stores sell ink in plastic packets, ready to use.

TOMATOES

Spanish explorers brought tomatoes back from the New World in the 16th century. Today, these vegetable-fruits are so popular throughout Spain and Portugal that it is hard to imagine either cuisine without them. For the best flavor, use in-season, sun-ripened tomatoes. For dishes in which tomatoes cook for any length of time

STOCKS

For the recipes in this book, use good-quality canned or frozen broth, taking care not to buy overly salted brands. Or prepare one of the following stocks when you have an afternoon to spare.

CHICKEN STOCK

5 lb (2.5 kg) chicken parts, fat removed

3 qt (3 l) water

1 yellow onion, peeled and chopped

1 carrot, peeled and chopped

12 fresh flat-leaf (Italian) parsley sprigs

1 teaspoon minced fresh thyme or ½ teaspoon crumbled dried thyme

1 bay leaf

❧ Place the chicken in a large stockpot and add all the remaining ingredients. Bring slowly to a boil, regularly skimming off any scum and froth from the surface. Reduce the heat to low and simmer, uncovered, until the meat has fallen off the bones and the stock is fragrant, 3–4 hours, periodically adding water to maintain the original level.

❧ Line a sieve or colander with cheesecloth (muslin) and strain the stock through it into a clean container. Refrigerate, uncovered, until cool. Before using, lift off the fat solidified on the surface with a spoon. Store in a tightly covered container in the refrigerator for up to 5 days or in the freezer for up to 2 months.

Makes about 3 qt (3 l)

FISH STOCK

2 lb (1 kg) fish heads, fish frames, small bony fish, and, if possible, shellfish shells

2 tablespoons olive oil

1 large yellow onion, coarsely chopped

2 cloves garlic (optional)

2 carrots, peeled and chopped

1 leek, including about 2 inches of the green tops, chopped

2 bay leaves

1 lemon slice

12 peppercorns

1 fresh thyme sprig

1 fresh flat-leaf (Italian) parsley sprig

1 fresh marjoram sprig

6–8 cups (48–64 fl oz / 1.5–2 l) water

salt to taste

❧ Rinse all the fish and shells well. In a stockpot over medium heat, warm the olive oil. Add the onion and the garlic, if using, and sauté for a few minutes. Add the rinsed fish and shells and sauté for a minute or two, stirring often. Then add the carrots, leek, bay leaves, lemon slice, peppercorns, herb sprigs, and water. Bring slowly to a boil, regularly skimming off any scum and froth from the surface. Reduce the heat to medium-low and simmer uncovered, skimming often, for 25 minutes.

❧ Line a sieve or colander with cheesecloth (muslin) and strain the stock through it into a clean saucepan. Return to high heat, bring to a boil, and cook to reduce and further intensify the flavor. Season with salt. Use immediately, or cover and refrigerate for up to 3 days or freeze for up to 3 months.

Makes 1½–2 qt (1.5–2 l)

and thus reduce to a purée, canned tomatoes are fine and convenient. They are available in whole peeled, diced, or puréed forms.

TO PEEL TOMATOES, use a small, sharp knife to score a shallow X in their bottoms. Using a slotted spoon or wire skimmer, immerse them in a pan of boiling water until the skins wrinkle and loosen, 20–30 seconds, then transfer them to a bowl filled with ice and water. When the tomatoes are cool enough to handle, peel away the skins with your fingertips or with the help of a knife.

TO SEED TOMATOES, whether skinned or not, cut them horizontally in half. Use your fingertip or the handle of a teaspoon to scoop out their seed sacs before slicing, chopping, or dicing as a particular recipes requires.

MEAT STOCK

6 lb (3 kg) meaty beef and veal shanks

2 yellow onions, coarsely chopped

1 leek, trimmed and coarsely chopped

2 carrots, peeled and coarsely chopped

1 celery stalk, coarsely chopped

1 cup (8 fl oz/250 ml) hot water

6 cloves garlic

4 fresh flat-leaf (Italian) parsley sprigs

10 peppercorns

3 fresh thyme sprigs

2 small bay leaves

❦ Preheat an oven to 450°F (230°C). Put the beef and veal shanks in a large roasting pan and roast, turning occasionally, until nicely browned, about 1½ hours. Transfer the shanks to a large stockpot, reserving the pan juices. Add cold water to cover generously and bring slowly to a boil, regularly skimming off any scum and froth from the surface. Reduce the heat to low and simmer, uncovered, for 2 hours, adding water as needed to keep the bones generously immersed. Skim the scum from the surface occasionally.

❦ Meanwhile, place the roasting pan on the stove top and add the onions, leek, carrots, and celery to the fat remaining in the pan. Brown over high heat, stirring often, until the vegetables caramelize, 15–20 minutes. Take care not to scorch them.

❦ When the shanks have simmered for 2 hours, add the browned vegetables to the stockpot. Pour the hot water into the roasting pan, bring to a simmer, and deglaze the pan, stirring to dislodge any browned bits. Add this liquid to the pot. Place the garlic, parsley, peppercorns, thyme, and bay leaves on a square of cheesecloth (muslin), bring the corners together, tie securely with kitchen string, and add to the stockpot.

WINE, PORTUGUESE

While the excellent wines of Spain tend to get more attention (see sidebar, page 125), Portuguese vintners have made great strides in the production of good table wines. Fine red wines are now produced in the Dão region southeast of Oporto, with others of great promise coming from north of the Dão in the Douro Valley. Just north of Oporto, a classified wine-growing region known as Vinho Verde, or "green wine," produces light, fruity, slightly effervescent wines of the same name. They must be drunk young, within two years.

For information on the country's famous port wine, see the sidebar on page 237, and on its nearly as well-known Madeira wine, see the sidebar on page 215.

Simmer over low heat, uncovered, for 6 hours longer (a total of 8 hours).

❦ Remove the stockpot from the heat and remove the solids with a slotted spoon or skimmer. Pour the stock through a sieve into a container. Line the sieve with cheesecloth and strain the stock again into a clean container. Refrigerate, uncovered, until cool. Before using, lift off the fat solidified on the surface with a spoon. Store in a tightly covered container in the refrigerator for up to 5 days or in the freezer for up to 2 months.
Makes 4–5 qt (4–5 l)

VEGETABLE STOCK

10 cups (2½ lb/1.25 kg) cut-up assorted vegetables such as leeks, celery, tomatoes, mushrooms, green beans, spinach, and Swiss chard

1 yellow onion, coarsely chopped

1 carrot, peeled and coarsely chopped

12 fresh flat-leaf (Italian) parsley sprigs

pinch of fresh thyme leaves

1 bay leaf

❦ Place the assorted vegetables, onion, and carrot in a stockpot. Place the parsley, thyme, and bay leaf on a square of cheesecloth (muslin), bring the corners together, tie securely with kitchen string, and add to the pot. Add cold water to cover the vegetables by 3 inches (7.5 cm), bring to a boil over high heat, and then immediately reduce the heat to low. Simmer, uncovered, until the stock is aromatic and flavorful, 1–1½ hours, adding water as needed to maintain the original level.

❦ Remove the stockpot from the heat and pour through a fine-mesh sieve into a clean container. Use immediately, or refrigerate, uncovered, until cool, then cover tightly and store in the refrigerator for up to 1 week or in the freezer for up to 2 months.
Makes 2–3 qt (2–3 l)

INDEX

ACKNOWLEDGMENTS

Joyce Goldstein dedicates this book in memory of Catherine Brandel, a wonderful cook and teacher who loved Spain.

Noel Barnhurst wishes to thank his photography assistant, Noriko Akiyama, and Suzanne Cushman, for her help with props. George Dolese thanks his associate Leslie Busch for her continued excellence in the kitchen. The photo team also thanks HGC Imports for their help in providing Portuguese food products.

Steven Rothfeld experienced the beauty of Spain and Portugal through the always-patient assistance of many individuals: Juanita Martinez and her colleagues at the Tourist Office of Spain in Beverly Hills and Madrid helped with itineraries and reservations at the country's superb paradors. Mariana Oom, of the Portuguese Trade & Tourism Commission in San Francisco, eased travel in her country. William A. Devin, of Unio Agraria Cooperativa, was an invaluable source of contacts in the worlds of wine, cheese, and tuna. José Manuel Perez and Marta Olmos graciously opened the door to Bodegas Perez Pascuas in Pedrosa del Duero. Javier Ortiz, director general of Conservas Ortiz, generously spent two days on the Basque coast explaining every aspect of the tuna trade. Mariano and Mar Sanz, of the Consorcio de los Quesos Tradicionales de España, acted as indispensable guides on a visit to Artegreso, a Manchego cheese maker. Special thanks to designer Kari Ontko and photography editor Sandra Eisert for sifting through hundreds of photographs and placing them so beautifully on the page. And finally, many thanks to associate publisher Hannah Rahill, who, in the spirit of Spain and Portugal's Golden Age of Discovery, made this unforgettable photographic journey possible.

Weldon Owen would like to thank the following individuals and establishments for their help and support: Wendely Harvey, Monique Balbuena, Desne Border, Linda Bouchard, Celeste Carrasco, and Ken DellaPenta; and in Spain, Jose Goméz and the rest of the staff at Parador de Ronda; Eduardo Cointreau and his staff at the International Cookbook Revue in Madrid; Casa de Carmona in Seville; and Augusto Higueras Sanz.

Time-Life Books is a division of Time Life Inc.
Time-Life is a trademark of Time Warner Inc. and affiliated companies

TIME LIFE INC.
President and CEO: Jim Nelson

TIME LIFE TRADE PUBLISHING
Vice President and Publisher: Neil Levin
Senior Director of Acquisitions and Editorial Resources:
Jennifer Pearce
Director of Design: Kate L. McConnell
Project Manager: Jennifer L. Ward

WILLIAMS-SONOMA INC.
Founder and Vice-Chairman: Chuck Williams
Book Buyer: Cecilia Michaelis

WELDON OWEN INC.
Chief Executive Officer: John Owen
President: Terry Newell
Chief Operating Officer: Larry Partington
Vice President International Sales: Stuart Laurence
Associate Publisher: Hannah Rahill
Consulting Editors: Sharon Silva, Norman Kolpas
Design: Kari Ontko, India Ink
Photo Editor: Sandra Eisert
Production Director: Stephanie Sherman
Production Manager: Chris Hemesath
Editorial Assistant: Dana Goldberg
Food Stylist: George Dolese
Associate Food Stylist: Leslie Busch
Illustrations: Marlene McLoughlin
Calligraphy: Jane Dill

THE SAVORING SERIES
conceived and produced by Weldon Owen Inc.
814 Montgomery Street, San Francisco, CA 94133
Telephone: 415-291-0100, Fax: 415-291-8841

In collaboration with Williams-Sonoma Inc.
3250 Van Ness Avenue, San Francisco, CA 94109

Separations by Colourscan Overseas Co. Pte. Ltd.
Printed in Singapore by Tien Wah Press (Pte.) Ltd.

Savoring is a trademark of Weldon Owen Inc.

p 2: *Berenjenas Rellenas a la Catalana* (stuffed eggplants) and *Batatas com Coentro* (potatoes with cilantro), recipes page 187. pp 4–5: At the base of Lisbon's massive Monument to the Discoveries, built to honor Prince Henry the Navigator, an elaborate mosaic depicts a mariner's compass.

pp 6–7: Strings of fresh peppers hang in a sunny outdoor market in Evora, a picturesque walled town on the Alentejan plain. pp 8–9: A young couple enjoys a *bocadillo*—and a laugh—outside Bilbao's boldly modern Museo Guggenheim, a titanium-sheathed showcase for contemporary art on the banks of the Nervión River. pp 12–13: A grove of olive trees flourishes under the Andalusian sun near Setenil, one of the region's *pueblos blancos*—"whitewashed towns."

A WELDON OWEN PRODUCTION
Copyright © 2000 Weldon Owen Inc.

First printed 2000
10 9 8 7 6 5 4 3 2 1

Library of Congress
Cataloging-in-Publication Data

Goldstein, Joyce.
  Savoring Spain & Portugal : recipes and reflections on Iberian cooking / Joyce Goldstein, recipes and text ; Chuck Williams, general editor ; Noel Barnhurst, recipe photography ; Steven Rothfeld, scenic photography ; Marlene McLoughlin, illustrations.
    p. cm.—(The savoring series)
    ISBN 0-7370-2042-3 (hc.)
    1. Cookery, Spanish.   2. Cookery, Portuguese.   I. Title: Savoring Spain & Portugal.   II. Williams, Chuck.   III. Title. IV. Series.
TX723.5.S7.G63 2000
641.5946—dc21   99-057163
                                                        CIP